"Excellent! An over-time analysis of the factors that impact elections from one of the few people able to do it. From class and culture to white identity, it is all there. Special attention is paid to the vote in 2012 and 2016. An original and creative contribution to our understanding of the dynamics of elections. Mandatory reading!"

—*William Crotty, Thomas P. O'Neill, Jr. Chair in Public Life and Emeritus Professor of Political Science, Northeastern University*

"This book offers a much-needed update on social class and voting behavior in presidential elections. Prysby gives careful thought on how to measure social class, and conducts a systematic analysis that is both well executed and convincing. This work makes a major contribution to the academic literature. Highly recommended to anyone who wants to understand how the relationship has changed between social class and voting behavior during the first two decades of this century."

—*Peter L. Francia, East Carolina University*

# RICH VOTER, POOR VOTER, RED VOTER, BLUE VOTER

This book examines the changing relationship between social class and voting behavior in contemporary America. At the end of the 20th century, working-class white voters were significantly more Democratic than their middle-class counterparts, as they had been since the 1930s. By the second decade of the 21st century, that long-standing relationship had reversed: Republicans now do better among working-class whites. While Trump accentuated this trend, the change began before 2016, something that has not been fully appreciated or understood.

Charles Prysby analyzes this development in American politics in a way that is understandable to a wide audience, not just scholars in this field. Drawing on a wealth of survey data, this study describes and explains the underlying causes of the change that has taken place over the past two decades, identifying how social class is directly related to partisan choice. Attitudes on race and immigration, on social and moral issues, and on economic and social welfare policies are all part of the explanation of this 21st century development in American political trends.

*Rich Voter, Poor Voter, Red Voter, Blue Voter: Social Class and Voting Behavior in Contemporary America* is essential reading for scholars, students, and all others with an interest in American elections and voting behavior.

**Charles L. Prysby** is a professor of Political Science at the University of North Carolina at Greensboro. He specializes in American elections, voting behavior, and political parties. His most recent book, coauthored with David Holian, is *Candidate Character Traits in Presidential Elections* (Routledge, 2015).

# RICH VOTER, POOR VOTER, RED VOTER, BLUE VOTER

Social Class and Voting Behavior in Contemporary America

*Charles L. Prysby*

Routledge
Taylor & Francis Group

NEW YORK AND LONDON

First published 2020
by Routledge
52 Vanderbilt Avenue, New York, NY 10017

and by Routledge
2 Park Square, Milton Park, Abingdon, Oxon OX14 4RN

*Routledge is an imprint of the Taylor & Francis Group, an informa business*

*Library of Congress Cataloging-in-Publication Data*
A catalog record for this title has been requested

ISBN: 978-0-367-33428-4 (hbk)
ISBN: 978-0-367-33429-1 (pbk)
ISBN: 978-0-429-31982-2 (ebk)

Typeset in Bembo
by Taylor & Francis Books

For Anita, Nicole, and Michelle

# CONTENTS

# TABLES

# PREFACE

I have been interested in social class and political behavior for a long time. When I was an undergraduate student at the Illinois Institute of Technology in the 1960s, I took a course in political science, and one of the assigned books for the course was Seymour Martin Lipset's *Political Man*. I found that book's discussion of the social bases of political behavior to be much more interesting than the engineering that I was studying. I decided that I would rather be a political scientist, so I changed my major and made plans to go to graduate school. Fortunately, that decision turned out well, as I went on to earn my Ph.D. at Michigan State University. My interest in social class and political behavior continued through graduate school, and I wrote my dissertation on working-class voting in Chile. However, my interests drifted away from social class and voting as my academic career progressed. I studied and wrote on contextual effects on political behavior, on various aspects of southern politics, and, most recently, on the role of candidate character traits in presidential elections. But the 2016 presidential election campaign rekindled my interest in social class and voting behavior. The media discussions of Donald Trump's appeal to white working-class voters led me to explore how social class is related to partisan choice in contemporary America. In writing this book, I have tried hard to make the arguments and the evidence comprehensible to a broad audience, not just political scientists interested in voting behavior. One reason that I have done so is because I think that some of the discussions of this topic in the mainstream media have been incomplete or even misleading. I hope that this study contributes to a more complete and accurate understanding of the changing relationship between social class and voting behavior.

I could not have completed this project without the help that I received from others. First of all, I am grateful for the support that the University of North Carolina provided. The University awarded me a research leave for the spring semester of 2019. Without that research leave, this book would not have been completed in a timely fashion. UNCG also provided funds for Kaylee Faw, an undergraduate political science major at UNCG, to work as a research assistant for me. Kaylee participated in all stages of the research and writing, from data collection and bibliographic work in the early stages to proofreading at the end. Her assistance was invaluable. Several fellow political scientists assisted me with this project, and I am pleased to thank them for their help. Bill Crotty, professor emeritus at Northeastern University, read several chapters and provided useful feedback. Peter Francia, a professor at East Carolina University, helped me to understand the role of labor unions in American politics. Two of my UNCG political science colleagues, David Holian and Susan Johnson, read and commented on parts of the manuscript, and I appreciate their contributions. Also, my wife, Anita, and my two daughters, Nicole and Michelle, read most of the manuscript to see if my arguments and presentation would make sense to a broad audience. Their suggestions helped me to make points clearer to those unfamiliar with the political science literature on this topic. Finally, my editor at Routledge, Natalja Mortensen, was very encouraging throughout this project. This was the second time that I have worked with her, and I am pleased that the second time has been as rewarding as the first time was. Naturally, any errors or shortcomings that remain in the book are my responsibility.

# 1

# A CHANGING CLASS ALIGNMENT?

Democrats are the party of the working man. At least that has been the popular image of the party, one that was forged in the 1930s New Deal realignment and that continued for decades afterwards. But this image may no longer be accurate. The 2016 presidential election seemed to indicate that the white working class now prefers the Republican Party. News coverage of the election emphasized Donald Trump's appeal to white working-class voters. According to numerous media accounts, many working-class whites, especially those in areas where good blue-collar jobs have been disappearing, found Trump's campaign message appealing. The Democratic Party found itself doing better among white middle-class voters than among white working-class voters, a reversal of a long-standing pattern. This might be viewed as the result of a unique appeal of Trump, who certainly was an unusual Republican candidate. However, this study finds that the appeal of the Republican Party to the white working class did not begin with Trump. He only accentuated a trend that actually began earlier this century, a development that was not clearly recognized or properly analyzed in earlier election years. To better understand these developments in American politics, we can first look at accounts of Trump's appeal in 2016, then examine what political analysts were observing about social class and voting prior to 2016.

## Donald Trump's Appeal in 2016

The 2016 presidential election was unusual from start to finish. Both candidates were judged very unfavorably by the electorate. The eventual winner was a wealthy businessman and celebrity who had no experience in government and who was thought to be unqualified by many within his own party. The loser had a lengthy and distinguished political resume and was widely endorsed by leaders in her party. The campaign was extremely negative, with each candidate relentlessly attacking the other's character. Trump claimed that Clinton was a crooked liar whom he would put in jail if he were elected. Clinton argued that Trump was a racist misogynist who was clearly unfit to be president. Trump prevailed even though his campaign was marked by a series of outrageous comments that provoked widespread criticism. Clinton lost even though she clearly won all three presidential debates, at least in the eyes of the voters. Pundits and political scientists predicted a Democratic victory throughout the fall, and while Trump did lose the popular vote by slightly over two percentage points, he won the electoral college vote by narrowly winning some key Midwestern states. Trump was, to put it mildly, a very atypical Republican candidate, who ran a very atypical campaign, and who won in a rather atypical fashion.

The unusual nature of the Republican candidate and his campaign led to considerable discussion of the source of his appeal. A frequent theme in these interpretations was Trump's appeal to white working-class voters, an appeal that Clinton seemed to lack. Several explanations were offered for Trump's ability to win support from the white working class. One popular explanation was that these working-class voters liked Trump's economic message. They were unhappy with their economic situation, believed that the economic policies pursued by the Obama administration were not helping them very much, and thought that Trump's proposed changes in American trade policies were what the country needed.

The geography of the Republican vote in 2016 suggests that Trump had a particular appeal to a certain set of blue-collar voters. Trump did only slightly better in the overall popular vote than did Mitt Romney—Trump won about 48.9 percent of the two-party vote, while Romney won about 48.1 percent—but Trump carried Pennsylvania, Ohio, Michigan, and Wisconsin, all states that Romney failed to win. Had Trump lost any three of those states, he would have lost the election. That easily could have happened, as he won three of the four by less than one percentage point. Media accounts of Trump voters in these states emphasized a common theme: Trump had strong support among voters who lived in communities that were in economic decline, areas where good manufacturing jobs had been lost. White working-class voters in these areas were disillusioned with their economic prospects, and many felt that bad trade policies had contributed to their worsening economic situation. These voters were described as feeling left behind and upset that the government did not care about their economic situation.

Reports of interviews with blue-collar workers illustrate these feelings. For example, Thomas Edsall (2016) talked with voters in one small city in Pennsylvania, Pottstown, and he found that voters were concerned over the loss of well-paying blue-collar jobs. This was a community where many people had been employed in manufacturing, but it now was an area where few of those jobs still existed. The presence of shuttered factories no doubt was a constant reminder to these people that the economic prospects had declined for workers who lacked a college education. Especially unhappy were men who liked to work with their hands and who at one time had been able to earn a good salary doing so. The decline of the industrial base in the area greatly reduced their opportunities to find manufacturing jobs. The top two employers in Pottstown now were the school district and the medical center, which were not the types of places that laid-off steelworkers or machinists were likely to find a good job.

Tim Reid (2016) reported similar sentiments among blue-collar workers in Canton, Ohio, a medium-sized city that once had a thriving steel industry. His interviews with members of the United Steelworkers union, usually a strong source of votes for Democrats, revealed considerable support for Trump. These blue-collar workers liked his opposition to free trade, which they saw as responsible for the loss of manufacturing jobs. Reid reported that Ohio had lost about 200,000 manufacturing jobs since the 2008–2009 Great Recession, so this was an issue of great concern to blue-collar workers in the state.

Other journalists and political commentators, often relying on a broader set of data, reported similar conclusions about Trump voters. A common argument was that working-class voters were concerned about declines in their real income and pessimistic about their future (Coontz 2016; Greenberg 2017). They felt that the recovery from the Great Recession produced largely low-paying jobs and that past trade policies were responsible for the loss of good-paying jobs (Confessore 2016a; Gest 2017). Some of these voters were exasperated with the economic policies of past Democratic and Republican administrations alike; they saw Trump as someone who would reverse what they saw as the disastrous economic policies of the past.

Economic grievances may be part of the story, but numerous accounts of support for Trump among white working-class voters stressed negative attitudes toward immigrants and minorities as a key factor. Trump certainly made immigration policy a key issue in his campaign, repeatedly calling for building a wall along the Mexican border to keep people from entering the country illegally, plus adding that he would make Mexico pay for it. He also called for a ban on immigration from Muslim countries, arguing that they were a threat to the U.S. Furthermore, he frequently characterized immigrants in derogatory terms, stating, for example, that many of the Mexican immigrants were rapists and criminals. Expressions of hostility toward blacks were more subtle in Trump's campaign, but they were nevertheless quite clear. In fact, well before he became a presidential candidate, he gained notoriety for his persistent claim that President Obama was not born in the United States. As a presidential candidate, Trump hired Steven Bannon, whose website had white nationalism as a central theme, to head his campaign. And many of Trump's tweets criticized prominent black leaders or celebrities and characterized black communities as economic and social disasters (Leonard and Philbrick 2018).

Not surprisingly, many political commentators argued that Trump's appeal was largely racist in nature (Confessore 2016b; McElwee 2016; Parker 2016). This explanation emphasized that many white voters felt that blacks and other minorities received preferential treatment, that high levels of immigration, particularly illegal immigration, made the nation worse off, and that the cultural identity of the country was being destroyed by the growth of racial and ethnic minorities. While these reasons applied to white Trump voters in general, working-class whites were believed to be more likely than middle-class whites to express these attitudes. Thus, while both economic dissatisfaction and racial resentment may have contributed to Trump's appeal to the white working class, many analysts found racial attitudes to be a more potent factor.

Trump's appeal to whites who were economically dissatisfied and/or anti-immigrant were part of a broader populist theme. He argued that the existing political elites had failed the country, particularly the large number of ordinary, working Americans, and he did not just blame Democrats. When he claimed that past trade deals and policies had cost the country millions of manufacturing jobs, he was criticizing Democrats and Republicans alike. Similarly, he argued that both parties had failed to stop the flood of illegal immigrants into the country. His theme was that the country was run by entrenched, powerful interests who cared little about the plight of ordinary Americans, that the country needed a strong leader who would represent those average citizens who were being ignored, and that he was the only one who was capable of doing that. All of this was a classic populist refrain, and according to some political analysts, it was one that was appealing to many white working-class voters.

The anti-establishment character of his campaign was fully displayed in his quest for the Republican nomination. At the start of the primary season, he had virtually no endorsements from prominent Republican leaders; indeed, many of them openly opposed Trump (Cohen *et al.* 2016). Nevertheless, he prevailed by winning most of the presidential primaries, starting with New Hampshire. A staple of his nomination campaign was a large rally, where he hurled inflammatory accusations, insulted his political opponents, and bragged about his accomplishments and abilities. Although controversial in their content, the rallies made good television news, so Trump received considerable free media time, much more than his Republican opponents were able to generate. His frequent tweets also generated free media coverage as well as being directly received by his many followers. Compared to his Republican opponents, Trump relied much more on these direct appeals to voters and much less on a traditional campaign organization.

## The Story Before Trump

Accounts in the popular media may have particularly stressed Trump's appeal to working-class whites in 2016, but well before 2016 a number of columnists and pundits argued that the white working class, which once was solidly Democratic, was moving toward the GOP. Among well-known national columnists, David Brooks has most frequently echoed the theme that Democrats no longer appeal to white working-class voters; he sees the Democratic Party as attempting to build a coalition of minority groups and well-off liberal whites (Brooks 2005; 2010; 2015). Declining Democratic support among white working-class voters was the theme of Thomas Frank's (2004) best-selling book, *What's the Matter with Kansas?*, which argued that white working-class voters, especially those in "Middle America," began supporting Republican candidates because of social issues. Their cultural conservatism on a variety of issues, often motivated by their religiosity, trumped their economic interests. Frank also argues that the Democratic Party failed to advance economic policies that would have benefitted these voters, a theme that he stresses in his most recent book, *Listen Liberal* (Frank 2016a). Arlie Hochschild's (2016) book, *Strangers in Their Own Land*, reports the results of her interviews of Tea Party supporters in Louisiana, many of whom were not economically well-off; her research, which was completed before Trump was a presidential candidate, concludes that many of these individuals felt that their blue-collar way of life was no longer respected, leaving them politically and socially alienated.

Moreover, the reasons offered for Republican success with the white working class prior to 2016 are similar to those discussed above for Trump's support among these voters. One theme was that working-class voters no longer viewed the Democratic Party as the champion of their economic interests (Frank 2016b). Trade policies that were unpopular among manufacturing workers, especially unionized ones, contributed substantially to this change in party images. So too did stagnating incomes and declining job opportunities for blue-collar workers. This does not necessarily mean that these voters began to see the Republican Party more favorably on economic issues, particularly since the Republicans also supported past trade policies that many blue-collar workers opposed, but the advantage that the Democrats once had in this area had diminished or disappeared.

Racial attitudes also were an important part of the explanation of declining Democratic support among white voters, particularly less-educated ones. Many of these voters viewed the Democratic Party as increasingly becoming the party of minority groups, and they felt that government policies all too often benefitted minority groups at the expense of whites. Hochschild (2016) used the metaphor of a long line of people patiently waiting for economic rewards that they believed they deserved. Many of the Tea Party supporters that she interviewed thought that blacks, immigrants, and other minority groups were cutting in line ahead of them. They saw the government as unfairly rewarding a variety of supposedly disadvantaged groups at the expense of ordinary, hard-working people. With Barack Obama as the Democratic candidate, it is not surprising that many scholars found racial attitudes to be important in the 2008 and 2012 presidential elections (Knuckey 2011; Knuckey and Kim 2015; Lewis-Beck, Tien, and Nadeau 2010).

Social conservatism also was identified as a source of Republican support among white working-class voters prior to 2016. The rise of the Christian Right in the 1980s and the continued salience of hot-button social issues, such as abortion or gay rights, into the 21st century provided reasons for some working-class voters to vote for Republican candidates. This was particularly true for areas where whites were strongly religious, such as the South and many parts of the Midwest. For example, one married couple interviewed by Hochschild (2016) in Louisiana stated that they supported the Republican Party primarily because of their strong anti-abortion attitudes, which trumped their pro-Democratic views on other issues. The impact of these social and moral issues on voting was enhanced by the development of clear policy differences between the two parties in this area in recent decades. The Republican identification of many white Christian conservatives had become so strong by 2016 that Trump was able to obtain strong support from both leaders and voters from the Christian Right, despite the fact that his credentials as a religious conservative were thin and his campaign statements and behavior often seemed inconsistent with traditional religious values (Bailey 2016; Holland and Conlin 2016).

Republican support among white working-class voters now seems particularly strong in rural or less-urbanized areas. This can be explained in part by the fact that whites in these areas, compared to those in heavily urbanized areas, are more likely to be socially conservative, more likely to have negative attitudes towards minority groups, and more likely to see their economic prospects as dismal. But there may be an additional factor in this relationship: rural and small-town voters may feel a more general resentment toward urban areas. Katherine Cramer's (2016) book, *The Politics of Resentment*, reports the results of her in-depth interviews with focus groups drawn from residents of rural areas of Wisconsin. She found that these rural citizens resented what they perceived as the tendency of urban elites to direct resources to urban areas, at the expense of those in rural areas, a perception that was prevalent even though the residents of rural areas of Wisconsin actually received more government services for their tax dollars than did those in urban areas. Furthermore, those rural voters saw urban residents as lacking a proper work ethic and good moral values.

In sum, even before Trump's candidacy, many widely read political analysts and commentators argued that the white working class was moving away from the Democratic Party. Disillusioned by their perceived economic prospects and by what they saw as a lack of concern with this on the part of both parties, disappointed by what they saw as Democrats catering to minority groups at the expense of whites, and dismayed by the social liberalism of Democrats, white working-class voters began to desert the Democratic Party well before 2016. Trump just accelerated an existing trend.

While many popular commentators and pundits stressed the movement of working-class whites toward the Republican Party for the reasons discussed above, political scientists have been more skeptical about the supposed desertion of working-class whites from the Democratic Party, especially prior to 2016. In a widely read and influential book, Bartels (2008, 64–97) systematically analyzed survey data through 2004 to test the arguments made by Frank in *What's the Matter with Kansas?* Comparing white voters in the bottom income tercile to those in the top tercile, Bartels found that the major claims made by Frank were unsupported by the evidence: compared to upper-income whites, lower-income white voters continued, even in recent years, to be: (a) more likely to vote Democratic; (b) more liberal on economic and social welfare issues; and (c) more likely to vote on the basis of economic rather than cultural issues. Stonecash (2000, 104–113) similarly compared upper and lower-income whites, and his analysis showed that the class difference in voting behavior among whites widened from the 1960s to the 1990s, especially in the South. Gelman

(2010, 43–57) found that although poorer states are more Republican, within each state, poorer voters are more Democratic. His analysis shows that pundits who infer that Democrats appeal more to wealthier voters from the state-level relationship between income and voting are simply committing an ecological fallacy.

That skepticism about working-class support for the GOP even extends to the 2016 presidential election, as some scholars argued that Trump did not appeal as strongly to working-class voters as many media stories indicated. Carnes and Lupu (2017) found that only one-third of Trump voters had incomes below the national median; furthermore, while many Trump voters lacked a college degree, that was true for all Republican primary voters, and it also was true that many of the non-college Trump voters had above average incomes. Similarly, Manza and Crowley (2017) concluded that Trump did not appeal particularly to economically insecure voters and that many of the arguments that such an appeal did exist were based on a faulty reading of the data.

The differences between the views of many media analysts and the findings of many political scientists results from several factors. First of all, media pundits and commentators often base their conclusions on casual empiricism and anecdotal evidence, whereas political scientists usually rely on systematic analyses of survey data on the electorate. A second reason for the differences in conclusions is due to differences in how social class is measured. Analysts and commentators in the popular press most frequently use education as their measure of social class, with those who lack a college degree defined as working class. This may be in part because education is routinely asked in public opinion polls and because it has a few simple categories. The problem with this definition is that many people who lack a college degree have occupations that would generally be considered middle class and that pay well. In fact, only about one-third of adults have a college degree, so classifying all of those without a four-year degree as working class would mean that two-thirds of Americans are working class, an overly broad categorization, and one that does not fit with the perceptions of most Americans, the majority of whom classify themselves as middle class. Political scientists are more likely to use income to measure social class, which is the approach used in this study. The question of how social class is best measured is examined in a subsequent chapter, but it is an important one for accurately determining class differences in voting. It also should be noted that many of the academic studies by political scientists discussed above do not use the most recent data, as it takes time for high-quality survey data to become available and to be analyzed. Thus, very recent shifts in the relationship between social class and voting behavior will not be reported in the scholarly literature as quickly as in the popular press. Indeed, some recent scholarly studies that analyze data from 2016 conclude that Trump did do relatively better among working-class whites (Sanders 2017; Stonecash 2017).

## Key Research Questions

The changing relationship between social class and voting behavior is just beginning to be thoroughly described and explained, and this study aims at advancing our understanding of this aspect of American electoral politics. In doing so, it focuses on the following questions:

*First, how much difference existed between the voting behavior of the white working class and the white middle class in 2016?* In answering this question, we need a good measure of social class. As I suggested above, defining those with a college degree as middle-class and those without a degree as working-class is problematic. This study uses income as the primary measure of social class, for reasons that I outline in the next chapter, but it makes certain adjustments to create a better measure than what is typically used, which should give us a better picture of true class differences in voting behavior. Also, whenever I refer to whites in this study, I mean non-Hispanic whites, as that is the focus of other studies on this topic.

*Second, how much change has occurred in the relationship between social class and voting among whites in recent years?* In answering this question, it is important to look at change in the difference between working-class and middle-class whites, not just at change in the absolute level of working-class support for Republicans. Whites in general have become more Republican over the past four decades. For example, Jimmy Carter won 47 percent of the two-party white vote in 1976, just three points lower than his 51 percent of the total vote. However, Hillary Clinton received only 42 percent of the white vote in 2016 even though she also won 51 percent of the total two-party vote. If we are analyzing class differences, the question is not whether white working-class voters are more Republican than they were in the past, but whether they are relatively more so compared to their middle-class counterparts.

*Third, why are white working-class voters now relatively more Republican in their voting?* This is a key question in this study, and it is one that requires careful analysis. Several attitudes are discussed above as possible reasons for this electoral pattern, and each of them is investigated in this study. To truly be a cause, any attitude that we identify must meet two tests.

First, it must affect the vote in the correct direction. For example, if economic dissatisfaction is suggested as a reason for white working-class voters to be more Republican, then it must be the case that those who are more dissatisfied are more likely to vote Republican. Moreover, this relationship must not be simply due to some confounding factors; there must be a causal relationship. As we shall see, some explanations for the relationship between social class and voting among whites that have been suggested in past studies or reports fail to meet this test.

Second, working-class voters must differ from middle-class voters on this attitude in the correct direction. For example, if racial resentment is suggested as an explanatory factor, then working-class whites must have higher levels of racial resentment than do middle-class whites. If there is no difference, then racial resentment cannot explain class differences in voting, regardless of how strongly it affects the vote. Again, we shall see that some suggested explanations for the relationship between social class and voting in the past fail to meet this test.

*Fourth, what is responsible for the change in the relationship between social class and voting behavior among whites?* In order for any of the factors identified above to be a reason for the change in the relationship between social class and voting among whites that has taken place in this century, one of two things must be true: (a) white working-class voters have become more conservative or more pro-Republican, relative to white middle-class voters, on the attitudes in question; or (b) existing class differences in these attitudes have increased in their influence on voting. For example, if social conservatism is a source of the increase in Republican support among the white working-class, then it must be that either: (a) working-class whites have become more conservative, relative to middle-class whites, on social issues; or (b) attitudes on social issues now have a stronger effect on the vote. If neither of the above is true, then social conservatism may help to explain why working-class voters currently are disproportionately Republican, but it will not explain why there has been a change in this relationship in recent years.

In this book, I tend to refer more to support for the Democratic Party among white working-class voters. However, as I have explained above, the concern in this study is with the difference between working-class and middle-class voters, not with the absolute level of support for either party from either social class. Thus, saying that in the past, working-class voters were more Democratic is equivalent to stating that middle-class voters were more Republican, and saying that working-class voters are now more Republican is no different from stating that middle-class voters are now more Democratic. I tend to refer to the relative decline of Democratic support from the white working class, rather than the relative increase in Democratic support from the white middle class, for two reasons. First, much of the literature on this topic focuses on the change in working-class support for Democrats among whites, as one can see from the books and articles cited earlier in this chapter. Second, in an absolute sense, there has been greater change in the behavior of white working-class voters. White middle-class voters have become relatively more Democratic, but there has been less absolute change in their vote. But even though I refer more to white working-class voters in this study, it is important to realize that I am implicitly talking just as much about white middle-class voters because my concern is with the difference between these two groups in their attitudes and behavior. Furthermore, whenever, I refer to whites in this study, I always mean non-Hispanic whites. This is consistent with the focus of both the existing scholarly literature and the stories in the popular press on this topic. That scholarly and popular focus reflects two facts. First, non-Hispanic whites are a large share of the electorate. Second, their voting patterns have changed considerably over recent decades. By contrast, the voting behavior of blacks has been very stable during that same time.

## Plan of the Book

The plan for the rest of this book is to first describe how social class has been related to party choice and how that relationship has changed in recent years, then to examine possible explanations for the change in that relationship. This involves determining how social class is best measured and identifying the possible reasons for increasing support for the Republican Party among white working-class voters. I outline below what topics are taken up in each of the chapters in this book.

In Chapter 2, I discuss how social class is best measured and examine the reasons for a relationship between social class and voting behavior. The discussion in this chapter will lay the foundation for subsequent chapters. Social class has been measured in various ways: occupation, income, education, and self-identification all have been used. As discussed above, using education as a measure of social class and focusing on the difference between those with and without a college degree leads to problematic conclusions. Occupation used to be a common measure of social class, but it is not used much now, largely because we lack the data that we need for an accurate measure. I argue that income is the best measure of social class currently available to us, but it needs to be adjusted for marital status and age, for reasons that will be explained.

The traditional expectation regarding social class and voting in both the United States and other industrial democracies is that working-class individuals prefer parties of the left and middle-class individuals favor parties of the right. This presumed relationship is based on the economic interests of working-class and middle-class voters. Working-class voters are expected to favor more liberal economic policies, while middle-class voters should support more conservative policies. These arguments for the relationship between class and party are examined in more detail in Chapter 2.

In Chapter 3, I examine how social class has been related to voting behavior in modern American politics, including recent changes in that relationship. For decades, the Democratic Party was widely viewed as the party of the working class. That image was established in the New Deal realignment of the 1930s, and it continued to be an accurate description throughout the 20th century. However, in the 21st century, the Republican Party began to do better among less-affluent white voters than it did among those who were more affluent, resulting in a reversal of the relationship that had characterized American politics for decades. That new pattern was most strongly evident in 2016, but it was developing before then.

Several explanations have been offered for the emerging Republican appeal to the white working class. One explanation is that lower-income whites are motivated by antipathy toward blacks, immigrants, and other minorities, who they see as culturally threatening. Conservative attitudes on social issues also have been identified as a reason for less-affluent whites to support the GOP, or for more-affluent whites to support the Democrats. A third explanation is that lower-income whites have become increasingly concerned about their economic situation and no longer view the Democratic Party as more likely to benefit them. Added to these more general reasons are some that are more specific to Trump, such as a desire for a strong leader or a distrust of all politicians. These explanations have been outlined above, and the following chapters will investigate them more thoroughly, including determining whether working-class whites truly are more conservative or more pro-Republican on these factors and whether attitudes on these factors truly influence voting behavior.

In Chapter 4, I examine the relationships between race, class, and the politics of white identity. Republican support from white working-class voters is due in large part to their attitudes on race, immigration, and related issues. Less-affluent whites are more negative in their attitudes toward blacks, immigrants, and other minority groups, and these attitudes affect their voting behavior. Trump made explicit appeals on this basis in 2016, but Republican appeals to white voters on the basis or racial issues predate Trump. This chapter will trace the evolution of how attitudes on race-related issues became intertwined with social class and political party and examine the depth of these feelings in current American politics. Considerable evidence indicates that these relationships became stronger during the Obama years.

In Chapter 5, I investigate the extent to which white working-class support for Republicans is due to their views on cultural and moral issues, such as abortion or gay rights. If less-affluent voters are more conservative on these issues than are more-affluent voters, and if attitudes on these issues affect the voting behavior of these voters, then this would strengthen working-class support for the GOP—or weaken middle-class support for Republicans. This chapter will examine how attitudes on cultural issues relate to social class and how they influence voting. Attitudes on these issues are related to religiosity, so this chapter also examines the relationship between social class and religious commitment among whites.

In Chapter 6, I analyze how economic anxiety and attitudes on economic issues have affected the relationship between social class and voting. In the past, working-class voters were more inclined to vote for Democrats because they saw Democratic policies as more economically beneficial to them. In recent years, many analysts have argued that many white working-class voters have become unhappy with their economic prospects and less likely to see Democrats as their economic champions, thus undercutting a fundamental reason for working-class support for the Democratic Party. Growing economic inequality and declining social mobility have fomented these feelings, and the Great Recession intensified this dissatisfaction. This chapter will analyze how social class is related to attitudes on economic issues and perceptions of the economic policies of the two parties, along with how these orientations influence voting behavior.

In Chapter 7, I integrate the various reasons for working-class support for the Republican Party that were discussed in the previous chapters into an overall explanation of the presidential vote in 2012 and 2016. The Republican candidates in these two elections were extremely different in their style and in their overt appeal to less-affluent voters, so similarities in voting behavior across these two elections should be quite interesting. Relying on survey data from these two elections, a multivariate analysis will examine the relative impact of the factors discussed above, along with some factors unique to each election, especially those involving Trump in 2016. This analysis will allow us to determine the relative contribution of economic anxiety, white identity, social conservatism, and other relevant attitudes to working-class support for the Republican Party.

Finally, in Chapter 8, I conclude the book by summarizing the findings of the book and discussing their implications for the future of American politics. As the nature of the party coalitions changes, the tensions within each party will change, and the dynamics of the party system will be altered. Future developments may depend on the relative importance of economic versus cultural factors. Working-class voters who now support the GOP because of their economic anxiety may desert the party if their economic situation does not improve, but those who support the GOP because of racial anxiety or moral conservatism are likely to remain Republican supporters. Future developments also are likely to be shaped by how the political parties and their candidates respond. Will Democrats shape their future appeals to more strongly emphasize the economic concerns of working-class voters? Will future Republican appeals deemphasize the politics of white identity? The answers to these and other questions will help to determine the future relationship between social class and party choice.

## References

Bailey, Sarah Pulliam. 2016. "White Evangelicals Voted Overwhelmingly for Donald Trump, Exit Polls Show." *Washington Post*, November 9.

Bartels, Larry M. 2008. *Unequal Democracy*. Princeton, NJ: Princeton University Press.

Brooks, David. 2005. "Meet the Poor Right." *New York Times*, May 15.

Brooks, David. 2010. "Midwest at Dusk." *New York Times*, November 4.

Brooks, David. 2015. "The Field is Flat." *New York Times*, March 27.

Carnes, Nicholas, and Noam Lupu. 2017. "It's Time to Bust the Myth: Most Trump Voters Were Not Working Class." *Washington Post*, June 5.

Cohen, Marty, David Karol, Hans Noel, and John Zaller. 2016. "Party versus Faction in the Reformed Presidential Nominating System." *PS: Political Science & Politics* 49(4): 701–708.

Confessore, Nicholas. 2016a. "How G.O.P. Elites Lost the Party's Base to Trump." *New York Times*, November 9.

Confessore, Nicholas. 2016b. "Trump Mines Grievances of Whites Who Feel Lost." *New York Times*, July 14.

Coontz, Stephanie. 2016. "Working-class Whites Give Trump the White House." *CNN*. November 11. www.cnn.com/2016/11/10/opinions/how-clinton-lost-the-working-class-coontz/index.html.

Cramer, Katherine J. 2016. *The Politics of Resentment: Rural Consciousness in Wisconsin and the Rise of Scott Walker*. Chicago: University of Chicago Press.

Edsall, Thomas. 2016. "Measuring the Trump Effect." *New York Times*, June 19.

Frank, Thomas. 2004. *What's the Matter with Kansas? How Conservatives Won the Heart of America*. New York: Metropolitan Books.

Frank, Thomas. 2016a. *Listen Liberal*. New York: Metropolitan Books.

Frank, Thomas. 2016b. "Millions of Ordinary Americans Support Donald Trump. Here's Why." *The Guardian*, March 7. www.theguardian.com/commentisfree/2016/mar/07/donald-trump-why-americans-support.

Gelman, Andrew. 2010. *Red State, Blue State, Rich State, Poor State: Why Americans Vote the Way They Do*. Expanded edition. Princeton, NJ: Princeton University Press.

Gest, Justin. 2017. "The Two Kinds of Trump Voters." *Politico*, February 8. www.politico. com/magazine/story/2017/02/trump-voters-white-working-class-214754.

Greenberg, Stanley. 2017. "The Democrats' Working-Class Problem." *The American Prospect*, June 1. https://prospect.org/article/democrats'-'working-class-problem'.

Hochschild, Arlie. 2016. *Strangers in Their Own Land: Anger and Mourning on the American Right*. New York: The New Press.

Holland, Steve, and Michelle Conlin. 2016. "Evangelical Leaders Stick With Trump, Focus on Defeating Clinton." *Reuters*, October 8. www.reuters.com/articles/us-usa-trump-evangelicals/ evangelical-leaders-stick-with-trump-focus-on-defeating-clinton-idUSKCN1280WE.

Knuckey, Jonathan. 2011. "Racial Resentment and Vote Choice in the 2008 U.S. Presidential Election." *Politics & Policy* 39(4): 559–582.

Knuckey, Jonathan, and Myunghee Kim. 2015. "Racial Resentment, Old-Fashioned Racism, and the Vote Choice of Southern and Nonsouthern Whites in the 2012 U.S. Presidential Election." *Social Science Quarterly* 96(4): 905–922.

Leonard, David, and Ian Prasad Philbrick. 2018. "Donald Trump's Racism: The Definitive List." *New York Times*, January 15.

Lewis-Beck, Michael S., Charles Tien, and Richard Nadeau. 2010. "Obama's Missed Landslide: A Racial Cost?" *PS: Political Science & Politics* 43(1): 69–76.

Manza, Jeff, and Ned Crowley. 2017. "Working Class Hero? Interrogating the Social Bases of the Rise of Donald Trump." *The Forum* 15(1): 3–28. https://as.nyu.edu/content/ dam/nyu-as/sociology/documents/manza-publications/Forum.pdf.

McElwee, Sean. 2016. "Yep, Race Really Did Trump Economics: A Data Dive on His Supporters Reveals Deep Racial Animosity." *Salon*, November 13. www.salon.com/2016/ 11/13/yep-race-really-did-trump-economics-a-data-dive-on-his-supporters-reveals-deep-racial-animosity/.

Parker, George. 2016. "How Donald Trump is Winning Over the White Working Class." *The New Yorker*, May 16.

Reid, Tim. 2016. "Ohio's Dirty Little Secret: Blue-Collar Democrats for Trump." *Reuters*, March 12. www.reuters.com/article/us-usa-election-trump-ohio-insight/ohios-dirty-little-secret-blue-collar-democrats-for-trump-idUSKCN0WC19Q.

Sanders, Elizabeth. 2017. "The Meaning, Causes, and Possible Results of the 2016 Presidential Election." *The Forum* 15(4): 711–740. www.degruyter.com/downloadpdf/j/ for.2017.15.issue-4/for-2017–0046/for-2017–0046.pdf.

Stonecash, Jeffrey M. 2000. *Class and Party in American Politics*. Boulder, CO: Westview Press.

Stonecash, Jeffrey M. 2017. "The Puzzle of Class in Presidential Voting." *The Forum* 15(1): 29–49. www.degruyter.com/downloadpdf/j/for.2017.15.issue-1/for-2017-0003/for-2017 -0003.pdf.

# 2

# CONCEPTUALIZING SOCIAL CLASS

Definitions matter. This is particularly true for studying how social class is related to political behavior. Different definitions of social class yield different results. Stories in the popular media most frequently use education as their measure of social class, with those who lack a college degree defined as working class and those with a four-year degree classified as middle class. Political scientists are more likely to use income to measure social class, most commonly dividing voters into two or three income groups. In the past, social scientists frequently used occupation to define social class: blue-collar or manual workers were considered working class; white-collar or non-manual workers were middle class. Each of these measures has its advantages and disadvantages. This chapter examines the relative merits of each of the possible measures of social class and explains why social class is expected to affect political behavior. For reasons that I outline below, this study relies on income as the primary measure of social class, especially for the analysis of the most recent elections, although I bring education and occupation into the analysis as well in order to provide a more complete picture. The discussion in this chapter provides a foundation for the remainder of the book, which analyzes how and why social class has been related to voting behavior and how that relationship has changed in recent years.

The basic idea of social class or socio-economic status is that people differ in their social and economic resources, which are important in determining how much control they have over their choices and opportunities in life. Those with greater resources have more ability to choose where they live, where they can send their children to school, what medical care they can receive, and so on. Social theorists sometimes distinguish between social class and socio-economic status, a distinction that in sociology goes back to Weber (1978, 302–307). Social classes are defined as groups of people who share highly similar economic conditions; they are groups that are relatively equal in their occupational situations, income, and wealth.

Socio-economic status, or SES, indicates an individual's rank in the stratification of society and puts emphasis on social prestige as well as on economic resources. Status is more subjective in nature than is social class. Moreover, SES does not necessarily imply that there are groups of people who are relatively equal; one can conceptualize SES as a ranking of people in society from extremely high to extremely low. However, the two terms often are used interchangeably, and that is the approach here. Scholars who use SES usually group people into a few groups, just as those who focus on social class do. In modern American society, social class and SES are highly intertwined, and the differences between the two are unimportant for the concerns of this study, which focuses on political behavior.

## Measuring Social Class

As I indicated above, there are different ways of defining or measuring social class. While there is a general idea of what social class means, there is no consensus among political scientists on how it is best defined or measured. Occupation, education, and income most commonly have been used. Self-identification also has been used. Each of these measures has its merits, which are discussed below.

### *Occupation*

Social class frequently has been defined in terms of occupation. This definition has its roots in the theories of Karl Marx, who conceptualized society as consisting of classes that were defined by their relationship to the means of production and distribution of goods and services. Marx's fundamental distinction was between the bourgeoisie, who owned the means of production and distribution, and the proletariat, who sold their labor to earn a living (Marx and Engels 1959). Max Weber also used this basic distinction, although he made more distinctions among these two groups (Weber 1978, 302–307). For example, those who sold their labor were a very diverse group, ranging from poorly paid laborers to highly paid, middle-class professionals. This suggests that those who are employed are best divided into at least two groups, a working class and a middle class, and that these two groups can be subdivided.

The conceptualization of society as divided into a working class and a middle (and upper) class was continued by more contemporary American sociologists, who also relied heavily on occupation to place individuals into classes. The difference between blue-collar or manual occupations versus white-collar or nonmanual occupations was an important one, but other factors played a role, and most sociologists had a more sophisticated conceptualization than just working class or middle class. One pioneering study divided the residents of a single city into upper, middle, and lower classes, and then divided each of these classes into an upper and lower part (Warner and Lunt 1941). This resulted in six social classes, ranging from upper-upper to lower-lower. Blue-collar workers fell somewhere in the lower class; white collar workers were somewhere in the middle class. The very small upper class was reserved for the extremely wealthy, often those with inherited wealth. Another well-known study of two U.S. cities classified people into seven social classes, ranging from upper-upper down to the very poor (Coleman and Rainwater 1978). About one-half of the people were classified as either middle or upper-middle class; these people held white-collar jobs that ranged from professional and managerial positions down to sales and clerical positions. The working class, which did not include the semi-poor or the poor, con-sisted mostly of those in manual occupations, but poorly paid sales and clerical workers also fell into this category. A more recent study classifies Americans into six social classes: capitalist, upper-middle, middle, working, working poor, and underclass (Gilbert 2011, 13–15). This study includes craftsmen in the middle class and places less-skilled clerical and sales workers in the working class. Classifications of social class based on occupation frequently use the occupation of the head of the household, with retired or disabled individuals categorized by their prior occupation.

In defining social classes in terms of occupation, social scientists have focused on a few key aspects of jobs: pay, skill or education required, degree of autonomy, and working conditions (Beeghley 2008, 103–105). As a generalization, blue-collar jobs pay less and are less secure than white-collar jobs. Nonmanual workers tend to be salaried, while manual workers tend to be paid by the hour, and hourly workers are more likely to be laid off or have their hours reduced. Differences in income and income security produce differences in the resources that affect one's life chances, making this an important factor. White-collar occupations also are assumed to require more education or skill, which typically translates into better pay. Individuals in these occupations usually have more autonomy or freedom from supervision at work. Blue-collar workers often have more rigidly defined tasks at work and are more tightly supervised. Finally, manual occupations often are unpleasant, or at least less desirable: they are physically demanding, dirty, and even dangerous. For these reasons, the distinction between manual and nonmanual workers has commonly been used to create a simple division of people into two classes: working and middle (Alford 1963, 73–79; Hamilton 1972, 152–156).

Of course, these generalizations about manual and nonmanual occupations have many exceptions. There are poorly-paid sales and clerical workers who have monotonous jobs with tight supervision from management. There are well-paid craftsmen who have considerable freedom to do their work as they see fit. The blue-collar versus white-collar division is a crude one that does not capture all of the relevant features of one's occupation. Moreover, this simple dichotomy glos-ses over differences within each class. One could easily divide the middle class into upper and lower groups, depending on occupational prestige and income. The working class could be similarly divided. Also, the very rich are usually placed in the middle class, even though they are truly upper class, simply because there are too few very rich respondents in most surveys to create a separate group for them. One also could consider the very poor to constitute an underclass, rather than being part of the working class, but there is no well-defined point at which a person's income is so low that the person cannot be considered working class. Besides the difficulty of deciding where to draw the line between the lower working class and the very poor, there normally are too few very poor respondents in a survey to allow us to analyze them as a separate group.

In spite of the simplicity of this blue collar/white collar division, it has been used as a measure of social class in much of the past research in political science, and it has been a useful dichotomy (Alford 1963; Hamilton 1972). Overall, it has been a meaningful way of classifying people as working class or middle class. It is not, however, used much in current research because adequate data on occupation are not collected and reported these days in most surveys of political behavior in this country, including the ones that I use in this study. The national exit polls do not ask about occupation. The American National Elections Studies (ANES) surveys of the American electorate are the data on the American electorate that are most widely used in political science and are the data that I rely on in this study. But while the ANES still asks about occupation in its surveys, it no longer reports detailed occupational information on its respondents, something that it once did. The Cooperative Congressional Elections Surveys (CCES) do report occupational information, but there is no information recorded for a sizable number of respondents, and some of the recorded information is too vague to determine the respondent's social class (e.g., sales, musician).

One reason why occupation is not used as much now to measure social class may be that it is becoming more difficult to meaningfully classify people as middle or working class based on their occupation. The movement to a service economy has created a wide variety of white-collar jobs, some of which are clearly upper-middle class, but some of which are working class, even lower working class. Many routine clerical and retail sales jobs are appropriately considered working-class, even though they technically are nonmanual positions. This has been recognized for some time; the Coleman and Rainwater (1978) study discussed earlier put poorly-paid clerical and sales workers in the working class, for example. What has changed is that there are many more such positions in our service economy and that more heads of households are in these positions than used to be the case. In fact, retail sales workers now outnumber all workers involved in construction and manufacturing combined (Teixeira and Rodgers 2000, 17). The simple division of workers into manual or nonmanual may be a less accurate measure of social class today than it once was.

Furthermore, some specific occupations are not easily classified as working class or middle class. Police officers, for example, have traditionally been considered blue-collar workers, and thus working class, but police departments in some cities have made these jobs more professional positions, with an emphasis on hiring college graduates. Musicians and artists are other examples of occupations that are difficult to classify as working or middle class; it probably depends on how successful the individual is. For example, a violinist with the Chicago Symphony Orchestra, where the minimum salary for performers is over $150,000, certainly would be middle class, even upper middle class, but a guitar player who earns a modest living playing in local venues most likely would not be.

To accurately classify occupations as working class or middle class, we probably need reasonably detailed information about the occupation. The Census Bureau, for example, used a three-digit occupational code in 2000, running from 001 (chief executive) to 983 (military, rank not specified), which provides considerable information. The 2010 census used a similar complex code that identified over 500 different occupations. Based on these codes, most individuals can be accurately identified as working or middle class. However, using just the major categories is less reliable. For example, transportation workers are usually classified as blue-collar workers, but this category (the 9000 series in 2010) includes not only bus drivers (code 9120) and truck drivers (code 9130) but also airline pilots (code 9030), a group that certainly is not working class. Another major category is sales workers, which includes cashiers, retail sales workers, insurance agents, and manufacturing representatives. The first two groups are easily classified as working class, but the other two are usually considered middle-class occupations. In fact, the last group includes many well-paid professional positions, such as representatives of pharmaceutical companies. Unfortunately, surveys rarely collect and report such detailed information on the occupation of the respondents these days.

Another complication with using occupation to determine an individual's social class is the widespread participation of women in the workforce. When sociologists were defining social class decades ago, they usually used the occupation of the head of the household, who most often was a man. If both a husband and wife worked, a less common situation even as late as the 1950s or 1960s, it was assumed that the occupation of the husband determined the social class of the household. But as households where both the husband and wife work have become common, we encounter cases where one spouse is in a blue-collar job and the other in a white-collar job, and not just a relatively menial clerical or sales position. Classifying these families as working class or middle class sometimes can be problematic. Where, for example, should we place a married couple where one person is a registered nurse and the other is a carpenter, or where one is a public school teacher and the other is an automobile mechanic?

In sum, occupation probably comes closest to how most people think about social class, even if there is some uncertainty or disagreement over where some occupations should be placed. The images that people generally have of working-class individuals are those in blue-collar jobs or in more routine and poorly-paid white-collar jobs; the images of middle-class people usually are of those in white-collar jobs, particularly ones that are more professional and better paid. Unfortunately, most recent surveys of political behavior lack useful information on occupation, so we are unable to include this measure of social class for much of this study, which focuses on voting behavior in this century. However, we do have occupational information on voters for earlier years, so we are able to bring occupation into the some of the analyses of class and voting in the 20th century, although even here we encounter the problem that the simple division between manual and nonmanual occupations may be a less accurate measure of social class near the end of the century than it was in earlier decades. Given the lack of good occupational data in recent surveys of political behavior, most current research into voting behavior uses either education or income, two factors that are related to occupation, to measure social class; these measures are discussed below.

## *Education*

Stories in the popular media usually use education to define social class. Those with a college degree are considered to be middle class; those without are working class. Although these stories are rarely explicit about the rationale, the underlying justification for using education to identify social class is that education strongly affects the type of occupation that a person holds. Thus, it is not education per se that determines social class. Rather, those with a college degree are presumed to have the knowledge and skills that are required for professional and managerial positions. Those with just a high school diploma most likely will qualify only for manual occupations or for more menial white-collar jobs. Occupation, income, and education are correlated in modern American society, so there is a sound justification for using education to measure social class. Moreover, education is relatively easy to use: the information is almost always collected by surveys of political behavior, and we can easily compare the college educated to the non-college across different surveys. However, using education to define or measure social class, especially by relying on just the college versus no-college distinction, has some serious problems, which are outlined below.

First of all, only about one-third of adults have a four-year college degree, so classifying all of those without a college degree as working class would mean that two-thirds of Americans are working class, an overly broad definition that does not fit with the thinking of most Americans, the majority of whom classify themselves as middle class (Newport 2017). In fact, many people who lack a college degree have occupations that would widely be considered middle class and that pay quite well. Over one-half of those who lack a college degree have some college education, in many cases a two-year associate's degree. These people tend to be better off than those with just a high school diploma, and many of them are quite successful individuals. While most professional positions require a college degree, if not an advanced degree, many people in the business world have middle-class sales or managerial positions even though they did not graduate from college. The same can be said for a number of successful entrepreneurs.

Included in the list of very successful entrepreneurs who lack a college degree are the following individuals, with the company that they founded or co-founded in parentheses: Bill Gates (Microsoft), Steve Jobs and Steve Wozniak (Apple), Mark Zuckerberg and Dustin Moskovitz (Facebook), David Geffen (DreamWorks), Evan Williams (Twitter), Michael Dell (Dell Computers), Theodore Waitt (Gateway Computers), Arash Ferdowsi (Dropbox), David Karp (Tumblr), Larry Ellison (Oracle), David Green (Hobby Lobby), John Mackey (Whole Foods), and David

Neeleman (Jet Blue), plus many others who founded companies that are not quite as well known (Toren 2011). Below this list of all-star businessmen are many other solidly middle-class business owners. A recent survey of small business owners revealed that the majority of them lacked a college degree (Juang 2017). Some of the small businessmen in this survey may have been owners of small shops or self-employed blue-collar workers, and these individuals might not be considered middle-class; but even accounting for these individuals, it is clear that a sizeable number of people who are successful in the business world never graduated from college. They could be successful real estate developers, home builders, restauranteurs, or owners of a variety of other businesses.

It is not just entrepreneurs who can achieve middle-class status without a college degree. Employees can be in this category too. There are a number of positions in the business world that do not require a college degree. Individuals without a degree can and do work their way up to managerial positions in some companies. Some solidly middle-class jobs in sales, such as a real estate agent or a manufacturer's representative, are held by people without a college degree. This was more common in the past then now, as companies today are more likely to look for college graduates to fill professional or managerial positions, but among older voters, it would not be odd to find individuals without a college degree who are or have been successfully employed in the business world. In addition to the business world, there are middle-class people in the arts—e.g., actors, artists, dancers, musicians—who lack a college degree. While it is safe to assume that most individuals with a college degree are middle class in terms of occupation and income, classifying all those without a college degree as working class does not fit the reality of American society.

Another problem with education as a measure of social class is that an individual without a college degree may be married to someone who has a college degree and a professional or managerial job to match. This is particularly likely to occur among older couples, where a college-educated man with a solidly middle-class managerial or professional position may be married to a woman without a degree, a situation that reflects the gender roles and expectations of an earlier era. However, it is the economic situation of the household, not the individual, that determines social class. Using the example above, the non-college spouse would be considered working class if we classify people on the basis of their educational attainment, but this surely would be an inaccurate placement of that individual. A similar problem would occur for a situation where a college-educated woman who is a stay-at-home mother is married to a blue-collar worker who does not have a college degree: should the woman in question be classified as middle class because she has a college degree, even though her husband is clearly working class?

Two more points are worth noting about education. First, among those who have clearly middle-class occupations, education is tied to the specific type of occupation that one has. It is possible to have a successful business career without a college degree, as the discussion above clearly shows, but one cannot be an attorney or a physician, for example, without an advanced degree. Even being a public school teacher almost always requires one to have a four-year degree. These differences in the types of occupations and employers may influence people's political attitudes and behavior. A small businessman without a college degree may be just as middle class, if not more so, than an elementary school teacher, but the difference in the type of occupation held by these two hypothetical individuals may result in differences in their political attitudes and their voting behavior. For that matter, among those with a college degree, there are differences in the type of occupation held by those with an advanced degree compared to those without one, and these differences are related to political attitudes (Pew Research Center 2016). Some evidence that the type of occupation is a relevant factor comes for research by Gelman (2010, 27). He found that professional workers became more Democratic over the past four decades, but managerial and administrative workers became more Republican. The different patterns of change for these two groups exist even though both are equally middle class, probably upper middle class in most cases, so they represent differences between the different types of occupations that middle-class people are in.

Finally, education undoubtedly has its own effect on political behavior, apart from any effect on an individual's income or occupation. Consider two cabinet-makers, both with the same income, but one with a college degree and the other with only a high school diploma. Even though these two individuals are equal in occupation and income, it is likely that they will differ in their political attitudes and behavior because of their different educational experiences. The same principle applies to two business managers who are equal in income and occupational prestige but who differ in educational attainment: the college-educated manager may have different political attitudes than his or her less-educated counterpart simply because of the college experience.

Considerable research has shown that education affects political awareness, interest, and participation, apart from any effects that it has on occupation or income. More education tends to lead to greater political awareness, knowledge, interest, and participation in politics (Conway 2000, 25–29; Delli Carpini and Keeter 1997, 142–199; Milbrath and Goel 1977, 98–102; Rosenstone and Hansen 2003, 135–136). College-educated individuals are more likely to vote, more likely to participate in politics in other ways, more likely to follow politics in the media, more likely to be better informed, and more likely to have a higher sense of political efficacy. Because college-educated voters have higher political awareness and knowledge, they also are more likely to perceive policy differences between political parties, which is an important factor in voting behavior.

Education also influences how individuals think about politics. Those with higher levels of education are more likely to comprehend politics in more complex terms. They are more likely to think in ideological terms and to use an ideological conceptualization to understand specific political actions, events, and policies (Campbell *et al.* 1960, 250–251; Lewis-Beck *et al.* 2008, 280–282). Less-educated individuals find it harder to see connections between different actions, events, and policies. They also are less likely to have ideologically consistent attitudes across different policy areas (Bishop 1976; Pew Research Center 2016). All of this suggests that it is useful to bring education into the analysis even if it is not being used as the primary measure of social class.

## Income

Income is frequently used by political scientists to measure social class. Although income has its limitations as a measure of social class, as will be discussed shortly, it is likely to be better than education as a measure of a voter's true economic situation. As I indicated earlier, social class is commonly conceptualized as encompassing the economic resources that affect one's chances in life. Income affects where people can live, what kind of house they can afford, what schools they can afford to send their children to, and many other aspects of their life chances and opportunities. Furthermore, income is more directly affected by government policy than is education, making it more politically relevant. The taxes one pays are largely affected directly or indirectly by one's income, not by one's education. Government social programs provide benefits that are tied to one's income, not one's education, and this includes both programs that are means tested (e.g., Medicaid) and those that are not (e.g., Social Security).

Income also has the advantage of helping us distinguish between people who are similar in occupation but clearly different in social class. For example, musicians would be middle class or perhaps even upper middle class if they are quite successful, but they probably would be considered working class if they earn only a modest income. The same would be true for individuals in a number of other occupations that display wide variance in income or prestige, even when the individuals in these occupations are equal in education. Such occupational groups include artists, chefs, construction managers, farmers, laboratory technicians, retail proprietors, restaurant owners, and sales representatives, among others.

Although income seems superior to education as a measure of social class, it is not without its problems. The most commonly used income measure, and the one used in this study, is last year's household income. Household income is obviously affected by the number of adults in the household: a two-adult household with an income of, say, $50,000 is not as well-off as a single individual with the same income. To correct for this problem, I adjust household income for marital status. When I dichotomize individuals into higher or lower-income groups, I do this by classifying them on the basis of whether they are above or below the median income for their marital status. For example, married individuals are classified as higher income if they have a household income that is above the median household income for a married couple; single people are high if they are above the median for single people. This is not a perfect solution, to be sure. For example, a married couple with an income equal to the median income for all married people may truly be economically better off than a single person whose income is equal to the median income for all single people. Nevertheless, it does in large part correct for the problem, and it certainly is better than using no correction whatsoever.

Income also is related to age. Young people in particular may have a low income because they are still pursuing their education or are in the early stages of their careers, but their economic prospects may be bright. Their income, especially last year's household income, often does not reflect their true economic situation. Most college or graduate students are unlikely to think of themselves as working class even if they have a low income, and this is especially true if their parents are middle class. In fact, very young adults with lower household incomes may actually be more likely to be middle class than those with higher incomes, simply because those who go directly into the labor force after high school are likely to be earning more than those who choose to go to college. In order to correct for this problem, the analysis in this study often will focus on individuals who are at least 30 years of age, on the assumption that these individuals are highly likely to have finished their education and started their career. Of course, there still are likely to be some life-cycle effects present among those over 30: those in their 50s probably are in their peak earning years, while those in their 30s probably are not. However, analyzing only those who are at least 30 does remove the biggest distortion that age has on income as a measure of social class.

It should be clear that whenever I exclude voters who are less than 30 years old in subsequent analyses that focus on the relationship between social class and voting behavior, it is only because I feel that it is difficult to assess social class for young voters. They are not excluded because I think that social class is unimportant for the political behavior of young people. It most likely is important. The problem simply is that it is difficult to measure social class for those who have not completed their education or have not really begun their career, at least if we are using the survey data that are available to us. Including young people in an analysis of the relationship between income and voting behavior is particularly problematic for recent elections because young voters are now more Democratic than older voters, something that was not necessarily true in earlier decades. Including them in an analysis of recent elections would be including a set of voters who are likely to be both Democratic and low in income, but not really working class despite their low income. The result would be to distort the true relationship between social class and voting behavior.

Even with adjustments for marital status and age, income is not a perfect measure of social class. For one thing, it ignores differences in the cost of living. For example, a married couple with an $70,000 income probably is economically much better off if they live in a small town than if they live in a major urban area. That income undoubtedly allows for a nice middle-class life in rural North Carolina, for example, but not so for San Francisco. Differences in wealth also are ignored, as is the possibility that last year's household income was atypically large or small. Despite these deficiencies, the adjusted household income that is used in this study seems to me to be the best measure of social class, given the data that we have for recent years, and it therefore is the one that I rely on most heavily in my analysis.

Among scholars who use income as their measure of social class, there is disagreement on what household income level constitutes working or middle-class status. Bartels (2008) defines those in the bottom one-third of the income distribution as working class. On the other hand, Williams (2017) classifies those in the middle third as working class, with those in the bottom third being poor and those in the top third as rich or elite. My choice is to use median income to distinguish working-class and middle-class voters, adjusting for marital status as explained above. There is no obvious income line to make this division, but I think that a relatively even division is as defensible as any other. It certainly seems better than using the bottom income tercile, which would mean that only one-third of the electorate would be working class; in reality, well over one-third of Americans call themselves working class (Newport 2017). And it seems superior to defining all those without a college degree as working class, which would put two-thirds of the electorate in the working class. Thus, in this study, I will use the terms lower-income (meaning below average) and working class synonymously, and the same for higher-income and middle-class. Of course, it undoubtedly is true that some people with above-average incomes might be considered working class by most people because of their occupation, just as some lower-income people might be widely regarded as middle class. For example, well-paid blue-collar workers may have above-average household incomes, particularly if their spouses are employed, yet they may consider themselves as working class, and most other people may also see them that way. Income, even adjusted as I do, is not a perfect measure of one's social class, a point that is important to keep in mind.

## Social Class Identification

Another way of measuring social class is to ask individuals how they classify themselves. This approach was pioneered by Centers (1949), who asked people whether they considered themselves to be upper, middle, working, or lower class. Nearly everyone was willing to place themselves into one of these four categories, and nearly 95 percent chose either the middle or the working class in 1945. There was a strong connection between class identification and occupation: 70 percent of white-collar workers said that they were middle class, and over 75 percent of blue-collar workers labeled themselves as working class. More recent work by Jackman and Jackman (1983) found similar patterns. They gave individuals five choices: poor, working, middle, upper-middle, and upper class; about 50 percent of their respondents identified as middle or upper-middle class, and almost 40 percent said that they were working class. They also found that subjective class identification was related to income, education, and occupation, although the relationship was far from perfect.

Allowing people to identify what social class they belonged in might seem to be a desirable approach. As we can see from the above discussion, occupation, education, and income all can be inaccurate indicators of a person's social class. People know their own economic situation better than do researchers, so they might be better able to take into account all of the factors that determines one's social class, which I defined at the start of this chapter as referring to the economic and social resources that affect the ability that people have to control their life choices. In fact, the authors of the seminal work in voting behavior, *The American Voter*, found that subjective class identification was a better predictor of political attitudes than was occupation (Campbell *et al.* 1960; 333–350), although among the objective measures of social class, occupation was a better predictor than was income or education.

However, using subjective class identification to measure social class has some problems. How people classify themselves reflects not only their objective economic situation but also their political and social attitudes. Among people who are all equally working class in their objective characteristics, such as occupation and income, those who call themselves working class will differ in their attitudes from those who call themselves middle class. The same is true for middle-class people. Thus, subjective class identification may be a good predictor of the vote in part because it incorporates political attitudes that directly affect voting. To the extent that subjective and objective measures of social class differ, the objective measures are closer to how most people define social class. For example, Centers (1949, 98–99) asked people to identify the characteristics of middle and working-class individuals, and almost all of the respondents cited various aspects of income, occupation, or education—all objective features. In the eyes of most people, individuals who are blue-collar workers with below-average incomes are not middle class even if they say that they are. While class identification is a useful variable for studying political behavior, it is not the best measure of social class as this concept is defined in this study.

## *Summary*

There is no consensus among political scientists about how social class is best measured. Income, occupation, education, and class identification all have been used. Each measure has certain strengths and weaknesses. Occupation may most closely correspond to how most people identify social class, but such data are lacking in recent surveys of the American electorate. My assessment is that income is the best measure of social class that we have available for recent survey data, and I have tried to present that argument above. Furthermore, income is a better measure if it is adjusted for marital status, which I do in this study. But even when adjusted, income is not a perfect measure of social class, so I often look at other measures as well to see if similar patterns are present.

Given that all of the measures discussed above have their limitations, one strategy might be to use an index of the above variables to measure social class. For example, Eulau (1962) combined occupation, income, and education into an overall objective measure of social class, which he dichotomized into working and middle class. Similarly, Francia and Bigelow (2010) used education and income to classify people as working class or middle class. I opted against such an approach for several reasons. First, adequate occupational data are not present in the most recent surveys, so it is not possible to use all three of the above indicators for the time period that this study focuses on. It would be possible to combine education and income into an overall measure of social class, but that method has two limitations. One is that it was easier to attain middle-class status without a college degree years ago than it was now, which makes using such an index for comparisons over a long period of time somewhat questionable. The other limitation is that education may have its own effects on political attitudes and behavior, separate from any effects on social class, a possibility that is discussed above.

Income is strongly related to education and class identification. Table 2.1 shows how lower and higher-income individuals differ in education and class identification. I combined the 2012 and 2016 ANES studies to create a large number of cases, and I adjusted household income for the number of adults in the household, using the method that I described earlier in this chapter: individuals are classified as high or low income based on whether they are above or below the median household income level for people with their marital status. Only adults over 30 years of age are included in this analysis because it is difficult to measure social class for young people, as I discussed above. To simplify the presentation, I divided education into just those with a college degree and those without, which is the distinction commonly used by analysts, and I classified the small number of individuals who said that they were upper or lower class as middle or working class, respectively. Unfortunately, these surveys do not have measures of occupation, so we cannot include that in this analysis, but data from earlier years indicate that income and occupation also are strongly related.

Whether we look at all adults or just at white adults, the results are similar. First of all, there is a strong but far from perfect relationship between income and class identification. A majority of those with low income consider themselves working class, but a sizable minority classify themselves as middle class. This is not surprising, given the high level of identification with the middle class among

**TABLE 2.1** Education and Social Class Identification by Income, 2012–2016

|  | Income Level | |
| --- | --- | --- |
|  | Low Income | High Income |
| *All adults, 30+ years old* | | |
| % with college degree | 18.5 | 50.8 |
| % identifying as working class | 58.1 | 27.5 |
| *White adults, 30+ years old* | | |
| % with college degree | 21.0 | 51.7 |
| % identifying as working class | 54.0 | 24.0 |

Source: ANES surveys, 2012–2016.

Americans that was discussed above. Higher-income people generally call themselves middle class, but about one-fourth do not. The relationship between income and education also is quite interesting. Those with a low income are unlikely to have a college degree: only about one-fifth do. But higher-income individuals are almost as likely to not have a degree as to have one. This supports my earlier discussion of how many people have been able to attain middle-class status without having a college degree.

## Reasons for Class Differences in Partisan Choice

A basic feature of American electoral politics for many years has been a connection between social class and partisan choice. Democrats were commonly identified as the party that favored the working class; Republicans were the party of business and upper-income groups. These images had their basis in reality. As we shall see in the next chapter, working-class voters have been disproportionately Democratic in their voting for decades after the New Deal realignment of the 1930s. This leads to the question of why this was so. Why did the Democratic Party appeal more to the working class and the Republican Party more to the middle class? Economic interests are usually seen as fundamental to this relationship between class and party, both in the U.S. and in other industrial democracies (Alford 1963, 34–40; Lipset 1960, 243–249). Working-class and middle-class voters differ in their economic interests in a way that makes parties of the left more attractive to working-class voters. In modern American politics, there are four economic policy areas that have contributed to class differences in partisan choice: management of the economy, particularly in terms of fighting inflation and unemployment; labor-management relations issues, particularly involving labor unions; social welfare and income security programs; and taxation policy.

When it comes to managing the economy, everyone favors a healthy economy, meaning that there is, among other things, low unemployment and low inflation. But there is considerable disagreement over which goal should take priority. Working-class and lower-income voters favor fiscal and monetary policies that are aimed more at reducing unemployment and keeping it low, even if that means accepting more inflation (Hibbs 1987, 138–141). Middle-class and upper-income voters put their emphasis on keeping inflation low, even at the expense of higher unemployment. In terms of general economic interests, this makes sense. Working-class individuals usually have less job security; they are more subject to being laid off than are middle-class people (Goldthorpe and McKnight 2006). Lower-income individuals usually are hurt more by a temporary loss of income, something that higher-income people can more easily weather. And lower-income people are more likely to be borrowers rather than lenders, so they are less affected by higher inflation, which might even make their loans easier to pay off. Higher-income people are more likely to be concerned about inflation reducing the real value of their savings or investments.

Besides fiscal and monetary policies, trade policies are likely to be viewed as affecting unemployment and inflation. Blue-collar workers in the manufacturing sector often are concerned about cheaper imported goods reducing employment in their area of manufacturing. White-collar workers have less to fear from foreign trade, and they may see cheaper foreign goods as economically beneficial. Of course, not all blue-collar workers are potentially threatened by imported goods: construction and transportation workers generally would not be, for example. Concerns about foreign trade causing a loss of manufacturing jobs in this country have been present for decades, but they seem to have increased in intensity in this century, even though there is widespread agreement among economists that trade is good for the economy (Binder 2019).

Class differences have been especially sharp when it comes to labor-management relations. Historically, blue-collar workers have been more supportive of labor unions, favoring laws that make it easier for workers to form a union and engage in collective bargaining. The history of labor unions in this country demonstrates that unionizing and engaging in collective bargaining, including striking, benefited blue-collar workers both during the Great Depression and in the post-World War II affluence of the 1940s and 1950s (Lichtenstein 2002, 20–97). Although unionization was largely a blue-collar phenomenon earlier in the 20th century, white-collar workers have become an increasing share of the unionized labor force (Aronowitz 1998, 139–158; Asher *et al.* 2001, 28–31). Public sector workers, both white and blue collar, also have increased their desire to form unions (Aronowitz 1998, 59–85). In addition to government policies regarding labor unions, working-class individuals favor more government restrictions on what employers can do in other areas of employment; they are more likely to favor stronger overtime policies and tougher occupational safety regulations, for example. In general, working-class people have felt that they need collective bargaining and governmental regulations to create better working conditions. There are some groups of white-collar workers, such as public school teachers, who might share these sentiments, but support for unions and for government regulation of the working environment is lower overall in the middle class, especially, of course, among those who are business owners or self-employed.

Social welfare and income security programs are another area where the economic interests of voters tend to divide along class lines. A higher minimum wage primarily benefits poorly-paid workers. More generous unemployment benefits are valued more by blue-collar workers since they are more likely to be laid off. Lower-income individuals generally benefit from more extensive social welfare programs, which tend to redistribute income downward. Means-tested social welfare programs, such as food stamps or Medicaid, obviously provide direct benefits to lower-income individuals, but so do programs that are not means-tested, such as Social Security or Medicare. When it comes to Social Security, for example, lower-income individuals tend to receive higher payments relative to their pre-retirement income than do upper-income individuals, and Social Security payments generally are a higher percentage of the retirement income of working-class people (Peters 2013, 316–317).

Finally, taxation policies obviously affect income groups differently. Income tax rates can be more or less progressive, and a more progressive income tax system clearly is more beneficial to those with a lower income. Income from investments can be taxed at a lower rate than income from salary or wages, a policy that obviously favors people who have substantial income from investments, something most working-class people do not. Sales taxes tend to be regressive; lower-income individuals spend a higher percentage of their income on items that are subject to a sales tax. Thus, tax policies can be evaluated in terms of where the tax burden is placed (Peters 1991, 167–170).

## Party Differences on Economic Issues

On all of the above economic matters, Democrats and Republicans have consistently disagreed. A comparison of the 2016 platforms of both parties is revealing, both in specific policy proposals and in what is emphasized. The Democratic Party platform begins with an emphasis on economic inequality. After pointing out how well the country recovered during the Obama administration from the Great Recession, the platform states that too many Americans have been left behind. To combat this situation, Democrats proposed to increase the minimum wage to $15.00 per hour and to do everything that can be done to build a full-employment economy. Regarding labor-management relations, the platform is strongly pro-union; it calls for abolishing so-called "right to work" laws and other measures that make it more difficult for unions to organize workers. Democrats proposed expanding Social Security and raising Social Security taxes on those earning over $250,000 per year in order to ensure that future benefits will be able to be paid. Finally, the platform calls for making wealthy Americans pay their fair share of taxes (Democratic Party 2016).

The 2016 Republican Party platform is a sharp contrast to the Democratic one. The Republican platform puts less emphasis on reducing economic inequality, especially through government programs, and more emphasis on achieving economic growth. Republicans argue that private investment is the key driver of economic growth and job creation. Their formula for economic growth is to encourage private investment through tax policies that reward such investment, including reducing the tax rate on corporations. The Republican platform also takes an entirely different position on unions, arguing for more worker freedom and for weaker regulations on employers in order to achieve greater economic growth. Regarding Social Security, the Republican platform pledges to preserve it, but it opposes tax increases as a method for doing so. For Medicare, the platform again promises to protect it, but it proposes doing so by raising the age of eligibility for younger voters and for giving them a fixed amount to purchase health insurance, rather than the direct cost coverage currently offered (Republican Party 2016).

The above party difference in economic and social welfare policies are not recent developments. They have been there for years. For example, if we look back at the party platforms from 1976, we find similar patterns, even though the political and economic circumstances were quite different forty years earlier. The 1976 Democratic Party platform begins with an emphasis on full employment, stating that the party is committed to the right of all Americans to be able to find a job with living wages. To achieve full employment, the platform argues for federal anti-recession programs that use public works projects, public employment, and grants to state and local governments to combat rising unemployment. The platform further argues that there has been a shift in the tax burden from the rich to the working people, a shift that should be reversed. There is a particularly strong pro-union section in the platform that calls for raising the pay standard for overtime work and for repealing the section of the Taft-Hartley Act that permits states to have open-shop laws. Democrats also recommended raising the minimum wage and indexing it to inflation. Finally, Democrats argued that the county needs a national health insurance system with universal coverage (Democratic Party 1976).

As was true in 2016, the 1976 Republican Party platform differs from its Democratic counterpart on these major economic policies. For one thing, there is little mention of unemployment. The platform begins by stating that inflation is the number one destroyer of jobs, that fighting inflation requires limiting government spending, and that the Democratic proposals for federal full employment programs ultimately destroy more jobs than they create. When it comes to health care, the Republican platform unequivocally opposes national health insurance. On labor-management relations, Republicans oppose strikes by public employees and support retaining the provision in the Taft-Hartley Act that permits states to have open-shop laws. On some issues where the Democratic platform takes a clear stance, such as raising the minimum wage or placing a higher share of the tax burden on wealthier Americans, the Republican platform is silent or ambiguous (Republican Party 1976).

Party platforms are not just idle promises. They reflect the policies pursued by Democratic and Republican administrations. The differences in the 2016 party platforms correspond to differences between the policies pursued by the two parties during the administrations of President Barack Obama and President Donald Trump, at least for Trump's first two years in office. During the first year of the Obama administration, Democrats responded to the Great Recession with a $800 billion stimulus bill, a bill that was criticized by Republicans as having far too much government spending (Ponder 2016, 227). Republicans favored stimulating the economy through tax cuts, not government spending, and they claimed that Democratic economic policies would lead to increased inflation. After Trump was elected president, Republicans were able to enact a large tax cut, which was widely criticized by the Democrats as being too favorable to the wealthy (Shear and Tackett 2017). The Trump administration also proposed substantial reductions of government regulation of business, particularly regarding the environment, arguing that removing these restrictions would promote economic growth (Lipton and Ivory 2017).

Differences in social welfare policies are equally visible. Obama campaigned in 2008 on the need for a national health care law, which Democrats were able to enact in 2010; Obamacare, as it was commonly called, probably was the signature achievement of his presidency, and it was one that was bitterly opposed by Republicans in Congress, who pledged to repeal it when in power (Rom 2012). While the GOP failed to fulfill its promise to repeal Obamacare after the 2016 election, even though they controlled both Congress and the White House, Republicans did weaken the law in several ways, which made it less effective than it otherwise would have been (Bacon 2018). Reflecting the concern with economic inequality in the Democratic platform, President Obama called for an increase in the minimum wage to $10.10 per hour in his second term, but by that time the GOP controlled Congress and was unreceptive to his proposal. President Trump made no such proposal to increase the minimum wage during his first two years in office, which was consistent with the Republican Party platform.

The Obama administration favored policies that would have made it easier for unions to organize, but congressional Republicans were able to prevent passage of his major legislative proposal, the Employee Free Choice Act (Francia 2010). President Obama also attempted to implement regulations to greatly expand the number of employees who would qualify for overtime pay, a policy championed by unions and opposed by many business groups, but this proposed change was blocked by the federal courts; the Trump administration subsequently declined to appeal the ruling, instead proposing a more modest increase in the number eligible for overtime (Wiessner 2019). The Obama administration was more successful in some other attempts to implement policies favored by labor unions. For example, the National Labor Relations Board issued rules that made it easier for unions to organize. This changed when President Trump took office: he appointed two individuals to the NLRB who were considered to be more pro-business, which resulted in changes in some of the NLRB rules (Johnson 2018).

Just as the 2016 party platforms reflect actual differences in the policies pursued during the Obama and Trump administrations, so do the 1976 platforms indicate differences in the policies of Presidents Jimmy Carter and Ronald Reagan. After winning the 1976 election, President Carter was faced with rising unemployment and a decade-long history of problems with inflation. Carter and congressional Democrats attempted to deal with both, but the priority was on combatting unemployment through both fiscal and monetary measures (Stein 1994, 218). When Reagan assumed office in 1981, the country was facing very high levels of unemployment and inflation; President Reagan put his emphasis on reducing inflation, although he broke with traditional conservative thinking by arguing that there was no necessary trade-off between fighting inflation and fighting unemployment. A centerpiece of Reagan's economic proposal was a large tax cut, which Reagan argued would generate enough economic activity to yield the same total tax revenue even with the lower tax rates, an argument that was part of Reagan's "supply side" economic approach.

Labor-management relations were an area where the Carter and Reagan administrations differed greatly. During Carter's administration, Democrats hoped to enact their proposed Labor Reform Act, a major legislative goal of organized labor. But even though Democrats controlled both houses of Congress, Senate Republicans were able to use the filibuster to prevent passage of the bill. The Reagan administration worked to weaken the power of unions. One of the most visible acts of President Reagan during his first term was his successful attempt to break the strike by the Air Traffic Controllers' union, an action that weakened the power of labor unions more generally (McCartin 2011).

Social welfare policies also differed from the Carter to the Reagan administration. President Reagan argued that federal social welfare expenditures needed to be lowered because the programs were wasteful and inefficient, ultimately hurt the poor by creating dependency on the programs, reduced incentives to work, and were more effectively run at the state level (Stein 1994, 280–281). Following this philosophy, Reagan proposed substantial cuts in Social Security in his first budget, an effort that congressional Democrats were able to stymie. In 1983, the Reagan administration, with bipartisan support in Congress, was able to enact scheduled increases in the eligible retirement age, so that it eventually would reach the age of 67 (Weaver 1985). The Reagan administration also tightened the eligibility requirements for Social Security disability payments, which initially resulted in nearly one-half million people losing their benefits; once again, congressional opposition prevented these changes from having their full intended effect (Weaver 1985). Another Reagan administration proposal would have shifted the federal food stamps program to the states; this too received a cool reception in Congress.

## Conclusions

The above discussion shows that working-class and middle-class voters generally have different economic interests. Working-class voters should be attracted to the Democratic Party because of its greater emphasis on keeping unemployment low, its stronger support for labor unions, its more liberal social welfare policy proposals, and its desire for a more progressive tax system. Middle-class voters should prefer the Republican Party because of its greater emphasis on fighting inflation, its weaker support for labor unions, its more conservative social welfare policy proposals, and its desire for a less progressive tax system. However, we must remember that what matters is how voters perceive their economic interests, and they may see their economic interests in a different light. Moreover, people favor economic policies that they think are fair, even if they do not see the policies as in their narrow economic self-interest. Finally, people vote on more than just economic issues. All of these are important points to keep in mind as we examine how and why social class affects partisan choice.

# References

Alford, Robert R. 1963. *Party and Society: The Anglo-American Democracies*. Chicago: Rand McNally.

Aronowitz, Stanley. 1998. *From the Ashes of the Old: American Labor and America's Future*. Boston: Houghton Mifflin.

Asher, Herbert R., Eric S. Heberlig, Randall B. Ripley, and Karen Snyder. 2001. *American Labor Unions in the Electoral Arena*. Lanham, MD: Roman and Littlefield.

Bacon, Perry. 2018. "Republicans Killed Much of Obamacare Without Repealing It." *FiveThirtyEight*, December 18. https://fivethirtyeight.com/features/republicans-killed-much-of-obamacare-without-repealing-it/.

Bartels, Larry M. 2008. *Unequal Democracy: The Political Economy of the New Gilded Age*. Princeton, NJ: Princeton University Press.

Beeghley, Leonard. 2008. *The Social Stratification of the United States*. 5th edition. Boston: Pearson.

Binder, Alan S. 2019. "The Free-Trade Paradox: The Bad Politics of a Good Idea." *Foreign Affairs* 98(1): 119–128.

Bishop, George F. 1976. "The Effect of Education on Ideological Consistency." *Public Opinion Quarterly* 40(3): 337–348.

Campbell, Angus, Philip E. Converse, Warren E. Miller, and Donald E. Stokes. 1960. *The American Voter*. New York: John Wiley & Sons.

Centers, Richard. 1949. *The Psychology of Social Classes: A Study of Class Consciousness*. Princeton, NJ: Princeton University Press.

Coleman, Richard P., and Lee Rainwater. 1978. *Social Standing in America: New Dimensions of Social Class*. New York: Basic Books.

Conway, M. Margaret. 2000. *Political Participation in the United States*. 3rd edition. Washington, DC: CQ Press.

Delli Carpini, Michael X., and Scott Keeter. 1997. *What Americans Know about Politics and Why It Matters*. New Haven, CT: Yale University Press.

Democratic Party. 1976. "1976 Democratic Party Platform." *The American Presidency Project*. www.presidency.ucsb.edu/documents/1976-democratic-party-platform.

Democratic Party. 2016. "2016 Democratic Party Platform." *The American Presidency Project*. www.presidency.ucsb.edu/documents/2016-democratic-party-platform.

Eulau, Heinz. 1962. *Class and Party in the Eisenhower Years*. New York: The Free Press of Glencoe.

Francia, Peter L. 2010. "Assessing the Labor-Democratic Party Alliance: A One-Sided Relationship?." *Polity* 42(3): 293–303.

Francia, Peter L., and Nathan S. Bigelow. 2010. "What's the Matter with the White Working Class? The Effects of Union Membership in the 2004 Presidential Election." *Presidential Studies Quarterly* 40(1): 140–158.

Gelman, Andrew. 2010. *Red State, Blue State, Rich State, Poor State: Why Americans Vote the Way They Do*. Expanded edition. Princeton, NJ: Princeton University Press.

Gilbert, Dennis. 2011. *The American Class Structure in an Age of Growing Inequality*. 8th edition. Los Angeles: Sage.

Goldthorpe, John H., and Abigail McKnight. 2006. "The Economic Basis of Social Class." In *Mobility and Inequality: Frontiers of Research in Sociology and Economics*, eds Stephen L. Morgan, David B. Grusky, and Gary S. Fields, 109–136. Stanford, CA: Stanford University Press.

Hamilton, Richard F. 1972. *Class and Politics in the United States*. New York: John Wiley & Sons.

Hibbs, Douglas A., Jr. 1987. *The American Political Economy: Macroeconomics and Electoral Politics.* Cambridge, MA: Harvard University Press.

Jackman, Mary R., and Robert W. Jackman. 1983. *Class Consciousness in the United States.* Berkeley: University of California Press.

Johnson, Katie. 2018. "Under Trump, Labor Protections Stripped Away." *Boston Globe*, September 3. www.bostonglobe.com/business/2018/09/02/under-trump-labor-protec tions-stripped-away/jbr9aClCWyca8SbQCdtKJP/story.html.

Juang, Mike. 2017. "A Secret Many Small-business Owners Share with Mark Zuckerberg." *CNBC.com*, July 19. www.cnbc.com/2017/07/19/survey-shows-majority-of-business-own ers-lack-college-degree.html.

Lewis-Beck, Michael S., William G. Jacoby, Helmut Norpoth, and Herbert F. Weisberg. 2008. *The American Voter Revisited.* Ann Arbor: University of Michigan Press.

Lichtenstein, Nelson. 2002. *State of the Union: A Century of American Labor.* Revised edition. Princeton, NJ: Princeton University Press.

Lipset, Seymour Martin. 1960. *Political Man: The Social Bases of Politics.* New York: Doubleday.

Lipton, Eric, and Danielle Ivory. 2017. "Trump Says His Regulatory Rollback Already Is the 'Most Far-Reaching'." *New York Times*, December 14.

Marx, Karl, and Friedrich Engels. 1959(1848). "Manifesto of the Communist Party." In *Basic Writings on Politics and Philosophy*, ed. Lewis S. Feuer, 1–41. New York: Anchor Books.

McCartin, Joseph A. 2011. "The Strike That Busted Unions." *New York Times*, August 2.

Milbrath, Lester W., and M. L. Goel. 1977. *Political Participation.* 2nd edition. Chicago: Rand McNally.

Newport, Frank. 2017. "Middle-Class Identification in U.S. at Pre-Recession Levels." *Gallup*, June 21. https://news.gallup.com/poll/212660/middle-class-identification-pre-recession-le vels.aspx.

Peters, B. Guy. 1991. *The Politics of Taxation: A Comparative Perspective.* Cambridge, MA: Blackwell.

Peters, B. Guy. 2013. *American Public Policy: Promise and Performance.* 9th edition. Los Angeles: CQ Press.

Pew Research Center. 2016. "Adults with Postgraduate Experience Most Likely to Have Consistently Liberal Political Values." April 26. www.people-press.org/2016/04/26/a -wider-ideological-gap-between-more-and-less-educated-adults/.

Ponder, Daniel E. 2016. "Back From the Brink: Obama's Economic Record." In *Debating the Obama Presidency*, ed. Steven E. Schier, 221–246. Lanham, MD: Roman and Littlefield.

Republican Party. 1976. "Republican Party Platform of 1976." *The American Presidency Project.* www.presidency.ucsb.edu/documents/republican-party-platform-1976.

Republican Party. 2016. "2016 Republican Party Platform." *The American Presidency Pro- ject.* www.presidency.ucsb.edu/documents/2016-republican-party-platform.

Rom, Mark Carl. 2012. "President Obama's Health Care Reform: The Inevitable Impossible." In *The Obama Presidency: Change and Continuity*, eds Andrew J. Dowdle, Dirk C. van Raemdonck, and Robeert Maranto, 149–161. New York: Routledge.

Rosenstone, Steven J., and John Mark Hansen. 2003. *Mobilization, Participation, and Democracy in America.* New York: Longman.

Shear, Michael D., and Michael Tackett. 2017. "With Tax Overhaul, Trump Fulfills a Campaign Promise and Flexes Republican Muscle." *New York Times*, December 20.

Stein, Herbert. 1994. *Presidential Economics: The Making of Economic Policy From Roosevelt to Clinton.* 3rd revised edition. Washington, DC: American Enterprise Institute.

Teixeira, Ruy, and Joel Rodgers. 2000. *America's Forgotten Majority: Why the White Working Class Still Matters*. New York: Basic Books.

Toren, Matthew. 2011. "Top Entrepreneurs Who Made Millions Without a College Degree." *Business Insider*, January 19. www.businessinsider.com/top-100-entrepreneurs-who-made-millions-without-a-college-degree-2011-1.

Warner, W. Lloyd, and Paul S. Lunt. 1941. *The Social Life of a Modern Community*. New Haven, CT: Yale University Press.

Weaver, R. Kent. 1985. "Controlling Entitlements." In *The New Direction in American Politics*, eds John E. Chubb and Paul E. Peterson, 307–342. Washington, DC: The Brookings Institution.

Weber, Max. 1978 (1922). *Economy and Society: An Outline of Interpretive Sociology*, eds Guenther Roth and Claus Wittich. Berkeley: University of California Press.

Wiessner, Daniel. 2019. "Trump Administration Proposes Overtime Pay Expansion." *Reuters*, March 7. www.reuters.com/article/us-usa-overtime/trump-administration-proposes-overtime-pay-expansion-idUSKCN1QO2UW.

Williams, Joan C. 2017. *White Working Class: Overcoming Class Cluelessness in America*. Boston, MA: Harvard Business Review Press.

# 3

# CLASS AND VOTING IN MODERN AMERICAN POLITICS

In 1976, Jimmy Carter won the presidential election with 51 percent of the two-party vote. He was the last Democratic presidential candidate to successfully hold together the old Democratic New Deal coalition of the South plus northern blue-collar workers and ethnic groups. Carter's winning Electoral College coalition consisted of every southern state save Virginia, plus a number of northeastern and midwestern industrial states. He won just one western state: Hawaii. In winning a slim majority of the popular vote, Carter captured 47 percent of the vote among whites. Among whites, he did well among ethnic groups and working-class voters, winning 55 percent of the vote from Catholics and 60 percent from blue-collar workers.[1]

Carter's Electoral College coalition was similar to the one assembled by John F. Kennedy in 1960, who also won a slim majority of the two-party vote. Of the 23 states carried by Carter, 18 of them were states won by Kennedy, who carried 25 states overall. The core elements of the New Deal coalition were critical to the presidential victories of both Kennedy and Carter, although there were differences between Kennedy's and Carter's electoral support. Carter won in the South by winning a high share of the votes from blacks, who were a significant share of the electorate. In 1960, blacks were largely disenfranchised in the South. Also, while Carter did relatively well among Catholics, Kennedy, who was positioned to be the first Catholic to be elected president, did extraordinarily well. When it comes to social class and voting, however, there is a similar pattern: both Kennedy and Carter won a majority of the votes of white working-class voters.

In 2016, Hillary Clinton also won 51 percent of the popular vote in the presidential election, but unlike Carter, she was unable to translate her popular vote victory into an Electoral College victory. Although Clinton received almost the same percentage of the popular vote as Carter did, the sources of her vote were quite different. A look at the Electoral College map shows quite different geographical patterns for these two elections. Clinton did poorly in the South, winning only Virginia, which coincidentally was the sole southern state that did not vote for Carter; on the other hand, she did much better than Carter in the West. Of the 20 states carried by Clinton in 2016, only seven were also won by Carter in 1976. The demographic pattern of support also was quite different for Clinton and Carter. Clinton won just 42 percent of the white vote, and among whites, she won only 40 percent of the Catholic vote and even less from the working class.[2] There was very little of the old Democratic New Deal coalition present in 2016. In particular, the old relationship between social class and voting behavior was now inverted.

This comparison of the 1976 and 2016 presidential elections illustrates three major changes in voting patterns that have taken place over the past several decades. First, the South has moved from being a region that was heavily Democratic, especially in congressional and state elections, to a region where Republicans are the majority party. That change already has been analyzed quite thoroughly by many scholars, and it is not one that is the focus of this study. Second, white voters have moved toward the Republican Party, especially in the South. That shift in voting patterns also has been the subject of considerable research, and it too is not the focus of this study. Third, among white voters, there has been a change in the relationship between social class and voting: working-class or lower-SES voters are no longer disproportionately Democratic. That change is the focus of this study. Changes in the relationship between partisan choice and region, race, or other factors are examined only insofar as they help to explain the changes in the impact of social class on voting behavior.

Table 3.1 compares the vote for Carter and Clinton among white major-party voters for several measures of social class or socioeconomic status (SES). Occupational data are not available for 2016, so we unfortunately cannot make that comparison to 1976, but data for income, education, and social class identification

**TABLE 3.1** Social Class and Presidential Voting, 1976 and 2016

|  | Presidential Candidate | |
|---|---|---|
|  | *Carter 1976* | *Clinton 2016* |
| % of the national two-party vote | 51.1 | 51.1 |
| % of the two-party vote among whites | 46.6 | 42.3 |
| White blue-collar workers | 59.5 | n.a. |
| Whites with below average incomes | 52.9 | 37.1 |
| Whites with only a high school educ. | 51.3 | 35.2 |
| Whites who identify as working class | 55.3 | 37.1 |

Source: The percent of the national two-party vote comes from the actual election results. The remaining figures were calculated from the ANES surveys of 1976 and 2016.

are available for both years. There is a sharp contrast in the vote of working-class people, however measured, between these two years. Carter won 47 percent of the vote of whites overall, but he won a majority of the votes of working-class individuals, regardless of which indicator we look at. Clinton won 42 percent of the white vote, but she only received between 35 and 37 percent of the vote of working-class whites, depending on the measure used. As I argued in the previous chapter, income probably is the best measure of social class that we have available now, especially given the lack of occupational information in recent surveys of voting behavior, but these figures indicate that other indicators of social class or SES produce similar results.

Clearly, much has changed in the 40 years from Carter's victory in 1976 to Clinton's loss in 2016. White working-class voters are now more Republican than their middle-class counterparts. Of course, one could also say that white middle-class people are relatively more Democratic. Regardless of how we state it, class differences in voting have changed. This tendency began before Donald Trump. In 2012, for example, Mitt Romney did better among white working-class voters, although not to the extent that Trump did in 2016. To better understand these changes in the relationship between social class and voting behavior, it will be useful to examine some historical background. We can begin with a brief historical sketch of how sharp class cleavages were established in American politics during the 1930s and 1940s, then look at this relationship in the last half of the 20th century, and finally focus on the developments in this century. As we shall see, there have been changes all along, but it is not until the 21st century that the white working class has become disproportionately Republican, relative to the white middle class.

## The New Deal Realignment

The New Deal realignment of the 1930s was one of the most critical electoral realignments in this country. A critical realignment of the electorate refers to a relative rapid, fundamental, and lasting change in the partisan loyalties of voters (Burnham 1970; Clubb, Flanigan, and Zingale 1980; Sundquist 1983). There is scholarly disagreement over exactly what constitutes a realignment, but no one disputes the fact that in the 1930s there were sweeping changes in the American electorate (Mayhew 2002; Sundquist 1983, 198–239). Prior to the 1930s, the Republicans were the majority party in the country; Democrats dominated in the South but were relatively weak elsewhere. Republicans won the presidential elections of 1920, 1924, and 1928 by substantial margins. The GOP also controlled Congress throughout the 1920s. The 1928 election was a landslide victory for Republican presidential candidate Herbert Hoover. He won 58 percent of the vote and a lopsided share of the Electoral College votes. All of this changed after 1929 as a result of the Great Depression. As the party in power, Republicans took the brunt of the blame for the economic catastrophe the nation was experiencing. In 1932, President Hoover was defeated by Democrat Franklin Delano Roosevelt, and Democrats took control of both houses of Congress. Roosevelt went on to be reelected three times, and Democrats retained control of Congress until 1946. What happened in the 1930s was more than just a temporary rejection of the Republican Party because of the abysmal state of the economy: there was a substantial and lasting change in how the parties defined themselves and how the voters aligned themselves with the parties. The Democrats became the majority party in the nation, and the New Deal coalition that was forged in the 1930s persisted for decades afterwards, albeit in a diluted form (Ladd with Hadley 1978, 88–128; Sundquist 1983, 240–268).

In the 1930s, the two parties divided sharply on economic issues. Prior to the 1930s, the federal government played only a small role in the national economy, something both parties endorsed. That changed under President Roosevelt and the Democrats, who favored a more active role for the federal government in combating the Great Depression. To put people back to work, the Roosevelt administration created projects that hired people to build and repair America's infrastructure. Under the Public Works Administration (PWA), Works Progress Administration (WPA), Civilian Conservation Corps (CCC), and Civil Works Administration (CWA), millions of workers were employed by the federal government (Lawson 2006, 119–132; Leuchtenburg 1963, 121–174; Morison 1965, 954–959). They built public buildings, dams, and bridges; they planted new forests, built roads, and improved national parks; they taught in public schools, wrote state guides, and catalogued public libraries; they even painted murals and performed plays. In addition to putting people back to work, a variety of financial measures were instituted by the Democratic administration to help stabilize the economy and speed the recovery. The Emergency Banking Act helped banks to reopen, and the Reconstruction Finance Corporation (RFC) improved their capital structure (Lawson 2006, 66–67; Leuchtenburg 1963, 71; Morison 1965, 954–959). The Emergency Farm Mortgage Act halted farm foreclosures, and the Agricultural Adjustment Act (AAA) sought to improve prices for farm products (Lawson 2006, 102–114). The Truth-in-Securities Act and the Glass-Steagall Banking Act reformed and regulated the stock market and banks (Leuchtenburg 1963, 60; Morison 1965, 954–959).

Some of the measures that were enacted early in the Roosevelt administration were designed to help pull the nation out of the Great Depression; these programs, such as the WPA or the CCC, were ended after that goal had been accomplished. But other programs enacted during the 1930s remained. Included in this category were several social welfare and income security programs, such as Social Security and Aid to Families with Dependent Children (commonly referred to as public welfare). The federal government was now providing benefits that it had never before provided. The federal government also took a more active role in managing the economy, with regulations of financial institutions and industry, and these policies continued after the Depression ended. For example, the Federal Deposit Insurance Corporation (FDIC), created in 1933 to guarantee small bank deposits, continued in existence as a prominent example of federal government involvement in the economy. The leftward movement of the Democratic Party contrasted with the Republican economic philosophy, which was that the federal government could not and should not do much to interfere in the workings of the free market. In the eyes of Republicans, the economic ills of the nation would best be cured by the actions of private businesses.

In the 1930s, Democrats and Republicans divided on more than just how to deal with the immediate problem of the Depression. They began to differ in their more general economic philosophies. Democrats supported permanent changes in federal government policy, including creating permanent social welfare programs, having the federal government engage in more regulation of businesses and the economy, and providing more support for labor unions. Republicans favored a more limited role for the federal government in the economy. As a result of these growing differences in policy, the two parties became more clearly distinguished in ideological terms: Democrats were liberal, Republicans conservative. At that time, these ideological terms referred primarily to economic philosophies.

While the Depression was the catalyst for the realignment of the 1930s, there were underlying sources of this development. American society was changing during the late 19th and early 20th century from a more agrarian to a more industrial society. These changes took place largely in the North. Cities grew. The industrial sector expanded. Large numbers of immigrants came into the cities and worked in factories. The economic policies that were suitable for a more rural and agrarian society were problematic for a more urbanized and industrial society. Even if there had been no Depression, similar changes in economic policy might well have been enacted, but undoubtedly not as quickly.

Labor-management relations became a more salient issue in an industrializing America. Industrial workers increasingly demanded the right to form labor unions and engage in collective bargaining with their employers. The Roosevelt administration responded to these demands with legislation that expanded and protected the right of workers to unionize, most notably the 1935 National Labor Relations Act (Roof 2011, 22–40). Industrialization also stimulated more demands for regulation of the industrial and financial sectors, particularly in the wake of the Depression. While a largely laissez-faire economic policy may have been suitable for 19th century America, increased government control over and regulation of business activity now seemed more appropriate. For example, the 1938 Fair Labor Standards Act established a federal minimum wage and set a standard working week of 40 hours, two measures that benefited many workers (Roof 2011, 30–32). A broader social safety net also was viewed more favorably by the electorate, especially industrial workers. Consequently, the income security measures established in the 1930s, such as Social Security or unemployment insurance, remained as permanent features of federal government public policy, and they were expanded in subsequent Democratic administrations by other measures, such as Medicare.

The policies of Roosevelt's New Deal were embraced by working-class voters. Class divisions were small in the 1920s, but they grew greatly in the 1930s and 1940s, at least in the North. Blue-collar workers were a core component of the Democratic New Deal coalition. At the same time, those of higher socio-economic status were strong supporters of the Republican Party. Gallup poll data show that in the 1936 presidential election, low-SES voters were about 30 points more Democratic than were high-SES voters, with those of middle SES about halfway between these two groups in their vote (Ladd with Hadley 1978, 69). Similarly, Gallup poll data on party identification from the early 1940s show that upper-income individuals were about 30 points more Republican than were lower-income individuals, with those of middle-income again about halfway between these two groups (Sundquist 1983, 216).

This sharp class division continued into the 1940s. In 1948, the division between working-class and middle-class voters was particularly strong. This was due in part to the fact that the recently passed Taft-Hartley Act, which was opposed by labor unions, was a salient issue in the presidential election (Roof 2011, 41–47). President Harry Truman harshly criticized the law in his reelection campaign, calling it a "shameful and vicious" law, and he reminded voters that the law was passed by a Republican Congress over his veto (Berelson, Lazarsfeld, and McPhee 1954, 217–218). Truman also vigorously defended other aspects of the New Deal, again contrasting his views with those of the Republicans and thereby making domestic economic issues salient in the election. The greater importance of economic issues in the 1948 election also may be due to the fact that it was the first presidential election after the end of World War II, which naturally dominated politics in the early 1940s.

Democratic economic policies were a major reason for the class differences in voting of the 1930s and 1940s, but other factors contributed as well. A sizable number of northern blue-collar workers were immigrants or first-generation Americans. Furthermore, these more recent immigrant groups came largely from southern and eastern Europe. They were Poles, Italians, Slavs, Greeks, Jews, and others. These more recent immigrant groups were largely Catholic, Eastern Orthodox, or Jewish in their religious orientations, and many of them felt that they were second-class citizens. They began to see the Democratic Party as the one that was more interested in integrating these newer ethnic groups into American society. Added to this mix were Irish Catholics, who largely immigrated earlier, settled in urban areas, and were already Democratic. The greater Democratic appeal to Catholics and other non-Protestant groups was not based primarily on theological differences between Protestants and Catholics or others. The cleavage was largely an ethnic one (Ladd with Hadley 1978, 46–53). Of course, the Democratic appeal to these newer ethnic groups overlapped with its appeal to those of lower SES because these non-Protestant ethnic groups were more likely to be blue-collar workers.

The realignment of the 1930s affected the North much more than the South.[3] Well before the 1930s, the South was solidly Democratic (Key 1977). That was a result of the Civil War, Reconstruction, and the effort of segregationist southern Democrats after the end of Reconstruction to reestablish their political control and to reassert white supremacy in the South. By the start of the 20th century, Democratic domination in the South was complete. Each of the eleven states of the Confederacy was thoroughly Democratic, and these southern Democrats were generally quite conservative. Blacks were discouraged and even prevented from voting through a variety of legal subterfuges, such as the literacy test or the poll tax, and sometimes by various forms of intimidation (Key 1977, 533–665). Republicans were a beleaguered minority throughout the South, unable to win any statewide elections and unable to have even a significant presence in state legislatures. The Democratic strength in the South remained after the 1930s realignment, which effectively combined the existing Democratic strength in the South with its newly acquired strength among northern working-class and ethnic voters to create the Democratic New Deal coalition.

The Democratic New Deal coalition began to break apart during the last half of the 20th century. The biggest change occurred in the South. The Democratic dominance slowly gave way to an emerging Republican majority. This appeared first in presidential elections, then moved down the ballot (Lublin 2004; Scher 1997). By the end of the 20th century, the GOP had a clear advantage in presidential, congressional, and state elections (Black and Black 2002; Lublin 2004). Conservative southern whites were the base of this new Republican majority. Democrats partly compensated for the loss of conservative white voters by winning an extremely high share of the vote from blacks, who became a more substantial portion of the southern electorate after the 1965 Voting Rights Act, along with other governmental actions, removed the barriers to black participation that had existed throughout the South (Bullock and Gaddie 2009; Bullock and Rozell 2018). A variety of factors were responsible for this transformation of southern politics, and they have been analyzed quite well by a body of literature that is too great to thoroughly cite here (Steed and Moreland 2006). These changes in the political character of the South are relevant for this study only to the extent that they affect the relationship between social class and voting behavior. As we shall see, there have been some important effects.

The split between white Catholics and Protestants in their voting, which reflected the ethnic differences between older and newer immigrant groups, also diminished over time. Some commentators concluded that Catholics had become so integrated into American society that they no longer were politically much different from Protestants (Fisher 2014, 57). However, the relationship between religion and voting is complicated by two factors: race and region. First of all, blacks are heavily Protestant, and after the 1960s, they began to vote in larger numbers and quite strongly for Democratic candidates. The effect of this shift was to increase Democratic voting among Protestants. Later, Latinos became a noticeable share of the electorate, especially in the 21st century. Latinos tend to be Catholic, and they lean toward the Democratic Party, although not to the extent that blacks do. The result of this change was to increase Democratic voting among Catholics. In the South, white voters, who are largely Protestant, began to move toward the Republican Party in the post-civil rights era. This increased Republican voting among Protestants. Thus, shifts in the overall electorate among blacks, Latino, and white southerners affected the difference in voting between Protestants and Catholics, sometimes working to reduce the difference, but sometimes to increase it.

In the Democratic New Deal coalition of the 1930s, the division between Catholics and Protestants in the North (i.e., the non-South) was largely an ethnic division between older and newer immigrant groups, essentially a division between those from the British Isles and northern Europe versus those from southern and eastern Europe (Irish Catholics were an exception to this pattern). Including blacks, Latinos, and white southerners in the analysis obscures the difference between white northern Catholics and Protestants. That difference still remains, although not to the extent that it once did. In the 1940s, there was around a 30-point difference in the presidential vote of white northern Catholics and Protestants: Catholics were around 70 percent Democratic, Protestants around 40 percent (Ladd with Hadley 1978, 118). That difference decreased somewhat during the 1950s, then jumped up in 1960 to about a 40-point difference, due of course to the fact that John F. Kennedy was the Democratic candidate. In becoming the first Catholic president, Kennedy captured over three-fourths of the vote of northern white Catholics (Ladd with Hadley 1978, 119). The Catholic-Protestant split declined in subsequent years, but it did not disappear. In the 2000 presidential election, for example, northern white Catholics were about 10 points higher in their vote for the Democratic candidate, Al Gore, than their Protestant counterparts, according to exit poll data for that year. In 2008, there was a similar 10-point difference in the presidential vote. That suggests some persistence in old ethnic differences, at least in the North. We should note, however, that around one-third of white northerners said that they had no religious affiliation or that they were some other type of Christian. We do not know the ethnic composition of these voters, but it is possible that if we did, it might affect our conclusions about ethnic differences in voting.

Another core element of the New Deal coalition that persisted throughout the latter half of the 20th century was the disproportionate appeal of Democrats to working-class voters. Although class divisions diminished after the 1940s, they remained a feature of American politics for decades afterwards. The image of the Democratic Party as the party of the working man persisted. That image still reflected reality. Democrats continued to win a greater share of the vote from working-class voters, even among white voters. However, there were ups and downs in this relationship, as well as some changes in the nature of the working-class vote. To better describe and explain these changes, the next section more carefully examines class differences in voting behavior from the 1950s through the 1990s.

## Class and Voting: 1950s to the 1990s

To examine the relationship between social class and voting for the second half of the 20th century, I examined the difference between working-class and middle-class voters, with social class measured in four different ways. I restricted the analysis to white, non-Hispanic voters because that is the focus of this study. For each measure of social class, I calculated the Democratic advantage among working-class voters, relative to middle-class voters, for both presidential vote and party identification. I included party identification in the analysis because it is a fairly stable partisan orientation that affects voting at all levels. In some years, the unique features of a presidential election might produce a change in the relationship between social class and presidential voting, even though there might be little change in the more fundamental relationship between class and partisan choice. For the presidential vote, I simply took the difference between the Democratic percentage of the two-party vote for the working class and the Democratic percentage for the middle class. A positive number indicates that working-class voters are more Democratic than are middle-class voters. For party identification, I calculated the Democratic advantage among the working class by taking the average of two figures: (a) the difference between the percentage of Democratic identifiers among working-class voters and the percentage among middle-class voters; and (b) the difference between the percentage of Republican identifiers among middle-class voters and the percentage among working-class voters.[4] Again, a positive number indicates that working-class voters are relatively more Democratic, or that middle-class voters are relatively more Republican. The data come from the American National Election Studies (ANES) surveys from 1952 through 1996.

I used four measures of social class: income, occupation, education, and class identification. In each case, I dichotomized voters as being either working class or middle class. I did not make finer distinctions in this analysis because I wanted to focus on the split between working-class and middle-class voters, a division that is the focus of many other studies. For income, I adjusted household income for marital status, for the reasons discussed in the previous chapter. Individuals are classified as above or below the median household income for people of their marital status, with those with below-average incomes considered to be working class. Also, when analyzing the effects of income, I look only at voters who are at least 30 years old, on the basis that last year's household income is a poor measure of social class for young voters, as discussed in the previous chapter. For occupation, I use the distinction between manual and nonmanual workers, with blue-collar workers defined as working class. For education, I compared those with a college degree to those with only a high school diploma or less. This leaves out those with some college education because this group is hard to classify. If we include them with those with a college degree, we probably have too broad of a definition of middle class, especially for more recent years. If we include them with those who lack any college education, we probably have too broad of a definition of working class. Comparing those with a college degree to those without any college education probably provides us with the clearest comparison of working-class and middle-class voters, but we need to keep in mind that a more ambiguous middle group is not included in the analysis. Finally, for class identification, most people consider themselves to be working or middle class, but a small number say that they are lower or upper class, and I classified these individuals as working or middle class, respectively.

Table 3.2 presents the results of the above analysis for the following presidential elections: (a) Dwight Eisenhower's two elections, 1952 and 1956; (b) the Kennedy and Lyndon Johnson elections, 1960 and 1964; (c) Richard Nixon's elections, 1968 and 1972; (d) the Carter election of 1976; (e) the Ronald Reagan and George Bush elections of the 1980s; and (f) Bill Clinton's elections, 1992 and 1996. I combined results for two or three elections in most cases because doing so yields a larger number of cases, thus reducing sampling error, and because this evens out some of the short-term effects on presidential voting that are present in individual elections. However, I left the 1976 election as a separate category because it did not seem to fit with either the elections that immediately preceded it or immediately followed it. As explained above, positive numbers indicate that working-class voters are relatively more Democratic; negative numbers indicate that middle-class voters are relatively more Democratic.

My focus in this analysis is on trends in the basic relationship between social class, not on change from one presidential election to the next. The relationship between social class and presidential voting varies across elections. The behavior of working-class and middle-class voters fluctuates in both absolute and relative terms, due to a variety of short-term forces, such as the nature of the candidates, the policies of the incumbent administration, and the salient issues in the election. I make some note of these patterns in the following analysis, but my primary attempt here is to identify general trends, ones that seem to represent more lasting effects of social class on partisan choice. Other scholars have speculated on the sources of these short-term variations in class polarization, and it is an interesting research question, but it is not the focus of this study (Campbell *et al.* 1960, 346–350; Lewis-Beck *et al.* 2008, 342–362). My concern is with identifying how the impact of social class on voting behavior has changed over time in more fundamental ways and how it might continue to change.

Looking first at the Eisenhower elections, we can see that the Democratic New Deal coalition remained a prominent feature of American politics in 1950s. Republican Dwight D. Eisenhower's victories in the presidential elections of 1952 and 1956 represented more of a personal victory for Eisenhower, due to his very favorable character traits, rather than a change in the underlying partisan loyalties of the American electorate. (Campbell *et al.* 1960). Democrats were in control of both houses of Congress for the last six years of the Eisenhower administration, for example, and they continued to command the partisan

**TABLE 3.2** Social Class Differences in Presidential Voting and Party Identification Among Whites, 1952–1996

| | 1952–1956 | 1960–1964 | 1968–1972 | 1976 | 1980–1988 | 1992–1996 |
|---|---|---|---|---|---|---|
| ***Democratic working-class advantage in presidential voting among white voters by:*** | | | | | | |
| **Income:** low v. high income | 5.3 | 7.1 | 3.1 | 12.7 | 7.5 | 9.2 |
| **Occupation:** manual v. nonmanual work | 18.6 | 18.7 | 5.9 | 18.5 | 3.9 | 5.5 |
| **Education:** high school v. college educated | 13.5 | 18.5 | 2.9 | 13.4 | 3.5 | 2.1 |
| **Class identification:** working class v. middle class | 11.7 | n.a. | 2.2 | 15.8 | 8.6 | n.a. |
| ***Democratic working-class advantage in party identification among white voters by:*** | | | | | | |
| **Income:** low v. high income | 7.2 | 8.7 | 7.3 | 9.3 | 9.6 | 11.8 |
| **Occupation:** manual v. nonmanual work | 12.2 | 15.4 | 9.6 | 11.1 | 11.8 | 7.6 |
| **Education:** high school v. college educated | 16.2 | 16.1 | 13.1 | 14.5 | 10.9 | 8.3 |
| **Class identification:** working class v. middle class | 13.8 | n.a. | 9.7 | 15.0 | 12.1 | n.a. |

Source: Figures were calculated from the ANES surveys, 1952–1996.

Note: The Democratic working-class advantage in the presidential vote is calculated as the difference between the Democratic percent of the two-party vote for the working-class group and the percent for the middle-class group in each category. For party identification, the Democratic working-class advantage in each category is calculated by averaging the Democratic advantage among working-class individuals and the Republican advantage among middle-class voters. In each case, a positive number indicates that working-class individuals are more Democratic than are middle-class individuals. See the text for details on the measures.

loyalties of a majority of the voters. Democrats continued in the 1950s to do better among white working-class voters, although the large class cleavages in voting of the 1930s and 1940s did diminish somewhat in the 1950s. Nevertheless, there still was a difference of almost 20 percentage points between blue-collar and white-collar workers in their presidential vote in the 1950s, and over a 10-point difference in party identification. The results of this analysis are consistent with the findings of Eulau (1962, 61–63), who analyzed class and party during the Eisenhower years using somewhat different measures of social class. One of the reasons for the decline in class divisions in the 1950s may be that party differences on economic issues were not as sharp as they were in the 1930s and 1940s. Many of the New Deal programs that were designed to get the country out of the Great Depression had been terminated by the 1950s. Many of the programs that remained, such as Social Security, developed strong support in the electorate. Even though he was a fiscal conservative, President Eisenhower accepted much of the New Deal economic and social welfare legislation (Smith 2013, 647–654). Additionally, the affluence of the post-World War II era probably helped to erase memories of Republicans as the party of Hoover and the Depression. Post-war affluence also may have diminished the intensity of class conflict in other ways (Ladd with Hadley 1978, 195–211).

It is interesting to note that the difference between higher- and lower-income voters in the 1950s was much smaller than the differences by occupation or education. What might seem to be a puzzling fact can be explained largely by one factor: unionization. Among blue-collar workers, those in a union household (i.e. at least one member of the household belonged to a union) were over 10 points more Democratic than those not in a union household. Moreover, unionized blue-collar workers generally earned more. In the ANES surveys of the 1950s, blue-collar workers in a union household were about 20 percentage points more likely to report an above-average income than those not in a union household. The result was that among blue-collar workers, there was no difference in voting between higher- and lower-income individuals because the higher-income voters were more likely to be in a union household. The union membership of the higher-income blue-collar workers pulled them toward the Democrats as much as the lower income did for the non-union blue-collar workers. This lack of any relationship between income and partisan choice among blue-collar workers blunts the overall relationship in the electorate between income and voting, which is stronger if only non-union members are analyzed. For white-collar workers, income did make a significant difference: those with above-average incomes were over 10 points more Republican in their presidential voting than those with below-average incomes. Among white-collar workers, those in a union household also were more Democratic in their voting, but there were relatively few voters in this category because unionization in the 1950s was largely restricted to the working class. In the ANES surveys of the 1952 and 1956 elections, there were as many blue-collar workers in a union household as not, but only a small percentage of white-collar workers were in a union household.

In sum, the most important division among blue-collar workers in the 1950s was whether they belonged to a union or someone in their household did. For white-collar workers, income was an important division, and income undoubtedly was strongly related to the type of white-collar work the individual did. Professional and managerial workers earned more than those in less prestigious nonmanual jobs. That also helps to explain the sizable differences in partisan choice by education. Those with a college education were very likely to be in professional or managerial positions, especially in the 1950s. Those with just a high school education or less were largely in blue-collar jobs, although in the 1950s it was easier than it is now for someone with no college education to obtain a white-collar job, even a managerial one. Of course, the educational difference reported in Table 3.2 is heightened somewhat by the fact that those with some college education are excluded from the analysis. If this group is lumped in with those with no college education, the educational differences in partisan choice are smaller.

Social class differences in voting in the early 1960s were quite similar to those in the 1950s. Both Kennedy and Johnson did significantly better among working-class individuals. As in the 1950s, the differences in voting are similar to those for party identification. For both aspects of partisan choice, there were substantial differences between manual and nonmanual workers and between those with a college degree and those with only a high school diploma or less. Differences by income were smaller. As in the 1950s, unionized blue-collar workers were more Democratic than those who were not. Of course, the Democratic share of the presidential vote was higher in the early 1960s than in the 1950s since both Kennedy and Johnson were elected, with Johnson winning in a landslide. But their victories were achieved because they both attracted a larger share of both working-class and middle-class voters, especially Johnson in 1964, thus leaving class differences similar to what they were in the 1950s.

The Nixon elections of 1968 and 1972 marked a sharp break in the relationship between social class and presidential voting. Working-class voters were only slightly more likely to vote for the Democratic candidates—Hubert Humphrey in 1968 and George McGovern in 1972—than they were to vote for Nixon, regardless of which measure of social class we look at. This led to speculation by some scholars that social class was no longer an important division in American politics. Ladd with Hadley (1978) concluded that the old New Deal class alignment had been inverted so that lower-SES individuals were now more Republican than higher-SES individuals, at least among white voters. Phillips (1970) predicted that increased Republican voting among once Democratic white working-class members would produce an "emerging Republican majority."

Claims that the disproportionate appeal of Democrats to working-class voters had ended proved to be premature. As we can see by examining the data after 1972, it does not appear that class differences were permanently disappearing. Differences between working-class and middle-class voters continued throughout the last quarter of the 20th century. The 1968 and 1972 presidential elections were exceptions to the overall relationship between class and voting; they more closely represented deviations from the established pattern rather than a transformation of the alignment between class and voting. For one thing, class differences in party identification during this time period were not that much different from what they were in the early 1960s, which indicates that underlying partisan loyalties were not undergoing substantial change. This means that 1968 and 1972 were deviating presidential elections more than they were realigning ones. Also, class cleavages in presidential voting returned to their previous levels in the 1976 presidential election, as was discussed earlier. Moreover, class difference in party identification continued to exist among whites after 1972.

The weak relationship between class and presidential voting in 1968 and 1972 can be attributed to some of the unique features of those two elections. The Vietnam War was a key issue in both elections, and it was one that split both parties and cut across class lines. Also, the 1968 election was complicated by the third-party candidacy of George Wallace, who attracted a considerable number of white working-class votes, especially in the South. Moreover, the Democratic presidential candidate in 1972, George McGovern was widely perceived to be very liberal, and he failed to earn the endorsements of unions that Democrats had typically received, two factors that contributed to his landslide loss to Nixon. Added to all of this was an ongoing dealignment of the electorate: partisan attachments were becoming weaker and voters were more willing to defect from their partisan loyalty in their presidential vote (Crotty 1984, 26–44; Nie, Verba, and Petrocik 1979, 47–73).

Social class differences in partisan choice were particularly strong in 1976, at least according to the ANES data. For both presidential voting and party identification, the difference between higher- and lower-income groups was much stronger than it was in the 1950s. Differences between the occupational and educational groups in 1976 are on a par with the earlier differences, and the same is true for class identification. Social class differences in presidential voting among whites then declined somewhat in the 1980s, particularly if we look at occupation and education. However, class differences in party identification remained reasonably strong, only slightly lower than what they were in the 1950s. That suggests that some of the decline in class voting was due to the appeal of Reagan and to short-term forces in those elections. Reagan was able to attract a number of working-class Democrats in both 1980 and 1984. That working-class support helped him to win over 55 percent of the two-party vote in 1980 and over 59 percent in 1984. But Reagan also did very well among middle-class voters, so class differences remained in voting, even if they were weaker than in earlier years.

Economic issues helped Reagan win in both years. In 1980, the combination of high inflation, high unemployment, and stagnating real incomes was the major factor in Carter's unsuccessful reelection effort (McDonald 1981; Plotkin 1981). By 1984, the economy was doing extremely well, which was a major factor in Reagan's landslide reelection. The contrasting economic records of the Carter and Reagan administrations may have diminished voter perceptions that the Democrats were the party better able to manage the economy, which had been a long-standing party advantage dating back to the 1930s. Nevertheless, there were some salient economic issues related to social class during the Reagan years. The Republican administration worked to weaken the power of labor unions, with Reagan's successful attempt to break the strike by the Air Traffic Controllers Union being the most visible action in this area (McCartin 2011). Significant cutbacks in social welfare programs also were a part of the Reagan administration's budget. Some of these cuts failed to make it through the Democratically controlled House, but some were successful. In general, Reagan pursued social and economic policies that were more beneficial to more-affluent voters (Weaver 1985). Of course, the economic prosperity for most of Reagan's presidency was applauded by voters of all social classes, and this was a major factor in both his reelection in 1984 and Bush's election in 1988.

Social class differences in presidential voting among whites in the 1990s were similar to those in the 1980s. Bill Clinton did much better among working-class voters than the Democratic candidates in the 1980s did, but he also did better among middle-class voters. Clinton averaged over 54 percent of the two-party vote in his two presidential elections; the three Democratic presidential candidates in the 1980s averaged under 44 percent. In absolute terms, working-class whites were more Democratic in their presidential voting in the 1990s than they were in the 1980s, but in relative terms, there was little change. Class differences in presidential voting among whites were only slightly larger in the 1990s than in the 1980s. Regarding party identification, the difference between the 1980s and the 1990s is mixed: there is a stronger relationship between income and party identification in the 1990s, but a weaker relationship for occupation and education.

A closer look at the data in Table 3.2 reveals an interesting pattern. Differences between higher- and lower-income voters were stronger in the 1980s and 1990s than they were in the 1950s and early 1960s, but differences between manual and nonmanual workers diminished in the later decades. This pattern is there for both presidential voting and party identification. It may seem odd that class differences increased over time when we focus on income, but decreased when we look at occupation, but there are some possible explanations for this seemingly contradictory pattern. One contributing factor is the role of union membership. As I pointed out earlier, unionized blue-collar workers are both more Democratic and more affluent than those not in a union. This resulted in little difference in voting between higher- and lower-income manual workers in the 1950s. However, in the 1990s, fewer workers were in a union, and while unionized workers were still more Democratic, their smaller numbers influenced the relationship between income and voting much less. We therefore find that among whites in the 1990s, more-affluent manual workers were more Republican than were less-affluent ones. Furthermore, if we look at higher-income blue-collar workers not in a union, they were even more Republican (the Ns in the analysis are small for this group, so we should be cautious about this conclusion). Thus, declining unionization in the labor force produced both weaker differences between blue-collar and white-collar workers, but greater differences between higher- and lower-income voters.

Another reason why occupation, at least in terms of manual versus nonmanual work, has declined in its effect on the vote may be the changing nature of both blue-collar and white-collar jobs. As was discussed in the previous chapter, the movement to a service economy has created a large number of nonmanual jobs that are relatively low skilled and low paying. If social class refers to the extent to which people possess the social and economic resources that determine their ability to control their life choices, then low-paying white-collar jobs are more accurately classified as working-class positions even though they are technically white-collar jobs. Blue-collar jobs also have changed over time. Fewer manual workers are in a traditional industrial setting. A significant number of blue-collar workers now are highly skilled, often with a community college education, and are relatively well paid. They also may have a high degree of independence in their work, with many even being in business for themselves. Although they are in manual positions, they may consider themselves, and be considered by others, to be middle class. Thus, the changing nature of jobs may mean that the division between manual and nonmanual work is a less reliable indicator of social class than it once was. Income may now be a better measure of social class.

It appears that we should consider both income and occupation as good measures of social class. Occupation may be a better measure in earlier years, but income may now be better, at least compared to the traditional occupational distinction of manual versus nonmanual work. Taking that approach, and looking at both presidential voting and party identification, we can compare class differences in the 1950s with those in the 1990s. For party identification, we see similar levels of class differences in partisan choice if we use income as the best measure of social class in the 1990s and occupation as the best measure for the 1950s. In both decades, Democrats had about a 12-point advantage among working-class individuals. On the other hand, using the same approach, we find that class differences in presidential voting declined substantially from the 1950s to the 1990s: Democrats had about a nine-point advantage among working-class voters in the 1990s (using income for this decade), compared to over an 18-point advantage in the 1950s (using occupation). Overall, it seems reasonable to conclude that class differences in partisan choice declined somewhat over the last half of the 20th century, but they still remained significant. At the end of the century, Democrats appealed more to working-class voters, Republicans more to middle-class voters, even among whites.

The above conclusions about the relationship between social class and voting differ from those of some studies that examine how social class has been related to voting over the past several decades. For example, Stonecash (2000) and Brewer and Stonecash (2007) conclude that social class differences in voting were greater in the 1990s than in the 1950s. However, these studies rely exclusively on income to measure social class.[5] While my data for income in Table 3.2 show a similar pattern, I think that looking at both occupation and income provides a more accurate assessment of how social class has been related to partisan choice, particularly for earlier years, as I have tried to explain in the above discussion. Unfortunately, we do not have good data on the occupation of respondents in the most recent surveys of political behavior, so we can no longer use the combination of occupation and income to measure social class. But as I argue above, income probably is the better measure of social class in recent years.

What these data do not show is a shift in the geographical nature of social class differences in voting. In the 1930s and 1940s, class differences in partisan choice were limited to the North. In the South, there was little difference between white working-class and middle-class voters. Both were strongly Democratic. That changed over time. As Republicans gained strength in the South, class differences emerged, particularly in the post-civil rights era (Gelman 2010, 46–48; Stonecash 2000, 106–110). Republicans gained support among both white middle-class and working-class voters, so much so that they commanded a large majority of the votes of all whites, but the GOP gained more among better-off voters (Nadeau *et al.* 2004).

In the North, changes in class differences are less clear. Occupational differences, which were large in the 1930s and 1940s, declined substantially from the 1950s to the 1990s, but differences between more and less-affluent voters increased (Gelman 2010, 46–48; Nadeau *et al.* 2004; Stonecash 2000, 106–110). Earlier we saw that in the 1950s, the difference between blue-collar and white-collar workers seemed to be a better indicator of social class, but that income seemed the better indicator by the 1990s. If this is true, then looking only at income may exaggerate the change in class differences in voting. Considering both income and occupation, a more reasonable interpretation of the data might be that there was some decline in class differences in voting in the North. Increasing class cleavages in the South partially compensated for decreasing cleavages in the North. The overall result was that the national pattern did not change that much over the last half of the 20th century, but there was much more underlying regional change.

I have left education out of this discussion to this point. As one can see from the data in Table 3.2, the difference between whites with a college degree and those with only a high school diploma or less in both presidential voting and party identification diminished from the 1950s to the 1990s. In fact, there was almost no difference in presidential voting in the 1990s between these two educational groups (remember that those with some college are excluded from this analysis). However, I think that this represents more than just a change in the relationship between class and party. Education is likely to affect voting behavior apart from any effects that it has on social class. As I discussed in the previous chapter, individuals who are equally middle class (or working class) in terms of occupation and income, but who differ in education, are likely to differ in their political attitudes and behavior. I explore the combined effects of income and education in a later chapter. At this point, it is sufficient to note that the relationship between education and voting weakened considerably during the last half of the 20th century. Also, I have not discussed class identification, partly because the data are not available for some of the time periods in Table 3.2, but more because I want to focus on objective measures of social class, for the reasons discussed in the previous chapter. The data that we have on class identification show that its relationship to voting over time is fairly consistent with the patterns for the other measures of social class.

## Class and Voting in the 21st Century

As we have seen, social class differences in voting declined somewhat in the last half of the 20th century, but differences were still clearly present. The relationship between social class and partisan choice among whites declined even more during the first decade of the 21st century, then actually reversed in its direction of association in the second decade. Among whites, middle-class voters are now more Democratic than are working-class voters. Table 3.3 presents data for the five presidential elections from 2000 to 2016. This table replicates the analysis

**TABLE 3.3** Social Class Differences in Presidential Voting and Party Identification Among Whites, 2000–2016

|  | 2000 | 2004 | 2008 | 2012 | 2016 |
|---|---|---|---|---|---|
| *Democratic working-class advantage in presidential voting among white voters by:* | | | | | |
| **Income:** low v. high income | 3.2 | 2.4 | 4.5 | -3.9 | -12.1 |
| **Occupation:** manual v. nonmanual work | -2.0 | -1.5 | n.a. | n.a. | n.a. |
| **Education:** high school v. college educated | -1.5 | -3.1 | -2.6 | -7.5 | -20.0 |
| **Class identification:** working class v. middle class | -1.8 | 5.4 | 7.8 | -0.2 | -8.3 |
| *Democratic working-class advantage in party identification among white voters by:* | | | | | |
| **Income:** low v. high income | 6.1 | 3.8 | 5.7 | 3.2 | -5.0 |
| **Occupation:** manual v. nonmanual work | 5.8 | -1.3 | n.a. | n.a. | n.a. |
| **Education:** high school v. college educated | 7.6 | -2.1 | 1.4 | 0.9 | -10.5 |
| **Class identification:** working class v. middle class | 8.6 | 2.7 | 7.6 | 4.0 | -0.1 |

Source: Figures were calculated from the ANES surveys and the national exit polls, 2000–2016.
Note: The Democratic working-class advantage in the presidential vote is calculated as the difference between the Democratic percent of the two-party vote for the working-class group and the percent for the middle-class group in each category. For party identification, the Democratic working-class advantage in each category is calculated by averaging the Democratic advantage in party identification among working-class individuals and the Republican advantage in party identification among middle-class voters. In each case, a positive number indicates that working-class individuals are more Democratic than are middle-class individuals. See the text for details on the measures.

reported in Table 3.2. I used the same four measures of social class: income, occupation, education, and class identification, although we unfortunately have occupational information only for 2000 and 2004. As I did previously, I examined both presidential voting and party identification and included only white, non-Hispanic voters in the analysis, as this is the focus of the study. In this table, I have reported the results for each election, so that we are able to more carefully examine change in recent elections.[6]

Class differences in voting among whites declined in the first decade of this century. Perhaps surprisingly, there were smaller differences between working-class and middle-class voters in the 2000 presidential election than there were in the 1990s. This was true even though the Democratic candidate, Al Gore, was vice-president under Clinton and thus might have been expected to have a similar base of support. Moreover, there were no prominent foreign policy issues that might have cut across class lines that year. The election was not an outlier in any other obvious way that might influence how class was related to voting. Class differences in presidential voting among whites remained low in 2004 and 2008, regardless of which measure of social class we examine. For the decade of the 2000s, lower-income white voters averaged slightly over three points more Democratic in their presidential voting than higher-income voters, a drop from the roughly nine-point difference that existed in the 1990s. There was even less of a working-class advantage for Democrats for both education and occupation. In fact, in both cases, working-class whites—i.e., manual workers and those with just a high school education—were slightly more Republican.

Class differences are somewhat stronger when it comes to party identification, particularly if we regard income as the best measure of social class. The Democratic advantage in party identification among white lower-income workers averaged about five points in the 2000s, down from about a 12-point advantage in the 1990s. There was an even weaker Democratic advantage among working-class voters when it comes to occupation and education (about a two-point advantage in both cases). The similarity of the patterns across all three presidential elections, along with the decline of class differences in party identification, indicate that the drop from the 1980s and 1990s represents a more fundamental change in the orientations of the American electorate.

Class differences among white voters were weak in the 2000s, but one could still say that the Democratic Party appealed somewhat more to white lower-income voters, even if the tendency was slight. In the next decade, one could not make that claim at all. In fact, the relationship between social class and voting was now the reverse of what it traditionally had been: white middle-class voters were now more Democratic in presidential voting than their working-class counterparts. The class difference was small in 2012: higher-income whites were only about four points more Democratic in their presidential vote. And Democrats retained a modest advantage among less-affluent whites regarding party identification, although it was a smaller advantage than they had in the previous election years.

In 2016, the inverted relationship between social class and presidential voting expanded. Trump had a 12-point advantage among less-affluent white voters, compared to more-affluent ones. That 12-point advantage exceeds the advantage that Democrat Bill Clinton had among those same voters in the 1990s. There was not only a significant shift in the relationship between class and voting between the 2012 and 2016 presidential elections: a similar shift took place for party identification. The spike up in Republican presidential voting among white working-class voters in 2016 most likely was due partly to unique factors associated with Trump, but the change in the patterns for party identification indicate that more fundamental partisan loyalties were changing as well. Chapter 7 more carefully analyzes voting in these two presidential elections to identify the continuities and the changes.

If we compare the pattern for presidential voting in Table 3.3 with that for party identification, we see that in each year, Democrats had a greater advantage (or a smaller disadvantage) among white working-class voters in party identification than in presidential voting. Using income as our measure of social class, the Democratic working-class advantage in 2000 was over six points for party identification, but only about three points for presidential voting. In 2016, the difference was even greater: Democrats had a 12-point disadvantage for presidential voting, but only about a five-point disadvantage for party identification. But the trends for both presidential voting and party identification are the same: a declining Democratic advantage among white working-class voters. The change for party identification appears to lag behind the change for voting. This could mean that the experience that voters have with the presidential candidates subsequently influences their party identification. If so, that raises the question of whether Trump's appeal to white working-class voters might influence their party identification in future years.

Although the focus of this study in on the behavior of white voters, it is worthwhile to look at class and voting for the entire electorate. After all, it is the entire electorate that determines the outcome of the election and the composition of the party coalitions. Table 3.4 presents data on the relationship between social class and both presidential voting and party identification from 1980 through 2016 for all voters. I have averaged data by decades, except for the most recent decade, when the difference between the two elections is stark. As we can see, Democratic presidential candidates in the 2000s appealed disproportionately to working-class voters almost as strongly as they did in the 1980s and 1990s. The data for party identification show the same thing. Lower-income voters in the first decade of this century were about 10 points more Democratic in their presidential voting than higher-income voters were, just as was the case in the 1980s and 1990s. Differences in party identification between more-affluent and less-affluent voters also remained fairly similar. The relative support for Democrats among white working-class voters declined over this three-decade period, but strong support from blacks and Latinos, who are more likely to be working class, compensated for that decline. Looking at the entire electorate, Democrats were about as much the party of the working class, and Republicans as much the party of the middle class, in the 2000s as they were in

**TABLE 3.4** Social Class Differences in Presidential Voting and Party Identification, 1980–2016

|  | 1980s | 1990s | 2000s | 2012 | 2016 |
|---|---|---|---|---|---|
| *Democratic working-class advantage in presidential voting among all voters by:* | | | | | |
| **Income:** low v. high income | 10.4 | 9.5 | 10.5 | 3.2 | -7.5 |
| **Occupation:** manual v. nonmanual work | 11.2 | 10.8 | n.a. | n.a. | n.a. |
| **Education:** high school v. college educated | 9.4 | 13.1 | 5.0 | 2.7 | -10.5 |
| **Class identification:** working class v. middle class | 14.0 | n.a. | 11.5 | 6.5 | 1.1 |
| *Democratic working-class advantage in party identification among all voters by:* | | | | | |
| **Income:** low v. high income | 10.4 | 14.0 | 9.9 | 6.8 | -2.3 |
| **Occupation:** manual v. nonmanual work | 13.5 | 11.4 | n.a. | n.a. | n.a. |
| **Education:** high school v. college educated | 12.2 | 14.6 | 6.4 | 6.4 | 0.3 |
| **Class identification:** working class v. middle class | 9.9 | n.a. | 13.8 | 8.0 | 5.5 |

Source: Figures were calculated from the ANES surveys, 1980–2016.
Note: The Democratic working-class advantage in the presidential vote is calculated as the difference between the Democratic percent of the two-party vote for the working-class group and the percent for the middle-class group in each category. For party identification, the Democratic working-class advantage in each category is calculated by averaging the Democratic advantage in party identification among working-class individuals and the Republican advantage in party identification among middle-class voters. In each case, a positive number indicates that working-class individuals are more Democratic than are middle-class individuals. See the text for details on the measures.

the 1990s. This is an important point to keep in mind whenever we highlight declining Democratic support among white working-class voters. The base of support for the Democratic Party in the 2000s was made up of minority groups more than was the case in the 1980s, but the base was nevertheless as much working class as it had been.

The stability of this relationship from the 1980s through the 2000s gave way to a sharp decline in Democratic appeal to the working class in the 2012 presidential election and an even sharper change in 2016. In 2012, Obama did only slightly better among less-affluent voters in the entire electorate. In 2016, Clinton did worse among lower-income voters in the entire electorate, despite her strong support from minorities. The decline in support for Democratic Party among white working-class voters had, by 2016, been so great that it altered the overall relationship between class and voting. For the first time in modern American political history, the GOP could legitimately claim that it was the party of the working class, at least in terms of voting in that presidential election. While some of this strong Republican appeal to working-class voters was due to the appeal of

Trump, these data also show that party identification shifted as well, to the point that there was virtually no difference in social class between Democrats and Republicans in 2016. Whether these recent trends will continue to be the case in future elections is a topic that we will explore later, after we determine what has been behind the changing relationship between social class and partisan choice.

## Conclusions

The relationship between social class and voting behavior has been changing. This may seem to be an obvious point, but it is one that at least a few studies, particularly in earlier years, have ignored. For example, Hawley (2014) concludes that there is little relationship between education and party identification, based on his analysis of data from the 2012 election. That indeed was the case in 2012, as Table 3.3 shows. But it was not the case before 2004, when less-educated voters were more Democratic, or in 2016, when the relationship between education and partisanship became inverted (see Tables 3.2 and 3.3). However, Hawley implies that the relationship that he found in 2012 describes a more stable pattern, not just the situation for a single election or two. The same willingness to infer more stable relationships about class and partisanship from the analysis of data from one election has appeared in some other studies as well. Of course, many scholarly studies that have examined data over time have recognized that the relationship between social class and voting behavior or partisanship is not static. Even so, there is scholarly disagreement about how much change has occurred in this relationship, so this chapter has attempted to paint as accurate a picture as is possible. This description of change in class divisions sets the stage for the next task: explaining why these changes have taken place.

Chapter 1 outlined the possible reasons why white working-class voters have moved toward the Republican Party. These reasons can be briefly recapped here. First, numerous commentators and scholars argue that white working-class voters like the GOP's stand on race-related issues. These voters see the Democratic Party as too interested in helping out minority groups, at the expense of deserving whites. Conversely, white middle-class voters prefer the Democratic Party's stand on these issues. Second, economic dissatisfaction among white working-class voters also has been suggested as a reason why they have left the Democratic Party, which they no longer see as pursuing policies that benefit them. Middle-class voters may now perceive the Democratic Party just as favorably as the GOP, if not more so, on a variety of economic issues. Third, conservatism on social and moral issues also may explain why working-class voters have moved toward the GOP, or why middle-class voters have moved toward the Democrats. Each of these three possible reasons will be explored in the following chapters.

As Chapter 1 pointed out, for any of these reasons to truly be an explanation of why white working-class voters are now relatively less Democratic than their middle-class counterparts are, or why white middle-class voters are now relatively less Republican, two tests must be met: (1) the proposed factor must affect the vote; and (2) there must be differences on this factor in the correct direction between working-class and middle-class voters. Furthermore, for the proposed factor to explain why there has been a change in the relationship between social class and voting among whites in this century, at least one of the following two conditions must be met: (a) white working-class voters have become more conservative or more pro-Republican, relative to middle-class voters, on the attitudes in question; or (b) existing class differences in these attitudes have increased in their influence on voting. These points guide the analysis reported in the following chapters.

## Notes

1  These figures were calculated from the 1976 ANES survey of the electorate.
2  These figures were calculated from the 2016 ANES survey of the electorate.
3  The South is defined as the eleven states of the old Confederacy. The North is defined as the rest of the country.
4  An example may help to clarify this method. Suppose that among working-class voters, 50 percent identify as Democrats, 10 percent as independents, and 40 percent as Republicans. Further suppose that among middle-class voters, 30 percent identify as Democrats, 20 percent as independents, and 50 percent as Republicans. This would mean that working-class voters are 20 points more Democratic than middle-class voters are, but only 10 points less Republican. Averaging these two differences results in a Democratic advantage of 15 points among working-class voters—or a 15-point Republican advantage among middle-class voters. If the percentage of independents is the same among both middle-class and working-class voters, then the difference in Democratic identification will equal the difference in Republican identification. The above method corrects for differences in the level of independent identification between the two social classes.
5  There also are methodological differences between my study and the ones cited here. These other studies do not adjust income for marital status and age, which I do, and that makes some difference. Also, I compare those with above-average incomes to those with below-average incomes, while these other studies compare those in the top income tercile to those in the bottom income tercile.
6  I relied on the American National Election Study surveys for these figures, but I compared the ANES data to the exit poll data for each year. For most years, the two sources yielded similar results for income and education, the only two variables available for the exit polls. However, in 2008, the two sources yielded quite different results, so for that year I reported the average of the two sources.

## References

Berelson, Bernard R., Paul Lazarsfeld, and William N. McPhee. 1954. *Voting: A Study of Opinion Formation in a Presidential Campaign*. Chicago: University of Chicago Press.

Black, Earl, and Merle Black. 2002. *The Rise of Southern Republicans*. Cambridge, MA: Harvard University Press.

Brewer, Mark D., and Jeffrey M. Stonecash. 2007. *Split: Class and Cultural Divides in American Politics*. Washington, DC: CQ Press.

Bullock, Charles S.III, and Ronald Keith Gaddie. 2009. *The Triumph of Voting Rights in the South*. Norman: University of Oklahoma Press.

Bullock, Charles S. III, and Mark J. Rozell. 2018. "African Americans' Role in Southern Politics." In *The New Politics of the Old South*. 6th edition, eds Charles S. Bullock III and Mark J. Rozell, 21–41. Lanham, MD: Roman and Littlefield.

Burnham, Walter Dean. 1970. *Critical Elections and the Mainsprings of American Politics*. New York: W. W. Norton.

Campbell, Angus, Philip E. Converse, Warren E. Miller, and Donald E. Stokes. 1960. *The American Voter*. New York: John Wiley.

Clubb, Jerome M., William H. Flanigan, and Nancy H. Zingale. 1980. *Partisan Realignment: Voters, Parties, and Government in American History*. Beverly Hills, CA: Sage.

Crotty, William. 1984. *American Parties in Decline*. 2nd edition. Boston: Little, Brown.

Eulau, Heinz. 1962. *Class and Party in the Eisenhower Years*. New York: The Free Press of Glencoe.

Fisher, Patrick. 2014. *Demographic Gaps in American Political Behavior*. Boulder, CO: Westview Press.

Gelman, Andrew. 2010. *Red State, Blue State, Rich State, Poor State: Why Americans Vote the Way They Do*. Expanded edition. Princeton, NJ: Princeton University Press.

Hawley, George. 2014. *White Voters in 21st Century America*. New York: Routledge.

Key, V. O., Jr. 1977 (1949). *Southern Politics in State and Nation*. New edition. Knoxville: University of Tennessee Press.

Ladd, Everett Caroll, Jr, with Charles D. Hadley. 1978. *Transformations of the American Party System: Political Coalitions from the New Deal to the 1970s*. 2nd edition. New York: W. W. Norton.

Lawson, Alan. 2006. *A Commonwealth of Hope: The New Deal Response to Crisis*. Baltimore: The Johns Hopkins University Press.

Leuchtenburg, William E. 1963. *Franklin D. Roosevelt and the New Deal*. New York: Harper and Row.

Lewis-Beck, Michael S., William G. Jacoby, Helmut Norpoth, and Herbert F. Weisberg. 2008. *The American Voter Revisited*. Ann Arbor: University of Michigan Press.

Lublin, David. 2004. *The Republican South: Democratization and Partisan Change*. Princeton, NJ: Princeton University Press.

Mayhew, David R. 2002. *Electoral Realignments: A Critique of an American Genre*. New Haven, CT: Yale University Press.

McCartin, Joseph A. 2011. "The Strike That Busted Unions." *New York Times*, August 2.

McDonald, Stephen L. 1981. "Economic Issues in the Campaign." In *A Tide of Discontent: The 1980 Elections and Their Meaning*, eds Ellis Candoz and Cecil V.Crabb, Jr, 139–156. Washington, DC: CQ Press.

Morison, Samuel Eliot. 1965. *The Oxford History of the American People*. New York: Oxford University Press.

Nadeau, Richard, Richard G. Niemi, Harold W. Stanley, and Jean-Francois Godbout. 2004. "Class, Party, and South/Non-South Differences: An Update" *American Politics Research* 32(1): 52–67.

Nie, Norman H., Sidney Verba, and John R. Petrocik. 1979. *The Changing American Voter*. Enlarged edition. Cambridge, MA: Harvard University Press.

Phillips, Kevin P. 1970. *The Emerging Republican Majority*. Garden City, NY: Anchor Books.

Plotkin, Henry A. 1981. "Issues in the Presidential Campaign." In *The Election of 1980: Reports and Interpretations*, ed. Gerald M. Pomper, 38–64. Chatham, NJ: Chatham House.

Roof, Tracy. 2011. *American Labor, Congress, and the Welfare State, 1935–2010*. Baltimore: The Johns Hopkins University Press.

Scher, Richard K. 1997. *Politics in the New South: Republicanism, Race, and Leadership in the Twentieth Century*. 2nd edition. Armonk, NY: M. E. Sharpe.

Smith, Jean Edwards. 2013. *Eisenhower in War and Peace*. New York: Random House.

Steed, Robert P., and Laurence W. Moreland (eds). 2006. *Writing Southern Politics: Contemporary Interpretations and Future Directions*. Lexington: University Press of Kentucky.

Stonecash, Jeffrey M. 2000. *Class and Party in American Politics*. Boulder, CO: Westview Press.

Sundquist, James L. 1983. *Dynamics of the Party System: Alignment and Realignment of Political Parties in the United States*. Revised edition. Washington, DC: The Brookings Institution.

Weaver, R. Kent. 1985. "Controlling Entitlements." In *The New Direction in American Politics*, eds John E. Chubb and Paul E. Peterson, 307–342. Washington, DC: The Brookings Institution.

# 4

# RACE, CLASS, AND THE POLITICS OF WHITE IDENTITY

Race has always been important in American politics. In the beginning, slavery was the key issue, one that divided the nation along regional lines and ultimately led to the Civil War. After the war, the question of slavery was settled, but the place of blacks in American society remained a divisive issue. Following the end of Reconstruction in the South, conservative southern Democrats regained power in each of the eleven states of the old Confederacy. Once in power, they established a system of white supremacy throughout the South. Legal segregation was installed, the so-called "Jim Crow" laws. Blacks were largely disenfranchised through the poll tax, literacy test, and even intimidation, if necessary. For the first half of the twentieth century, the South was solidly Democratic, and southern Democrats successfully defended their positions on race relations. Neither northern Democrats nor Republicans seriously challenged the policies of southern white supremacy. This began to change in the 1950s, as there were more aggressive challenges to the status quo in the South. By the 1960s, the civil rights movement was forcing change in discriminatory racial policies. The key pieces of federal legislation were the 1964 Civil Rights Act, which outlawed segregation and discrimination in many aspects of society, and the 1965 Voting Rights Act, which instituted a variety of legal measures to ensure that blacks would be able to register and vote. Added to these landmark acts were additional federal laws, some important Supreme Court decisions, and a constitutional amendment that banned the use of the poll tax. The civil rights conflicts of the 1960s shaped the current party system, creating a clear division between Democrats and Republicans on the question of race in American politics. A half-century after the civil rights era, race and race-related issues were in the center of the political stage during the 2016 presidential election. During the election campaign, a number of commentators argued that support for

Donald Trump was driven by racial resentment and concerns about white identity (Confessore 2016; McElwee 2016; Parker 2016). According to these media pundits, many white voters felt that blacks and other minorities received preferential treatment, that high levels of immigration, particularly illegal immigration, made the nation worse off, and that the cultural identity of the country was being harmed by the growth of racial and ethnic minorities. Scholarly studies after the election echoed these conclusions. Sides, Tesler and Vavreck (2018) found that attitudes toward blacks and other minority groups were potent forces affecting the presidential votes of whites. Hooghe and Dassonneville (2018) concluded that both racial resentment and hostility toward immigrants were important determinants of the Trump vote. Other analyses came to similar conclusions (Abramowitz and McCoy 2019; Schaffner, MacWilliams, and Nteta 2018).

If racial resentment and white identity were important determinants of the presidential vote in 2016, they also may help to explain why Trump drew his support disproportionately from the white working class. In order to establish that, we must show not only that these attitudes affected the vote in 2016, but also that there were significant differences between working-class and middle-class whites on these issues. Moreover, the previous chapter showed that the movement of the white working class toward the Republican Party began before Trump, which leads to the question of whether race-related attitudes help to explain social class differences in voting behavior in earlier presidential elections, or whether these effects were unique to 2016. Finally, we can look at change in these relationships over time. For attitudes on race-related issues to explain why the relationship between social class and voting behavior among whites has changed in this century, then either or both of the following must be true: (a) working-class whites have become more conservative, relative to middle-class whites, on race-related issues over the past two decades; or (b) race-related issues have become more important determinants of voting behavior over the past two decades.

Before analyzing the data on the relationships between social class, attitudes on race-related issues, and voting behavior in order to answer the above questions, it will be useful to understand how conflict over race has developed since the 1960s, which is what the next section discusses. Then we will look at survey data to examine attitudes on race-related issues, including how these attitudes are related to both social class and partisan choice and how these relationships have changed in recent years. Finally, this chapter will look at attitudes on immigration, which represents a new dimension of conflict over race, ethnicity, and white identity. The focus of all of the analysis that follows is on whether attitudes on issues of race and immigration help to explain the change in the relationship between social class and partisan choice that has taken place in this century.

## Race in American Politics Since the 1960s

Conflict over civil rights issues in the 1960s created clear differences between the two major parties on this issue dimension. Prior to then, it would have been difficult for most voters to see significant differences between Democrats and Republicans on civil rights. Republicans were the party of Lincoln, so they had a historical claim to be the party of racial equality, and the GOP party platforms in the 1950s contained strong civil rights statements (Republican Party 1952; 1956). However, Republicans seemed reluctant to really push for federal government action in this area. President Dwight Eisenhower did order troops to Little Rock, Arkansas, in 1957 to enforce the desegregation of the public schools that had been ordered by the federal courts, an action that received considerable national media attention. But Eisenhower did so reluctantly, and he generally was at best unenthusiastic about the Supreme Court's 1954 *Brown v. the Board of Education* decision declaring that segregated public schools were unconstitutional (Scher 1997, 196–206). Many Northern Democrats, such as Hubert Humphrey, were strong advocates of federal government action to end legal segregation and discrimination, but in the South, where segregation was concentrated, Democrats controlled state governments and strongly defended existing racial arrangements (Black and Black 2002, 40–57; Lamis 1984, 7–19; Scher 1997, 193–230). If voters were unclear about how the political parties differed on civil rights issues in the 1950s, it was because the parties did not provide unambiguous signals to the electorate on this topic (Carmines and Stimson 1989, 37–55).

That changed in 1964. In March, the Congress passed the landmark Civil Rights Act. President Lyndon Johnson championed that legislation, but he needed bipartisan support to get it enacted. In the Senate, the bill passed by a vote of 73 to 27 (Library of Congress 2019). Of the 73 Senators voting for the legislation, 27 were Republicans and 46 were Democrats. Among those who voted against the act, there were six Republicans and 21 Democrats, almost all from the South. Thus, support for this landmark civil rights bill cut across party lines. The six Republican senators who opposed the legislation included Barry Goldwater, who became the Republican presidential nominee later that year. Goldwater's nomination led to a sharp contrast between the two presidential candidates in 1964, a contrast that began to establish lasting differences between the parties on racial issues. President Johnson fully supported the Civil Rights Act. Senator Goldwater not only opposed it; he pursued a "southern strategy" in his campaign, which emphasized his opposition to federal government civil rights action as part of his general conservatism. The result was that he carried the five states of the Deep South, but the only other state that he won was his home state of Arizona. The difference between the Democratic and Republican candidates in 1964 continued in subsequent presidential elections (Scher 1997, 100–117). Richard Nixon followed a similar "southern strategy" in his 1968 and 1972 presidential campaigns (Mayer 2002, 69–122). So did Ronald Reagan in 1980 and

1984 (Mayer 2002, 150–200). From 1980 on, the Republican presidential candidate always did better in the South than in the North, something that was accomplished by winning a hefty share of the southern white vote.

Race became an issue that changed the party alignments. First of all, voting was more strongly along racial lines after the 1960s. The 1965 Voting Rights Act, also championed by President Johnson, led to dramatic increases in black voter registration and turnout in the South (Bullock and Gaddie 2009). Blacks now viewed the national Democratic party as the one that supported federal government action to eliminate discrimination, and they began to vote overwhelming for Democratic candidates. Southern whites moved toward the Republican Party. This transformation of southern politics was not accomplished overnight. Shifts in voting behavior were more gradual, occurring first at the presidential level, then moving down the ballot to congressional and then state legislative elections (Lublin 2004, 33–65). By the end of the 20th century, Republicans were clearly the majority party in the South, and party support was along racial lines: blacks voted overwhelmingly for Democrats; whites voted solidly for Republicans (Black and Black 2002, 244–256). Racial divisions were strong in the North as well. Blacks staunchly supported the Democratic Party, while whites leaned toward the GOP, although not as strongly as southern whites did.

Among whites, attitudes on race-related issues began to shape ideological and partisan orientations. The basic question was how far the federal government should go in attempting to secure equal treatment for blacks. Goldwater's 1964 candidacy provided an ideological justification for opposing extensive federal action. Attitudes on civil rights policies became tied to more general ideological orientations: liberals favored strong federal government efforts to achieve racial equality; conservatives opposed aggressive civil rights actions (Carter 1996). Similar divisions were established along party lines. Democrats favored more extensive civil rights actions; Republicans wanted more limited efforts. These changes occurred both among voters and among political elites (Carmines and Stimson 1989, 55–83). Voting on civil rights issues in the Congress became more divided along party lines after the 1960s. Party platforms similarly diverged on these issues. So did presidential campaigns (Mayer 2002). Moreover, attitudes on race influenced attitudes on other issues that are indirectly tied to race, such as social welfare or criminal justice issues (Carmines and Stimson 1989, 115–137). In sum, attitudes on race and race-related issues achieved a central position in American electoral politics after the 1960s.

The growing importance of racial issues in voting and partisanship may have worked to weaken the relationship between social class and voting behavior that existed in the 1950s in at least two ways. First of all, there are the potential crosscutting effects of racial issues. Huckfeldt and Kohfeld (1989) argue that as voters began to vote more on the basis of racial issues, this reduced the influence of economic issues through a simple substitution effect. The connection between social class and partisan choice that was established during the New Deal realignment was built on economic issues. As Chapter 3 outlined, this was the situation in the North in the 1950s: party differences were largely in terms of economic issues, which then translated into social class differences in partisanship. But as racial issues began to rival economic ones as important cleavages in American politics after the 1960s, some northern white Democrats were pulled toward the Republican Party, and some white Republicans shifted toward the Democrats, with the result that social class differences in voting were reduced. Even without any relationship between social class and attitudes on racial issues, the increased effect of racial issues on partisanship tended to decrease the influence of economic issues and thus diminish the relationship between social class and voting behavior.

In the South, a different dynamic was unfolding, as Chapter 3 explained. The development of two-party competition after the 1960s in the South allowed class cleavages to emerge in the region. Southern voting prior to the 1960s was largely unrelated to social class. Middle and working-class whites both strongly supported the Democrats as the party of segregation and white supremacy. The civil rights movement of the 1960s changed that: southern whites moved toward the GOP, with those who were conservative on civil rights issues being the most likely to shift their party allegiance (Knuckey 2001; 2005; Valentino and Sears 2005). At the same time, economic issues began to influence voting behavior more than in the past, and white southerners who were more conservative on economic issues were now more likely to vote for Republicans (Lublin 2004, 172–216). With southern whites now voting on the basis of both economic and racial issues, class cleavages developed in a region that previously did not have them (Shafer and Johnston 2006, 173–176; Nadeau et al. 2004). Middle-class whites moved toward the Republicans more than did working-class whites not because they were more conservative on civil rights issues, but because they were more conservative on economic issues. Nevertheless, the importance of racial issues in the South muted what might have been stronger class differences in voting behavior.

Huckfeldt and Kohfeld (1989) argue that group conflict was another dynamic that reduced class differences in voting among whites. As blacks began to vote in much higher numbers, especially in the South, and as they began to vote heavily for Democrats, they became a larger share of the Democratic electorate. This frequently fomented conflict between blacks and whites, thereby increasing tensions within the Democratic biracial coalition. Some whites, believing that the Democratic Party was becoming too concerned with the political interests of blacks, began to leave the party. This pattern of behavior was more likely to occur in areas with a relatively high percentage of blacks in the electorate (Glaser 1994). The result is that counties that have the highest share of blacks in their electorates have become the ones with the lowest level of Democratic voting among whites (Gelman 2010, 190–193).

For racial issues to produce a reversal, rather than just a weakening, of the traditional relationship between social class and partisan choice, there has to be more than just crosscutting effects of racial issues. More conservative attitudes on these issues among working-class whites would be required to make them more Republican than middle-class whites are. Some studies suggest that this is the case. In particular, some research has found that attitudes on racial issues are related to education (Schuman *et al.* 1997, 231–234). Specifically, college-educated whites tend to be more liberal on civil rights questions. Since education is related to social class, working-class whites should have more conservative attitudes. But other research has found little relationship between socio-economic status and attitudes on racial issues (Kinder and Sanders 1996, 90). This indicates that our analysis needs to consider both how strongly attitudes on racial issues affect the vote and how much these attitudes are related to social class.

While racial issues have been important in American electoral politics since the 1960s, considerable research has determined that these issues have become more potent after the nomination and election of Obama in 2008. In fact, several studies conclude that Obama lost votes in 2008 because of his race (Kinder and Dale-Riddle 2012, 105; Lewis-Beck, Tien, and Nadeau 2010; Piston 2010). After his election, the presence of a president who was a black Democrat further galvanized the relationship between race and party. White voters, especially those who were less educated, began to perceive sharper differences between the political parties on racial issues. Attitudes on racial issues began to affect voting behavior more, not less, after 2008, even though Obama avoided emphasizing racial issues while he was president (Abramowitz and McCoy 2019; Kinder and Dale-Riddle 2012; Tesler 2016).

## Racial Issues and Voting Behavior

The political changes summarized above generated an enormous body of research on race, racial attitudes, and political behavior in the U.S. The consensus of this research is that the old questions of segregation and racial superiority have largely disappeared from American politics. The new questions focus on whether blacks have an equal opportunity for success, why blacks tend to be economically worse off than whites, and what the federal government should do about this. On one side of the argument is the belief that there is not much discrimination in American society, that the failure of blacks to prosper as much as whites is due to a lack of effort among blacks, and that the federal government should not provide special help to blacks. The opposing view is that substantial discrimination remains, that historical circumstances and unequal treatment prevents blacks from getting ahead, and that the federal government needs to do more to ensure racial equality.

Numerous researchers have used the concept of racial resentment (also referred to as symbolic racism or modern racism) to capture the above views (Kinder and Sanders 1996; Sears *et al.* 2000). Those with high levels of racial resentment believe that blacks do not face significant discrimination and that their failure to be more successful is because they do not embrace values of hard work and determination that whites generally subscribe to. Put simply, blacks would be

more successful if they just tried harder. People with low levels of racial resentment believe that blacks still face discrimination and that more government effort
is needed to rectify the situation. A commonly used method for measuring racial
resentment in surveys is to construct an index from the following four statements
that individuals are asked to agree or disagree with: (1) Irish, Italians, Jewish and
many other minorities overcame prejudice and worked their way up. Blacks
should do the same without any special favors; (2) Generations of slavery and
discrimination have created conditions that make it difficult for blacks to work
their way out of the lower class; (3) Over the past few years, blacks have gotten
less than they deserve; and (4) It's really a matter of some people not trying hard
enough; if blacks would only try harder they could be just as well off as whites
(Tesler 2016, 21). These questions have been asked by the American National
Election Studies (ANES) for several past elections, which allows us to look at the
relationships over time.

I formed an index of racial resentment from the above four questions. Each
question had a five-point response scale that ran from strongly agree to strongly
disagree. I scored each item so that a higher score represented a more conservative
position, took the mean score for the set of questions, and scaled the scores to run
from 1.0 to 4.0 in order to make them comparable to other variables that will be
used later in the analysis. The four items are all correlated fairly strongly, so putting
them together into a single index makes sense. The index of racial resentment also
correlates well with other questions about race, including a question about whether
the government should provide special help to blacks. This question was a seven-
point scale running from providing no special help to blacks to making every effort
to help blacks. It also has been asked in the ANES surveys for some time, and I
make use of this question as well in the following analysis. This question directly
asks about the desirability of government aid to blacks, which is what the racial
resentment index indirectly measures.

Attitudes on racial issues are strongly related to the presidential vote in 2016.
Trump did much better among whites with higher levels of racial resentment.
Table 4.1 shows this relationship. For simplicity of presentation, I trichotomized
the racial resentment scale so that there were roughly three equal groups of
whites. As the table shows, Trump received less than 20 percent of the vote of
whites with a low level of racial resentment, but he won close to 90 percent of
the vote of whites with a high level of racial resentment. A very similar pattern
appears in Table 4.2, which shows the relationship between attitudes on government aid to blacks and the presidential vote in 2016. As described above, this
question was a seven-point scale running from feeling that blacks should get no
special help to feeling that the government should make every effort to aid
blacks. To simplify the analysis, I collapsed the seven-point scale into three
groups: (a) those who favored providing some special help to blacks (the three
most liberal categories on the seven-point scale); (b) those with a neutral attitude
(the middle position on the scale); and (c) those who opposed providing any

**TABLE 4.1** Presidential Vote by Feelings of Racial Resentment, 2016

| | Racial Resentment | | |
|---|---|---|---|
| *Presidential Vote:* | *Low* | *Medium* | *High* |
| % for Clinton | 82.0 | 35.8 | 11.4 |
| % for Trump | 18.0 | 64.2 | 88.6 |
| Total | 100% | 100% | 100% |
| (N) | (607) | (531) | (664) |

Source: ANES 2016 survey.
Note: Only white, major-party voters are included in the table. See the text for details on the variables.

**TABLE 4.2** Presidential Vote by Attitudes Toward Government Aid to Blacks, 2016

| | Government Aid to Blacks | | |
|---|---|---|---|
| *Presidential Vote:* | *Should help blacks* | *Neutral opinion* | *No special help for blacks* |
| % for Clinton | 84.4 | 58.4 | 16.3 |
| % for Trump | 15.6 | 41.6 | 83.7 |
| Total | 100% | 100% | 100% |
| (N) | (405) | (356) | (886) |

Source: ANES 2016 survey.
Note: Only white, major-party voters are included in the table. See the text for details on the variables.

special help to blacks (those in the three most conservative categories). In this case, there are not similar numbers of voters in each of the categories; far more respondents were on the conservative end of the scale. Still, the relationship looks much like the one in Table 4.1. Trump did poorly among those with a liberal attitude on this issue but extremely well among those with a conservative attitude on this issue. All of this is consistent with the conclusions reached by many political analysts and scholars, namely that Trump's support was driven by racism or racial conservatism (Abramowitz and McCoy 2019; McElwee 2016; Mutz 2018; Schaffner, MacWilliams, and Nteta 2018; Sides, Tesler, and Vavreck 2018).

A frequently articulated view in the media in 2016 was that racial attitudes played a much greater role in 2016 than in previous presidential elections. To test that hypothesis, I looked at the relationship between the presidential vote and feelings of racial resentment in previous years. In each case, I divided scores on the racial resentment index into three approximately equal groups, just as I did in the analysis for Table 4.1. In addition to 2016, I analyzed data from 2012, an election that was quite different from 2016. Racial issues did not have the salience in the 2012 campaign that they did in 2016, and Mitt Romney certainly was not perceived as hostile to minorities in the way that Trump was. I also looked at 2008 and at the two presidential elections before Obama's election. As noted above, several scholars found that racial attitudes played a greater role in American electoral politics after Obama's election than they did before then, so comparing 2016 with the four previous presidential elections should show this change. I combined the data for George W. Bush's two elections, 2000 and 2004, to create a larger number of cases, since the ANES surveys for these years had fewer respondents than was the case for the other years. Unfortunately, the questions for the racial resentment index were not asked in the ANES surveys conducted during the 1990s, so it was not possible to include those years in this analysis. The analysis results are in Table 4.3. According to these data, racial issues have increased in importance in presidential elections in this century, just as some scholars have claimed. They already were quite important in the Bush elections, but they became even stronger in the Obama elections, and then even stronger in 2016.

I also analyzed the relationship over time between attitudes on racial issues and presidential voting using the question about government aid to blacks that is described above. The question about government aid to blacks has been asked for a longer period of time than the questions about racial resentment, so I not only ran the analysis for all of the years in Table 4.3, but I also added 1996 so that we could have a somewhat longer time perspective on the relationship. The results of this analysis are in Table 4.4. The pattern here is quite similar to what we observed for Table 4.3. Attitudes on government aid to blacks were strongly related to the vote among whites well before Trump and Obama. Those with conservative attitudes have been much more likely for some time to vote for the Republican candidate than those with liberal attitudes have been. In 1996, for example, the Republican presidential candidate, Bob Dole, did 45 points better among those with a more conservative position on this issue than he did among those with a more liberal position. This already strong relationship became even

**TABLE 4.3** Presidential Vote by Feelings of Racial Resentment, 2000–2016

| Presidential Vote: | Racial Resentment | | |
| --- | --- | --- | --- |
| | Low | Medium | High |
| 2016: % for Trump | 18.0 | 64.2 | 88.6 |
| 2012: % for Romney | 23.2 | 65.1 | 78.4 |
| 2008: % for McCain | 25.4 | 60.2 | 76.0 |
| 2000–2004: % for Bush | 37.2 | 62.2 | 72.0 |

Source: ANES surveys, 2000–2016.
Note: Only white, major-party voters are included in the table. Figures are the percent of the major-party vote for the Republican candidate. See the text for details on the variables

**TABLE 4.4** Presidential Vote by Attitudes Toward Government Aid to Blacks, 1996–2016

| | Government Aid to Blacks | | |
| --- | --- | --- | --- |
| Presidential Vote: | Should help blacks | Neutral opinion | No special help for blacks |
| 2016: % for Trump | 15.6 | 41.6 | 83.7 |
| 2012: % for Romney | 15.7 | 20.3 | 73.3 |
| 2008: % for McCain | 21.7 | 45.5 | 70.9 |
| 2000–2004: % for Bush | 29.3 | 52.0 | 68.5 |
| 1996: % for Dole | 14.8 | 38.7 | 60.5 |

Source: ANES surveys, 1996–2016.
Note: Only white, major-party voters are included in the table. Figures are the percent of the major-party vote for the Republican candidate. See the text for details on the variables.

stronger during the Obama years, as existing research has indicated, and then strengthened even more in 2016. Trump won over 80 percent of the vote of whites with a conservative attitude on this issue, but not even one-sixth of the vote of those with a liberal attitude.

A well-established principle in the research on issue voting is that for voters to cast a ballot on the basis of a public policy issue, they need to have both an opinion on an issue and a perception of candidate differences on the issue (Campbell *et al.* 1960, 168–187; Lewis-Beck *et al.* 2008, 161–200). Fortunately, the ANES surveys have been asking respondents where they would place the presidential candidates on several policy issues for a number of years. One of the issues that they have asked these questions about is the seven-point scale regarding federal government aid to blacks that is discussed and analyzed above. As a simple way of looking at perceptions of the candidates, I took the mean score on the seven-point scale for perceptions of both the Democratic and the Republican presidential candidates for the same election years included in Table 4.4 (1996–2016), and I also included the mean score for the self-placement of respondents on this scale.

Table 4.5 presents the results of the analysis. Three points are obvious. First, voters have been perceiving substantial differences between the candidates on racial issues for some time. The perceived candidate differences were on average greater in 2016 than in 2012, again not surprising considering the difference between the campaigns in these two years, but they were sizable prior to Trump. Second, perceived differences between the parties are greater after 2008 than before, just as many scholars argue. The final point that stands out in the table is that white voters on average place themselves much closer to the Republican Party than they do to the Democratic Party. What may be surprising is that white voters, while still perceiving themselves closer to Trump than to Clinton, were not nearly as close to Trump as they were to Romney in 2012.

What stands out in all of the analyses in this chapter is that the relationship between racial attitudes and voting for 2016 also existed in earlier years, although

**TABLE 4.5** Voter Attitudes and Perceptions of Candidate Positions on Government Aid to Blacks, 1992–2016

| | Mean Scores on the Aid to Blacks Scale | | |
| --- | --- | --- | --- |
| | Self-placement of voters | Placement of the Dem. candidate | Placement of the Rep. candidate |
| 2016 | 4.75 | 2.59 | 5.66 |
| 2012 | 5.27 | 2.75 | 5.47 |
| 2008 | 5.13 | 2.86 | 4.92 |
| 2000–2004 | 4.90 | 3.23 | 4.82 |
| 1996 | 4.97 | 3.23 | 4.97 |

Source: ANES surveys, 1996–2016.
Note: Only white, major-party voters are included in the table. The aid to blacks scale runs from 1 to 7, with a lower score indicating more support for government aid to blacks. See the text for further details on the variables.

not as strongly as in 2016. Feelings of racial resentment were strongly related to the presidential vote in 2012, for example. The relationship is somewhat stronger in 2016, not surprising given the focus on race in that campaign, but 2016 is not a sharp deviation from the two Obama elections, 2008 and 2012. Racial issues were far more prominent in the 2016 campaign, but the impact of racial attitudes on the vote did not increase as much as some observers inferred from the behavior of the candidates in 2016. Furthermore, feelings of racial resentment were clearly related to the presidential vote before the Obama years, although the relationship clearly strengthened during his administration. Moreover, further analysis shows that feelings of racial resentment are related to party identification just as strongly as to the presidential vote in these earlier years. All of this supports the conclusions that many researchers came to well before 2016: both the parties and the voters have divided along racial lines in the post-civil rights era, and these divisions have been clear at least since the 1980s. This division intensified during the Obama years, and then grew even stronger in 2016. However, even if the Republicans had nominated someone else in 2016, feelings of racial resentment undoubtedly would have shaped the votes of whites, although probably less than was true for Trump.

Attitudes on racial issues have been important in American electoral politics for some time. But do they help to explain the increasing appeal of the Republican Party to white working-class voters? In particular, were white working-class voters in 2016 more likely to support Trump because they had more conservative attitudes on racial issues? To help answer this question, I calculated the mean scores for working-class and middle-class whites on the two measures of racial attitudes used above: the racial resentment index and the question about government aid to blacks. The racial resentment index runs from 1.0 to 4.0, with a high score indicating greater racial resentment. The question about government aid to blacks is a seven-point scale, with a higher score indicating a more conservative attitude. I also included one additional item: the mean score on the feeling thermometer toward blacks, which runs from one to 100 degrees, with a high score indicating greater warmth toward blacks. For social class, I used the adjusted household income measure that is described in Chapter 2. As I argued there, I think that household income, appropriately adjusted, is the best measure of social class that is available in recent surveys. I only analyzed voters who are at least 30 years old, on the basis that income is a poor measure of social class for very young voters, as discussed in Chapter 2. These mean scores are presented in Table 4.6. On both the racial resentment index and the question about aid to blacks, lower-income voters are somewhat more conservative. The social class differences on these two measures are real but quite modest, about 0.2 points. To give some idea of how much of a difference this is, on the question about aid to blacks, 58 percent of working-class whites had a conservative attitude (i.e. they chose one of the three most conservative positions on the seven-point scale), compared to 53 percent of middle-class whites. This modest difference on racial attitudes suggests that while racial attitudes probably contributed to Trump's disproportionate success among white working-class voters, they do not fully explain it. Interestingly, there are no appreciable differences by social class on the feeling thermometer toward blacks.

Further analysis of these data show that the reason why middle-class voters are more liberal on racial issues is because they are more educated on average. Income has little effect on these attitudes once education is controlled for. While I have argued earlier in this study that income is the best indicator of social class that we currently have, especially given the lack of good occupational information in recent surveys of the electorate, education may have effects on attitudes apart from its relationship to social class, a point discussed in Chapter 2. Thus, two individuals who have equally high incomes and equally good managerial

TABLE 4.6 Racial Attitudes by Social Class, 2016

| Racial Attitude | Working-class Voters | Middle-class Voters |
| --- | --- | --- |
| Mean score on the racial resentment index | 2.88 | 2.65 |
| Mean score on the aid to blacks scale | 4.93 | 4.72 |
| Mean score on the feeling thermometer toward blacks | 67.5 | 68.7 |

Source: ANES 2016 survey.
Note: Only white, major-party voters are included in the table. The racial resentment index runs from 1 to 4, with a higher score indicating higher resentment. The aid to blacks scale runs from 1 to 7, with a lower score indicating more support for government aid to blacks. The feeling thermometer runs from zero to 100, with a higher score indicating a warmer feeling. See the text for further details on the variables.

jobs, but who differ in education, are likely to differ in their attitudes on racial issues. The same would be true for individuals who are equally working-class in terms of income and occupation but who differ in education. As Chapter 2 showed, there are many whites who lack a college degree but who are middle-class, even upper middle-class, in terms of income and occupation, so recognizing the potential effects of education apart from social class is important.

Attitudes on racial issues appear to provide at least some explanation of why working-class whites were more likely to vote for Trump than were middle-class whites in 2016. Racial attitudes had a strong effect on the vote in 2016, and working-class whites were somewhat more conservative on these attitudes. Do racial attitudes also help to explain the change in the relationship between social class and voting behavior that was described in the previous chapter? As Chapter 3 showed, class differences in voting declined from the 1990s to the early 2000s, then in the 2010s actually became inverted, so that Republicans now do better among the white working class. To investigate this question, I calculated mean scores for lower and higher-income whites on both the index of racial resentment and the seven-point scale that asked about government aid to blacks for the same election years used in Table 4.4 (1996–2016), which showed how these attitudes on racial issues were related to the vote. Table 4.7 presents these data.

As we can see, social class differences in racial attitudes were greater in 2016 than in previous years. In fact, on the question about government aid to blacks, social class differences prior to 2016 were almost nonexistent. While this may seem surprising, given many reports in the popular press about the intolerance of working-class individuals, some existing research has come to the same conclusion (Kinder and Sanders 1996, 90). It also is interesting, and perhaps surprising, that whites were not more racially resentful or racially conservative overall in 2016 than they were in 2012; in fact, just the opposite is the case. Racial

**TABLE 4.7** Attitudes on Racial Issues by Social Class, 1996–2016

|  | Racial Resentment Index | | Aid to Blacks Scale | |
|  | Working-class Voters | Middle-class Voters | Working-class Voters | Middle-class Voters |
|---|---|---|---|---|
| 2016 | 2.88 | 2.65 | 4.93 | 4.72 |
| 2012 | 3.06 | 2.93 | 5.32 | 5.25 |
| 2008 | 3.00 | 2.93 | 5.23 | 5.25 |
| 2000–2004 | 3.00 | 2.83 | 4.91 | 4.91 |
| 1996 | n.a. | n.a. | 4.94 | 5.01 |

Source: ANES surveys, 1996–2016.
Note: Entries are mean scores. Only white, major-party voters are included in the table. The racial resentment index runs from 1 to 4, with a higher score indicating higher resentment. The aid to blacks scale runs from 1 to 7, with a higher score indicating a more conservative attitude. See the text for further details on the variables.

resentment was lower in 2016 than in 2012. The same is true for the question about government aid to blacks. It seems that racial resentment or racial conservatism increased slightly from 2004 to 2012, but it then decreased between 2012 and 2016. But while whites were less racially resentful in 2016 than in previous years, their feelings of racial resentment were more clearly related to social class, and that is the important fact for explaining class differences in voting.

The analysis so far can be summarized fairly quickly. First, racial attitudes have affected voting and party identification for some time. The impact of these attitudes on presidential voting was somewhat stronger in 2016 than in previous elections, but the impact has been substantial for some time, and it has been increasing over time. Second, social class differences on racial issues among whites have been very small up to 2016, so their direct effect on class differences in voting in earlier years has been modest at best. Somewhat larger class differences on racial issues emerged in 2016, helping to explain Trump's disproportionate appeal to working-class whites. But even in 2016, the social class differences on racial issues among whites were modest, which contradicts some stories in the popular media about how Trump's support came heavily from working-class whites largely because they were much more hostile to blacks and other racial or ethnic minorities.

## Immigration Issues and Voting Behavior

Racial issues have been important in American politics for a long time. Current immigration issues are new to the main stage. It has been in this century that the issues have become salient and that the parties have clearly divided on the issues. This change is a result of the significant increase in immigration into this country. In 1970, less than 5 percent of the U.S. population was foreign born, which was the low point for the 20th century (Pew Research Center 2019). That number increased to about 8 percent in 1990, to 11 percent in 2000, and to nearly 14 percent in 2015, which is the high point so far for this century (Pew Research Center 2019; Zong, Batalova, and Burrows 2019). A significant number of these immigrants are residing in the country without the legal authorization to do so. Unauthorized immigrants are estimated to be around 11 million people, which is about one-fourth of all foreign-born residents (Pew Research Center 2019; Zong, Batalova, and Burrows 2019). As the number of immigrants, legal and illegal, has grown, both in absolute numbers and as a share of the U.S. population, concerns about immigration have intensified among whites. Contributing to this concern is the fact that most recent immigration has come from Latin America, Asia, or the Middle East (Zong, Batalova, and Burrows 2019).

Trump made immigration a cornerstone of his 2016 campaign, arguing that immigration had hurt the country and that drastic action was needed to deal with the situation. His portrayal of immigrants was frequently inflammatory, such as his unsupported claims that many Mexican immigrants were criminals or rapists and that thousands of Muslims in New Jersey celebrated the fall of the World Trade

Center towers on September 11, 2001 (Carroll 2015; Lee 2015). His policy proposals were controversial: he repeatedly promised that he would build a wall along the Mexican border, adding that Mexico would pay for it; he called for a ban on Muslim immigrants, claiming that they were potential terrorist threats; and he proposed to deport large numbers of illegal immigrants (Corasaniti 2016). Given Trump's campaign statements on this issue, it is not surprising that research shows that attitudes on these issues affected voters in 2016. For example, an analysis of vote switching between 2012 and 2016 found that it was affected by attitudes on immigration (Reny, Collingwood, and Valenzuela 2019). People who voted for Obama in 2012 but then switched to Trump in 2016 were motivated in large part by anti-immigration attitudes. Those who switched from Romney in 2012 to Clinton in 2016 were characterized by pro-immigration attitudes. Similarly, Hooghe and Dassonneville (2018) found that anti-immigrant attitudes increased the likelihood of a Trump vote in 2016.

While immigration issues were particularly prominent in 2016, they were present in previous presidential elections. Several questions on this topic divide the American electorate. One question is how many immigrants to let in, a question that has become more salient given the substantial immigration into the country over the past few decades. Another question is which types of immigrants should be favored, particularly in terms of their level of education or job skills. A third question is what to do with immigrants who are living in the U.S. without legal authority, another question that has become more salient with the growth of this group in recent decades. Underlying positions on these policy issues are views about immigrants and what contributions they make to the society (Hainmueller and Hopkins 2015). Those who feel that immigrants contribute to the economy and society are more likely to oppose both reducing the level of immigration and deporting large numbers of unauthorized immigrants. Those who feel that immigrants are a burden tend to have opposite opinions. Attitudes about whether immigrants contribute to the economy or are a burden are related to opinions about which types of immigrants should be favored. Immigrants who are well-educated or skilled workers are more likely to be viewed as economically beneficial (Hainmueller and Hopkins 2015).

Of course, attitudes regarding immigration are not solely based on economic assessments. One divisive question concerns the estimated 11 million immigrants who are residing illegally in the U.S. Surveys have found that white Americans have less favorable attitudes towards these unauthorized immigrants than they do toward those who are here legally (Levy, Wright, and Citrin 2016). Not surprisingly, some Americans are concerned about the fact that so many people have been able to enter the country and stay without legal permission. Some of the hostility toward illegal immigrants may reflect feelings that all people should obey the laws, including entering the country in a legal manner. It also could be that many Americans have stereotypes of illegal immigrants that differ from those of legal immigrants.

After the attacks of 9/11, questions about Muslim immigrants took on a new tone. Muslims are often portrayed as hostile to the U.S., and they are more likely to be viewed as potential terrorists (Kalkan, Layman, and Uslaner 2009). Not surprising, research studies have found that white Americans have more unfavorable views of Muslim-Americans than they do of Hispanic-Americans or Asian-Americans (Sides and Gross 2013). Of course, Muslims also are a religious minority that many see as poorly fitting into American culture and society (Kalkan, Layman, and Uslaner 2009). Nevertheless, attitudes toward Muslims are best predicted by attitudes toward other immigrants, suggesting that there is an underlying orientation toward immigration in general that plays out in specific situations.

The dominant interpretation that political analysts have offered about the attitudes of white Americans toward immigrants is that these attitudes largely reflect concerns about the status of whites (Cox, Lienesch, and Jones 2017; Mutz 2018; Sides, Tesler, and Vavreck 2018). This interpretation stresses that the growing number of nonwhites in the country is a matter of concern for many whites because they fear that their status as the dominant racial group in the society is being threatened. Masuoka and Junn (2013) explain attitudes toward immigration through what they term a racial prism of group identity. Social groups understand their place in society by identifying how they are positioned relative to others. Whites tend to define themselves as having the traits that make them true Americans, and they tend to have stereotypes of other racial groups that are more negative. Opposition to immigration among whites is motivated by a desire to protect both the status of their group and what they see as national values. Immigrants are seen as not fully embodying these values, thus threatening American culture. These concerns about white identity and cultural displacement are more important determinants of attitudes toward immigration and immigrants than the other issues about immigration discussed above, such as whether immigrants entered legally or how much they will contribute to the economy. Thus, attitudes about immigration issues are highly correlated and share a common denominator. Therefore, it makes sense to consider overall attitudes toward immigrants in our analysis, rather than treat each question about immigration as a separate issue, even if some people make some distinctions among these questions.

The Pew Research Center has been studying public opinion on immigration for over two decades. Since the mid-1990s, they have asked respondents in their surveys whether immigrants strengthen the country or are a burden. Their data show a growing belief that immigrants strengthen the country. The change in opinion is enormous. In 1994, only about 31 percent had a positive view of immigrants, with 63 percent having a negative view. In 2016, these numbers had basically reversed: 59 percent now were positive and only 33 percent negative (Jones 2016). However, there was a growing partisan divide on this issue. Differences between Democrats and Republicans on immigration were small in the 1990s and early 2000s, but they began to grow after 2006 (Jones 2016).

Because the immigration issues are relatively new, we lack substantial data over time on attitudes toward immigration. The ANES surveys asked a number of questions on this topic in 2012 and 2016, but fewer questions were asked in earlier years, especially the 1990s. For this reason, I focused most of the following analysis on attitudes in the two most recent presidential elections. In 2016, the ANES survey asked respondents to agree or disagree with the following three statements: (1) Immigrants are generally good for America's economy; (2) America's culture is generally harmed by immigrants; and (3) Immigrants increase crime rates in the United States. Respondents also were asked how likely it was that recent immigration levels will take jobs away from people already here. I combined the above four items, which all were highly correlated, into an index of attitudes toward immigrants. The index is scaled from 1.0 to 4.0, with a higher score representing a more unfavorable attitude toward immigrants. In 2012, The ANES survey asked a somewhat different set of questions about immigration. For that year, I created an index of attitudes toward immigrants from five questions, which all were highly correlated.[1] That index also is scaled from 1.0 to 4.0, with a higher score representing a more unfavorable attitude toward immigrants.

Table 4.8 displays the presidential vote in 2012 and 2016 by attitudes toward immigration. For simplicity of presentation, I collapsed the voters into three approximately equal groups on the basis of their scores on the index of attitudes toward immigration for each year. There is a very strong relationship in 2016: Trump received about 86 percent of the vote from those who were in the most unfavorable third of the population in their attitudes toward immigration, but only about 19 percent from those in the most favorable third. The relationship for 2012 is not as strong as it is for 2016, but it nevertheless is quite strong. Just as we found for attitudes on race, attitudes on immigration divided voters along partisan lines before Trump's candidacy, but Trump accentuated that existing pattern.

Fewer questions were asked about immigration prior to 2012, but one question that was asked in earlier years was what the desirable level of immigration should

**TABLE 4.8** Presidential Vote by Attitudes Toward Immigrants, 2012–2016

| Presidential Vote: | Attitude Toward Immigrants | | |
|---|---|---|---|
| | Favorable | Mixed | Unfavorable |
| % for Trump, 2016 | 19.2 | 71.0 | 86.2 |
| (N) | (516) | (527) | (492) |
| % for Romney, 2012 | 25.5 | 64.9 | 79.0 |
| (N) | (920) | (1,035) | (944) |

Source: ANES surveys, 2012 and 2016.
Note: Only white, major-party voters are included in the table. See the text for details on the variables.

be. This question is nicely correlated with other attitudes about immigration, and it has been used considerably in previous research. This question offered respondents five choices, ranging from wanting much more immigration to wanting much less. However, very few respondents favored an increase of any sort in immigration, so I combined those who wanted a large increase and those favoring a small increase in order to create a large number of cases; even so, only a small minority of voters in each year were in favor of any increase, large or small, in immigration, so it makes sense to focus our attention on the difference between those who favor keeping immigration levels the same and those who want them lowered. That seems to be the key point of conflict on this issue.

I analyzed the relationship between attitudes on this issue and the presidential vote, using the same election years that are in the analysis reported in Table 4.4 (1996–2016). The results, which are in Table 4.9, show a striking change over time. In 1996, attitudes on immigration were unrelated to the presidential vote, just as the Pew Research Center found, using different data (Jones 2016). But by the start of the 21st century, a relationship emerged, with those who wanted immigration levels to go down being more likely to vote Republican. Bush, for example, won almost two-thirds of the vote from those wanting much less immigration, but only a little over one-half of the vote from those wanting immigration levels to remain the same. That moderate relationship grew over the years, to the point that in 2016, Trump won nearly 90 percent of the vote from those who wanted considerably lower levels of immigration, but only around one-third of the vote from those who favored keeping immigration at the current level.

Attitudes on immigration also are related to social class. Lower-income whites are more negative in their feelings toward immigrants than are higher-income whites. Table 4.10 shows the difference between lower-income and higher-income whites on the index of immigration attitudes for 2012 and 2016, the two years for which I was able to construct this index. As I explained above, it was necessary to use

**TABLE 4.9** Presidential Vote by Desired Immigration Level, 1996–2016

| Presidential Vote: | Desired Immigration Level | | | |
|---|---|---|---|---|
| | Increased | Same as Now | Decreased Somewhat | Decreased Considerably |
| 2016: % for Trump | 14.9 | 35.9 | 72.4 | 88.4 |
| 2012: % for Romney | 39.8 | 49.7 | 63.7 | 72.4 |
| 2008: % for McCain | 47.0 | 52.4 | 60.7 | 65.1 |
| 2000–2004: % for Bush | 39.9 | 53.8 | 61.2 | 62.0 |
| 1996: % for Dole | 47.8 | 46.9 | 49.1 | 46.3 |

Source: ANES surveys, 1996–2016.
Note: Only white, major-party voters are included in the table. Figures are the percent of the major-party vote for the Republican candidate. See the text for details on the variables.

**TABLE 4.10** Attitudes Toward Immigration by Social Class, 2012–2016

| Mean Score on the Index of Attitudes toward Immigrants: | Working-class Voters | Middle-class Voters |
|---|---|---|
| 2016 | 2.36 | 2.08 |
| 2012 | 2.67 | 2.40 |

Source: ANES surveys, 2012 and 2016.
Note: Only white, major-party voters are included in the table. The index of attitudes toward immigrants runs from 1 to 4, with a higher score indicating less favorable attitudes. See the text for details on the variables.

somewhat different questions to construct the index in each year, so the mean scores are not directly comparable. Specifically, the lower mean scores in 2016 do not necessarily mean that attitudes toward immigrants became more favorable between 2012 and 2016. Nevertheless, for each year, the index should be a good measure of relative attitudes toward immigrants, so the difference between lower-income and higher-income whites in each year should be a good indication of social class differences in these attitudes. As Table 4.10 shows, there are clear class differences in attitudes toward immigrants: working-class voters are considerably more negative in their attitudes. Moreover, class differences in immigration attitudes were just as strong in 2012 as they were in 2016.

Finally, we can examine social class differences on the question about the desirable level of immigration, which is the one question that was asked by the ANES in earlier years. Table 4.11 shows the percent of voters who wanted a much lower level of immigration, broken down by social class, for 1996 to 2016. While I chose to report the percent who wanted a much lower level, similar class differences are present if we look at all of those who wanted a reduction in immigration, even a small reduction. In 1996, social class differences on this question are small, but in the 21st century, significant class differences are present. From 2000 on, working-class whites are more likely to want a substantial

**TABLE 4.11** Desired Immigration Level by Social Class, 1996–2016

| % Wanting Much Less Immigration | Working-class Voters | Middle-class Voters |
|---|---|---|
| 2016 | 35.3 | 25.6 |
| 2012 | 31.9 | 22.3 |
| 2008 | 21.5 | 20.5 |
| 2000–2004 | 29.4 | 19.0 |
| 1996 | 28.8 | 25.8 |

Source: ANES surveys, 1996–2016.
Note: Only white, major-party voters are included in the table. See the text for details on the variables.

decrease in immigration. Furthermore, the size of the difference between lower-income and higher-income whites is about the same across the years, with the exception of 2008, when class differences were remarkably small. There is an overall increase in this century in the proportion of whites who want much less immigration, but the extent of the social class difference remains about the same in 2016 as it was in 2000–2004.

This analysis shows that attitudes toward immigrants help to explain why working-class whites have become more Republican than their middle-class counterparts. It seems clear that attitudes toward immigration influence the vote and that working-class voters are more conservative on these issues. While social class differences in attitudes on this issue do not seem to have changed much since 2000, the impact of these attitudes on the vote has increased. That helps to explain the change in social class voting in this century, namely that working-class whites have become more Republican than their middle-class counterparts. Furthermore, attitudes on immigration are related to attitudes on racial issues. Whites with higher levels of racial resentment tend to have more anti-immigrant attitudes (Abramowitz and McCoy 2019).

## Conclusions

Adding together the findings for racial attitudes with the findings for immigration attitudes, we can see that these questions of white identity are one significant reason why the relationship between social class and voting behavior has changed in this century. First of all, these issues have increased in salience. The attitudes of whites on race and immigration affect their vote more now than they did two decades ago. In the case of race, attitudes on these issues have influenced the vote of whites for some time, but the effect has strengthened in this century, reaching its greatest effect (at least so far) in 2016. For immigration, attitudes on these issues only began to affect the vote of whites in this century, but here too the effect has increased over time, also reaching its highest level in 2016. Moreover, class differences on these issues have become greater in this century. In 1996, there was little difference between working-class and middle-class whites on immigration; now there is a substantial difference. For race-related issues, class differences also were very weak at the start of the century, and they have increased to moderate differences. The combination of the increase in the impact of these issues plus the growth of class differences on the issues has contributed to the change in the relationship between social class and partisan choice among whites. Issues of race and immigration have pulled working-class whites toward the Republican Party and middle-class whites toward the Democratic Party over the past two decades. But since class differences on race and immigration are relatively modest, they hardly explain most of the change in the relationship between class and voting behavior.

One caveat needs to be stated here. The analysis presented in this chapter has only looked at the bivariate relationships between the vote and attitudes on racial or immigration issues in order to make the presentation simple. The bivariate relationships might reflect the influence of other variables not included in the analysis. These possible confounding variables could be producing simple associations that do not represent the causal effect of the variables examined here. Also, attitudes on racial issues are related to attitudes on immigration issues, so when we examined the relationship between racial attitudes and the vote, we were also getting the effects of immigration attitudes, and vice versa. In Chapter 7, the results of a multivariate analysis of the vote in 2016 and 2012 will be presented so that the independent effect of each variable can be assessed. As we will see, those results are consistent with the analysis in this chapter. For now, the simple two-variable tables will suffice to make the basic points clear, and the reader can rest assured that the analysis presented in this chapter is not misleading.

## Note

1 The 2012 questions asked: (1) What government policy should be toward unauthorized immigrants now living in the U.S.; (2) Whether people who were illegally brought into the U.S. as children under the age of 16, who have lived in the U.S. five years or longer, and who have graduated from high school should be allowed to become U.S. residents; (3) Whether state laws should require state and local police officers to determine the immigration status of a person if they find that there is reasonable suspicion that he or she is an undocumented immigrant; (4) Whether the number of immigrants from foreign countries who are permitted to come to the U.S. to live should be increased, decreased, or kept the same; (5) How likely it is that recent immigration levels will take jobs away from people already here.

## References

Abramowitz, Alan, and Jennifer McCoy. 2019. "United States: Racial Resentment, Negative Partisanship, and Polarization in Trump's America." *Annals of the American Academy of Political and Social Science* 681 (January): 137–156.

Black, Earl, and Merle Black. 2002. *The Rise of Southern Republicans*. Cambridge, MA: Harvard University Press.

Bullock, Charles S. III, and Ronald Keith Gaddie. 2009. *The Triumph of Voting Rights in the South*. Norman: University of Oklahoma Press.

Campbell, Angus, Philip E. Converse, Warren E. Miller, and Donald E. Stokes. 1960. *The American Voter*. New York: John Wiley.

Carmines, Edward G., and James A. Stimson. 1989. *Issue Evolution: Race and the Evolution of American Politics*. Princeton, NJ: Princeton University Press.

Carroll, Lauren. 2015. "Fact-checking Trump's Claim That Thousands in New Jersey Cheered When World Trade Center Tumbled." *Politifact*, November 22. www.politifact.com/ truth-o-meter/statements/2015/nov/22/donald-trump/fact-checking-trumps-claim -thousands-new-jersey-ch/.

Carter, Dan T. 1996. *From George Wallace to Newt Gingrich: Race in the Conservative Counterrevolution, 1963–1994*. Baton Rouge: Louisiana State University Press.

Confessore, Nicholas. 2016. "Trump Mines Grievances Of Whites Who Feel Lost." *New York Times*, July 14.

Corasaniti, Nick. 2016. "A Look at Trump's Immigration Plan, Then and Now." *New York Times*, August 31.

Cox, Daniel, Rachel Lienesch, and Robert P. Jones. 2017. "Beyond Economics: Fears of Cultural Displacement Pushed the White Working Class to Trump." *PRRI/The Atlantic Report*. Public Religion Research Institute, May 9. www.prri.org.

Gelman, Andrew. 2010. *Red State, Blue State, Rich State, Poor State: Why Americans Vote the Way They Do*. Expanded edition. Princeton, NJ: Princeton University Press.

Glaser, James M. 1994. "Back to the Black Belt: Racial Environment and White Racial Attitudes in the South." *Journal of Politics* 56(1): 21–41.

Hainmueller, Jens, and Daniel J. Hopkins. 2015. "The Hidden American Immigration Consensus: A Cojoint Analysis of Attitudes toward Immigrants." *American Journal of Political Science* 59(3): 529–548.

Hooghe, Marc, and Ruth Dassonneville. 2018. "Explaining the Trump Vote: The Effect of Racist Resentment and Anti-Immigrant Sentiments." *PS: Political Science and Politics* 51(3): 528–534.

Huckfeldt, Robert, and Carol W. Kohfeld. 1989. *Race and the Decline of Class in American Politics*. Urbana: University of Illinois Press.

Jones, Bradley. 2016. "Americans' Views of Immigrants Market by Widening Partisan, Generational Divides." Pew Research Center. www.pewresearch.org/fact-tank/2016/04/15/americans-views-of-immigrants-marked-by-widening-partisan-generational-divides/.

Kalkan, Kerem Ozan, Geoffrey C. Layman, and Eric M. Uslaner. 2009. "'Bands of Others'? Attitudes toward Muslims in Contemporary American Society." *Journal of Politics* 71(3): 847–862.

Kinder, Donald R., and Allison Dale-Riddle. 2012. *The End of Race?*. New Haven, CT: Yale University Press.

Kinder, Donald R., and Lynn M. Sanders. 1996. *Divided by Color: Racial Politics and Democratic Ideals*. Chicago: University of Chicago Press.

Knuckey, Jonathan, 2001. "Racial Resentment and Southern Republican Voting in the 1990s." *American Review of Politics* 22 (summer): 257–277.

Knuckey, Jonathan. 2005. "Racial Resentment and the Changing Partisanship of Southern Whites." *Party Politics* 11(1): 5–28.

Lamis, Alexander P. 1984. *The Two-Party South*. New York: Oxford University Press.

Lee, Michelle Ye Hee. 2015. "Donald Trump's False Comments Connecting Mexican Immigrants and Crime." *Washington Post*, July 8.

Levy, Morris, Matthew Wright, and Jack Citrin. 2016. "Mass Opinion and Immigration Policy in the United States: Re-Assessing Clientelist and Elitist Perspectives." *Perspectives on Politics* 14(3): 660–680.

Lewis-Beck, Michael S., William G. Jacoby, Helmut Norpoth, and Herbert F. Weisberg. 2008. *The American Voter Revisited*. Ann Arbor: University of Michigan Press.

Lewis-Beck, Michael S., Charles Tien, and Richard Nadeau. 2010. "Obama's Missed Landslide: A Racial Cost?." *PS: Political Science & Politics* 43(1): 69–76.

Library of Congress. 2019. "The Civil Rights Act of 1964: A Long Struggle for Freedom." www.loc.gov/exhibits/civil-rights-act/civil-rights-act-of-1964.html.

Lublin, David. 2004. *The Republican South: Democratization and Partisan Change*. Princeton, NJ: Princeton University Press.

Masuoka, Natalie, and Jane Junn. 2013. *The Politics of Belonging: Race, Public Opinion, and Immigration*. Chicago: University of Chicago Press.

Mayer, Jeremy D. 2002. *Running on Race: Racial Politics in Presidential Campaigns, 1960–2000*. New York: Random House.

McElwee, Sean. 2016. "Yep, Race Really Did Trump Economics: A Data Dive on His Supporters Reveals Deep Racial Animosity." *Salon*, November 13. www.salon.com/2016/11/13/yep-race-really-did-trump-economics-a-data-dive-on-his-supporters-reveals-deep-racial-animosity/.

Mutz, Diana C. 2018. "Status Threat, Not Economic Hardship, Explains the 2016 Presidential Vote." *Proceedings of the National Academy of Sciences*. www.pnas.org/cgi/da/10,1073/ pnas.1718155115.

Nadeau, Richard, Richard G. Niemi, Harold W. Stanley, and Jean-Francois Godbout. 2004. "Class, Party, and South/Non-South Differences: An Update." *American Politics Research* 32(1): 52–67.

Parker, George. 2016. "How Donald Trump is Winning Over the White Working Class." *The New Yorker*, May 16.

Pew Research Center. 2019. "Facts on U.S. Immigrants, 2017." www.pewhispanic.org/2019/06/03/facts-on-u-s-immigrants-trend-data/.

Piston, Spencer. 2010. "How Explicit Racial Prejudice Hurt Obama in the 2008 Election." *Political Behavior* 32(4): 431–451.

Reny, Tyler T., Loren Collingwood, and Ali A. Valenzuela. 2019. "Vote Switching in the 2016 Election: How Racial and Immigration Attitudes, Not Economics, Explain Shifts in White Voting." *Public Opinion Quarterly* 83(1): 91–113.

Republican Party. 1952. "Republican Party Platform of 1952." *The American Presidency Project*. www.presidency.ucsb.edu/documents/republican-party-platform-1952.

Republican Party. 1956. "Republican Party Platform of 1956." *The American Presidency Project*. www.presidency.ucsb.edu/documents/republican-party-platform-1956.

Schaffner, Brian F., Matthew MacWilliams, and Tatishe Nteta. 2018. "Understanding White Polarization in the 2016 Vote for President: The Sobering Role of Racism and Sexism." *Political Science Quarterly* 133(1): 9–34

Scher, Richard K. 1997. *Politics in the New South: Republicanism, Race, and Leadership in the Twentieth Century*. 2nd edition. Armonk, NY: M. E. Sharpe.

Schuman, Howard, Charlotte Steeh, Lawrence Bobo, and Maria Krysan. 1997. *Racial Attitudes in America*. Revised edition. Cambridge, MA: Harvard University Press.

Sears, David O., John J. Hetts, Jim Sidanius, and Lawrence Bobo. 2000. "Race in American Politics: Framing the Debates." In *Racialized Politics: The Debate About Racism in America*, eds David O. Sears, Jim Sidanius, and Lawrence Bobo, 1–43. Chicago: University of Chicago Press.

Shafer, Byron E., and Richard Johnston. 2006. *The End of Southern Exceptionalism: Class, Race, and Partisan Change in The Postwar South*. Cambridge, MA: Harvard University Press.

Sides, John, and Kimberly Gross. 2013. "Stereotypes of Muslims and Support for the War on Terror." *Journal of Politics* 75(3): 583–598.

Sides, John, Mark Tesler, and Lynn Vavreck. 2018. *Identity Crisis: The 2016 Presidential Election and the Battle for the Meaning of America*. Princeton, NJ: Princeton University Press.

Tesler, Michael. 2016. *Post-Racial or Most-Racial? Race and Politics in the Obama Era*. Chicago: University of Chicago Press.

Valentino, Nicholas A., and David O. Sears. 2005. "Old Time There Are Not Forgotten: Race and Partisan Realignment in the Contemporary South." *American Journal of Political Science* 49(3): 672–688.

Zong, Jie, Jeanne Batalova, and Micayla Burrows. 2019. "Frequently Requested Statistics on Immigrants and Immigration in the United States." Migration Policy Institute. www.migrationpolicy.org/article/frequently-requested-statistics-immigrants-and-imm igration-united-states.

# 5

# CULTURAL ISSUES, CLASS, AND VOTING

Issues of race, immigration, and white identity were prominent in the 2016 presidential election. Both pundits and scholars identified this set of issues as a major reason why Trump did so well among white working-class voters. Cultural issues, on the other hand, were rarely cited as a reason why white working-class voters were drawn to Trump. Yet in earlier years, cultural issues were considered to be important in explaining the appeal of the GOP to the working class. For example, Thomas Frank (2004) highlighted cultural issues as central to Republican success among less-affluent voters in middle America in his best-selling book, *What's the Matter with Kansas?*. Among political scientists, Brewer and Stonecash (2007) examined how cultural issues and social class divided Americans. The focus on these issues in earlier elections indicates that they should be considered in any attempt to analyze and explain the changing relationship between social class and voting behavior in contemporary America.

The analysis of how cultural issues have affected the relationship between social class and partisan choice in this century will proceed in four stages. First, this chapter will outline the emergence of cultural issues in modern American politics during the last few decades of the 20th century. Second, it will describe how attitudes on cultural issues are related to religious orientations. Third, this study will analyze the effect of cultural divisions on voting behavior and party identification. Fourth, it will examine how these cultural divisions are related to social class. The data analysis will again rely on the American National Election Studies (ANES) surveys of the American electorate. As we shall see, cultural issues have been and continue to be part of the story behind the changing relationship of social class to voting behavior.

## Cultural Issues since the 1960s

By cultural issues, I mean issues with a strong moral component, usually related to religious beliefs, and often related in some way to sex or gender. The term cultural issues sometimes is used more broadly to refer to most noneconomic domestic issues, including ones involving racial or criminal justice questions. The focus here is on a more tightly defined set of issues, ones that are tied to conceptions of morality and are influenced by religious orientations. These often are highly emotional wedge issues that can be used to attract voters from the opposite party. Conflict over these issues pits those who want to protect traditional moral values against those who have more progressive and secular views.

At the top of the list of these issues is abortion, which has been a highly divisive issue since the 1970s. More recently, questions of the rights of gay and lesbian individuals have been hotly debated. Further down the list are concerns about sexual behavior and depictions of sex in the media, questions about the role of women and the changing nature of family life, and disagreements about the proper relationship between church and state. None of these issues was particularly salient in the 1950s. Presidential candidates hardly mentioned them. That changed in the latter part of the 20th century, and in the 21st century all of these cultural issues have divided the parties, and the conflicts have become sufficiently intense for some analysts to call them culture wars (Hunter 1991; Nolan 1996).

Abortion quickly became a controversial and widely debated issue after the Supreme Court in 1973 declared in *Roe v. Wade* that a woman had a constitutional right to have an abortion. Prior to then, almost every state greatly restricted abortion (Craig and O'Brien 1993, 74–77). Three states completely prohibited it. The majority of states allowed abortion only to preserve the life of the mother. Most of the remaining states also permitted abortion when it was necessary to protect either the mental or the physical health of the mother. Only four states permitted it for any reason. There were movements to liberalize the abortion laws in a number of states in the 1960s, but these attempts did not greatly engage the public (Blanchard 1994, 22–28).

The Court did not establish an absolute right to an abortion in *Roe v. Wade* or its companion case, *Doe v. Bolton*. Rather, it stated that during the first trimester of a pregnancy, the decision about an abortion was to be left to the woman and her doctor; the state could not intrude into this doctor-patient relationship. But in the second trimester, the state could make some reasonable restrictions, and in the third trimester, the state could greatly restrict abortions so long as the mother's health was not endangered. This trimester scheme was based on when the fetus would become viable, which was determined to be sometime during the second trimester (Blanchard 1994, 28–30; Craig and O'Brien 1993, 24–32; Hull and Hoffer 2010, 170–179). Left unclear was exactly what restrictions states could enact at each stage.

Not surprisingly, the Court was widely attacked for its decision. The case was sweeping in its effect: it invalidated the laws concerning abortion in most of the states. Moreover, the Court based its decision on a constitutional right to privacy, a right that is not explicitly listed in the Constitution, but one that was asserted by the Court in a 1965 decision, *Griswold v. Connecticut* (Craig and O'Brien 1993, 26–32). The result was that *Roe v. Wade* stimulated considerable political activity. Opponents and supporters of the Court's decision organized and engaged in political actions to achieve their goals (Blanchard 1994, 51–101; Craig and O'Brien 1993, 35–96; Munson 2018, 40–56). They attempted to nominate and elect favorable candidates, lobbied legislatures, filed court cases, and engaged in direct participatory action, such as demonstrations. Some anti-abortion groups used confrontational and even violent methods, which revealed how intensely some individuals felt about this matter (Blanchard 1994, 85–95).

Anti-abortion or "pro-life" groups pushed Congress and the state legislatures to adopt the most restrictive laws possible. Some of the restrictions adopted included: (a) having strict standards for clinics that provided abortions, standards that many clinics would have difficulty meeting; (b) requiring informed consent and a waiting period for a woman seeking an abortion; (c) requiring parental consent for minors seeking an abortion; (d) permitting private hospitals to refuse to perform abortions; and (e) banning the use of state funds to pay for abortions (Craig and O'Brien 1993, 78–96). Pro-abortion or "pro-choice" groups fought against such restrictions, often by challenging the constitutionality of these laws in federal courts. Some of these laws were struck down by the courts, but many restrictions were upheld in some key Supreme Court cases, such as *Webster v. Reproductive Health Services* and *Planned Parenthood of Eastern Pennsylvania v Casey* (Hull and Hoffer 2010, 228–258). In the *Casey* decision, the Court ruled that states may restrict access to abortions so long as they do not create an undue burden on the right to have one, a decision that made it easier for states to enact such restrictions (Epstein and Walker 2019, 389–396).

The major battlegrounds in the abortion war were the state legislatures and the federal courts, but Congress and the President were involved too. One major action by Congress was the enactment of the Hyde Amendment in 1976, which prohibited the use of federal funds to pay for abortions, except when the mother's life would be in danger (Craig and O'Brien 1993, 118–119). This greatly limited the access to abortion by women covered by Medicaid. In 2003, Congress passed a bill that banned "partial birth" abortions, a rare but highly controversial procedure, and the Supreme Court upheld the constitutionality of that law in a 2007 decision, *Gonzales v. Carhart* (Hull and Hoffer 2010, 294–320).

Since presidents appoint federal judges, groups on both sides of the issue fought to elect a president who favored their position on abortion. Indeed, pro-life groups hoped that a change in the ideological makeup of the Court would lead to a reversal of *Roe v. Wade*, a possibility that worried pro-choice groups. That made abortion an issue in presidential elections. Even in election years when other issues, such as the economy, dominated the news, attitudes on abortion nevertheless influenced the vote (Abramowitz 1995; Hansen 2014, 109). Concerns about abortion undoubtedly helped Donald Trump win a high percentage of the votes of religious whites in 2016. They were willing to vote for him despite his weak credentials as a committed Christian because he promised to appoint judges who were opposed to abortion, a promise that he appeared to keep with his first two Supreme Court appointments and with other judicial appointments.

The attitudes of voters toward abortion remained closely divided into the 21st century. Years of discussion and debate failed to produce a consensus on this issue. Gallup poll data show modest change over the past four decades in the attitudes of Americans on abortion. For example, in 1976, 21 percent of the people said that abortion should never be allowed, and 22 percent said that it should always be allowed; in 2018, 18 percent said never, and 29 percent said always (Jones 2018). The proportions of Americans who identified as being pro-life and pro-choice was very stable from 2000 to 2018: the averages for this time period are 46 percent pro-life and 47 percent pro-choice (Jones 2018). There have been year-to-year fluctuations in the numbers, but no long-term trend. There appears to be some increase in favorable attitudes toward abortion since the 1970s, but the population still remains divided. In fact, a 2018 Gallup poll found that 48 percent of the respondents said that abortion was morally wrong (Jones 2018).

Attitudes toward abortion may not have shifted very much, but there has been a dramatic change in how these attitudes are related to partisanship. Democrats and Republicans have grown farther apart on this issue. In the 1970s, attitudes toward abortion cut across party lines: there were many pro-life Democrats and pro-choice Republicans, both in the electorate and among elected officials (Munson 2018, 91–92). But the parties began to clearly divide on this issue in the 1980s. Conservative Christian groups became more active in the Republican Party and pushed for a strong anti-abortion stance. Pro-choice groups moved toward the Democrats. The positions on abortion of party activists, candidates, and elected officials became more and more polarized, especially at the national level. Democratic and Republican presidential candidates began to take clearly opposing positions on abortion (Hansen 2014, 72–73). The electorate followed suit. Public opinion data from the Pew Research Center show how divided along party lines Americans have become: in 2019, 59 percent of Republicans said that abortion should be illegal in all or most cases, while 64 percent of Democrats said that abortion should be legal in all or most cases (Hartig 2018).

In the 21st century, gay rights began to rival abortion as a prominent cultural issue. Conflict over the legal rights of gays and lesbians certainly was present in the last few decades of the 20th century. Many observers see the 1969 Stonewall riots in New York City, which erupted as a reaction to a police raid on a gay bar, as the spark that ignited a more visible and aggressive gay rights movement (Grinberg 2019). The goal of the movement was to provide gay individuals with the same legal protections against discrimination that other protected groups had. There was some success in achieving this goal in the 1970s and 1980s, but public opinion remained unfavorable to gays and lesbians (D'Emilio 2007; Rom 2007). Nevertheless, by the 1990s, there was significant progress: many states had decriminalized homosexuality and repealed anti-sodomy laws, many businesses and other organizations had become more open to gay employees, and the popular media began to depict gay individuals more favorably (Brewer and Stonecash 2007, 106–108; Hansen 2014, 34–36). That paved the way for more significant legal changes in this century. In contrast to abortion, public opinion on this issue changed drastically over the past few decades, more than most people expected. Changes in public policy have been equally surprising.

Perhaps the most divisive question was whether same-sex couple should be allowed to legally marry. The answer in every state at the start of the 21st century was that they should not. Many states had passed constitutional amendments to that effect. Moreover, Congress in 1996 passed the Defense of Marriage Act by wide margins in both houses; the law stated that for federal purposes a marriage was defined as the union of a man and a woman and that states could refuse to recognize same-sex marriages that took place in a state where they were legal (Rimmerman 2007; White 2003, 109–110). In fact, there were no such states at the time. The first state to legally allow gay marriage was Massachusetts in 2003, when its Supreme Court declared that its state constitution gave individuals the right to enter into same-sex marriages. A few states subsequently legalized same-sex marriage, through either court decisions or legislative action, but as late as 2012 only nine states had done so (Pew Research Center 2015). In that year, President Barack Obama declared his support for same-sex marriage, making him the first president to do so. Much changed in the next few years, largely through federal court actions that culminated in a 2015 Supreme Court case, *Obergefell v. Hodges,* in which the Court determined that same-sex couples had the same constitutional right to marry as opposite-sex couples (Oyez 2015). The change in the legal status of gay marriage reflected change in public opinion: in 2001, only about one-third of Americans supported making same-sex marriage legal; that number rose to over one-half in 2015 and to over 60 percent in 2017 (Pew Research Center 2019).

There were other gay rights issues besides marriage. In 1993, President Bill Clinton proposed allowing gays and lesbians to serve in the armed forces. Opposition to this proposal forced Clinton to enact a more limited "don't ask, don't tell" policy in which gays and lesbians in the armed services would not openly state their sexual orientation, but would not be asked about it either (Hansen 2014, 34–35). That policy remained in effect until 2011, when it was repealed during the Obama administration and replaced with a policy allowing gays to serve openly. Another issue was whether employers could discriminate against gay individuals. In 2000, only 11 states had laws that prohibited private sector employers from discriminating on the basis of sexual orientation, although many more states did protect state employees; by 2015, 22 states protected private and public sector employees from such discrimination (McAnallen 2015). Federal protections were weaker, however. No federal law specifically prohibits employment discrimination on the basis of sexual orientation. The U.S. Equal Employment Opportunity Commission ruled in 2015 that such discrimination violated the 1964 Civil Rights Act, but the impact of that ruling is still unclear (Arana 2019). Public opinion has become more accepting of gays in the workplace over the past few decades. Gallup poll data show that in 1982 about 60 percent of Americans thought that gays and lesbians should have equal rights when it came to job opportunities; in 2019, over 90 percent felt that way (Gallup 2019). Similarly, support for allowing gays to serve in the military went from about 50 percent in 1982 to over 80 percent in 2019 (Gallup 2019).

Despite the growing consensus on the right of gays to marry, serve in the armed forces, and not be discriminated against by employers, some issues remain. One question is whether individuals can refuse on religious grounds to provide certain services to gay or lesbian couples. A highly publicized case involving this issue concerned a Colorado bakery, whose owner refused to create a wedding cake for a same-sex marriage ceremony on the grounds that doing so would violate his religious convictions (Oyez 2017). The gay couple filed a complaint with the Colorado Civil Rights Commission, which found that the bakery had violated the state's anti-discrimination act. State courts upheld the commission's decision, so the bakery appealed to the U.S. Supreme Court. In *Masterpiece Cakeshop v. Colorado Civil Rights Commission*, the Court ruled in favor of the bakery, but did so on narrow grounds, leaving unanswered the broader question of whether the right to freely exercise one's religious beliefs trump anti-discrimination laws (Liptak 2018). Thus, while some old issues have become settled legal questions, newer issues have emerged, indicating that feelings about gays were still mixed.

More recently, issues involving the rights of transgender individuals have been in the public spotlight. One highly emotional issue is whether individuals can use a public bathroom that corresponds to their gender identity. This question created a widely publicized controversy in North Carolina in 2016, when the Republican state legislature passed a law that required individuals to use the single-sex multiple occupancy public bathrooms in government buildings, including public schools, that corresponded to their biological sex, as documented on their birth certificate (Bitzer and Prysby 2018). Public outcry over the legislation, often identified as the state's "bathroom bill," dominated the state's politics with national headlines and actions against the state, including businesses cancelling job expansions in the state, boycotts and cancellations by performers such as Bruce Springsteen and Pearl Jam, and the National Basketball Association (NBA) pulling its All-Star Game from Charlotte. The controversy led to lawsuits and to the defeat of the Republican governor in 2016. The issue was finally settled in 2019 when the new Democratic governor reached a settlement with the federal courts that prohibited the state from banning individuals from using a public bathroom that matched their gender identity (Levin 2019).

Other issues involving sex, gender, and family life emerged out of the sexual revolution of the 1960s. Prime time television shows became more explicit in their sexual content, something evident in any comparison of the situation comedies of the 1950s with those in more recent decades (Brewer and Stonecash 2007, 93–94; Gunter 2002; White 2003, 66–67). The same change took place in movies, theatrical productions, and other artistic performances (Brisbin 2001; Gunter 2002). Conservative groups opposed the more explicit sexual content in the mass media and called for the government to take action. One example of such a controversy took place in 1989 when Senator Jesse Helms led an effort to ban the National Endowment for the Humanities from funding obscene art, a move prompted by some controversial art created with NEH funding, such as the photographic work of Robert Mapplethorpe (Eck 1996). Another instance occurred in 1992, when Vice President Dan Quayle publicly criticized the title character in a popular television show, *Murphy Brown*, for having an out-of-wedlock baby (White 2003, 66). His criticism received considerable attention and led to a public battle with the actress Candice Bergen, who played the character in the show.

Heated debates over sex education in the public schools took place in many states and localities in the latter part of the 20th century. A movement to move sex education from its staid 1950s emphasis on reproductive biology to a more modern treatment of sexual behavior emerged and had an impact in some states. Rising concerns over premarital sex among adolescents, unwed teenage mothers, and sexually transmitted diseases in the 1960s stimulated interest in reconsidering the sexual education curriculum (Moran 2000, 162–193). Reform groups wanted to provide more complete information about sexual behavior to students, including discussing controversial topics, such as premarital sex or homosexual behavior. Such proposals were often criticized for undermining proper moral values (Irvine 2002, 35–62; Moran 2000, 178–187). Conservatives wanted schools to teach that sex outside of marriage was wrong. In their eyes, failing to stress a strong moral message would effectively condone or even encourage premarital sex (Irvine 2002, 11–130. When AIDS began to attract public concern in the 1980s, this reinforced the difference between liberals and conservatives on this issue. Liberals favored sex education that would provide information about safe sexual methods, while conservatives argued that the only safe approach was sexual abstinence before marriage (Moran 2000, 205–216).

States and localities control the public school curriculum, so conflict over sexual education in the public schools played out largely at the state and local level. However, there were instances where this spilled over into national politics. Increasing concern over teenage pregnancy rates led reform groups to join with liberal members of Congress to pass the Adolescent Health Services and Prevention Act of 1978, which aimed at providing sex education and family planning services to teenagers (Moran 2000, 200–2005). Conservatives opposed the legislation, and in President Ronald Reagan's first term, they were able to pass the Adolescent Family Life Act, which emphasized chastity to prevent teenage pregnancy (Irvine

2002, 89–91). In 1994, Surgeon General Joycelyn Elders stated, in response to a question that she received while speaking at a conference, that it might be desirable to teach about masturbation in public schools. Her suggestion received considerable attention in the media, and plenty of criticism from conservative groups, including congressional Republicans. President Clinton subsequently fired Elders, a decision that was prompted by the intense criticism of her remarks (Irvine 2002, 1).

The modern feminist movement, which originated in the 1960s, also created controversies regarding family life. Betty Freidan's best-selling book, *The Feminist Mystique*, is widely credited with inspiring this movement. One of the most visible political battles over the role and rights of women concerned the proposed Equal Rights Amendment to the Constitution, which would have unequivocally established equal rights for men and women. The ERA passed Congress in 1975 and was sent to the states for ratification. However, conservative opposition in a number of states prevented it from being ratified by 1982, which was the deadline for ratification. The ERA was passed by 35 states, just three shy of the 38 necessary for ratification (Brewer and Stonecash 2007, 123–125). The positions of the two parties on this issue changed during the 1970s. At the beginning of the decade, the Democrats and Republicans did not differ much, but by the end of the decade, they clearly did. The GOP refused to endorse the ERA in its 1980 platform, a change from previous years, while the Democratic Party platform included a strong pro-ERA endorsement (Wolbrecht 2000, 3). Party differences on issues of women's rights continued throughout the remainder of the 20th century, and the images of the parties in the electorate reflected these differences (Wolbrecht 2000).

Public opinion on this issue has changed considerably since the 1970s and now seems broadly supportive of an equal role for women (Hansen 2014, 38–39). Nevertheless, there still are underlying conflicts. For example, in the 2016 ANES survey, over 30% of the respondents said that when women complained about discrimination, at least half of the time they were causing more problems. A similar percentage said that when women demanded equal treatment, at least half of the time they were seeking special favor. These attitudes are politically relevant. Some studies of the 2016 presidential vote conclude that Trump voters were motivated in part by feeling of sexism (Shaffner 2016; Sides, Tesler, and Vavreck 2018, 185–189).

Finally, questions regarding the separation of church and state became more salient and more divisive starting in the 1960s. In 1962, the Supreme Court ruled in *Engle v. Vitale* that reciting prayers in public schools, a practice that was widespread at the time, violated the Constitution (Jurinski 1998, 6–7). It was a controversial decision that generated a conservative outcry against "judicial activism" (DelFattore 2004, 77–81). Other highly visible controversies about the applicability of the Establishment Clause of the Constitution to educational institutions include the type of government aid that can be given to parochial schools and whether evolution can be taught in public schools (Flowers 1994, 81–102).

Other areas besides education have generated conflict over the separation of church and state (Greenawalt 2006). One question that has frequently been in the public eye is whether religious displays on public property, such as a nativity scene at Christmas, violate the Constitution. In a 1984 case, *Lynch v. Donnelly*, the Supreme Court ruled that a nativity scene on public property was not unconstitutional because it was part of a larger Christmas display that included Santa Claus, a Christmas tree, and other non-religious holiday items (Flowers 1994, 123). Five years later, the Court ruled that a nativity scene on the steps of a Pennsylvania county courthouse was unconstitutional because it was a stand-alone display (Flowers 1994, 123–124). Other church-state controversies involve religious freedom in the workplace, either for workers or employers. A recent Supreme Court case involving this issue is *Burwell v. Hobby Lobby Stores*, in which the Court said that certain types of privately owned corporations did not have to comply with the Affordable Care Act requirement that employers must cover birth control as part of any health insurance plan that they offer to employees, if the employers object because of religious beliefs regarding contraception (Goldstein *et al.* 2019, 643–664).

On all these cultural issues, differences between Democrats and Republicans became sharper after the 1970s. Whether it was abortion, gay rights, the role of women, or the place of religion in public life, Republicans were the party that supported traditional conservative moral values, while Democrats were the party that was more liberal and secular on these issues. Differences developed first among elected officials and party activists, then spread to the electorate. Growing party differences on cultural issues were apparent in the party platforms, the positions of the presidential candidates, congressional voting, the attitudes of party activists, and the attitudes of party identifiers (Layman 2001).

## Cultural Issues and Religion

New religious divisions in American politics developed in the latter part of the 20th century. The previous religious division was primarily between Protestants and Catholics, and it traces back to the early 20th century. As Chapter 3 explained, this religious division was largely an ethnic, not a theological, divide. It reflected the fact that Catholics and other non-Protestant groups were more recent immigrants, largely from southern and eastern Europe. These newer immigrant groups often felt discriminated against, and they came to see the Democrats as the party that was more interested in integrating them into American society. In the North, the Democratic New Deal coalition of the 1930s was based on the working-class and on Catholics, along with smaller non-Protestant groups, such as Jews and members of the various Eastern Orthodox churches. Catholics also tended to be urban blue-collar workers, so religion and social class divisions reinforced each other. The religious divisions in the North did not extend to the largely Protestant South, which remained Democratic after the 1930s realignment, as it had been throughout the 20th century.

The emergence of cultural issues after the 1960s produced a religious division in American society that was based more on religious commitment, rather than on religious affiliation (Green 2007, 48–60). Highly religious Catholics and Protestants now had a common political ground: both generally opposed abortion, gay rights, more open depictions of sexual behavior, changing styles of family life, and the strict separation of church and state. Those who are more religious are more likely to believe that traditional moral values are absolutes, not something that should change with the times. They also are more likely to believe that government should act to protect those traditional values. Hence, they oppose making abortions easier to obtain, allowing gays to marry, having sexual education in the public schools that seems to encourage premarital sex, prohibiting any displays of religion in public schools, and other public policies that appear to restrict the practice of religion or undermine traditional moral values (Green 2007, 67–81; Hansen 2014, 54). Along with this new religious division that is based on religious commitment, there is a new division along denominational lines, at least among whites: evangelical Protestants tend to be more conservative on these cultural issues, as compared to mainline Protestants or Catholics (Masci 2018; Oldfield 1996, 56–68; Wilcox and Robinson 2011, 56–64).[1]

Religious divisions in the electorate went hand-in-hand with the development of an organized Christian Right movement. Beginning in the late 1970s, a variety of organizations that represented conservative evangelical views were created with the aim of influencing public policy. One of the first of these organizations was the Moral Majority, formed by the televangelist Jerry Falwell. The Moral Majority was active in the 1980 presidential election, and it claimed to have played a key role in the election of Ronald Reagan, but it later ran into financial difficulties and was disbanded in 1989 (Wilcox and Robinson 2011, 43). Another prominent leader in the Christian Right movement was Pat Robertson, who hosted the 700 Club, a televised religious talk show that frequently focused on political issues (Wilcox and Robinson 2011, 45). Robertson ran for the Republican presidential nomination in 1988, coming in second in the Iowa caucuses before performing more poorly in later nomination contests (Oldfield 1996, 125–172). After his failed presidential bid, Robertson formed the Christian Coalition, which was quite active in the early 1990s. The organization distributed millions of voter guides in evangelical churches before election day, usually endorsing Republican candidates (Wilcox and Robinson 2011, 48–49). A number of other Christian Right organizations attempted to influence public policy on cultural and moral matters at the national, state, and local levels (Oldfield 1996, 101–102; Wilcox and Robinson 2011, 78–89). The activities of these organization helped to cement this new religious division in American politics.

We can examine the relationship between religious commitment and attitudes on cultural or moral issues by looking at attitudes on some of these issues, using recent ANES survey data. Abortion surely has been one of the most salient issues, and the ANES surveys have asked the same question about abortion for years. Specifically, respondents are asked whether abortion should: (a) never be allowed;

(b) allowed only in cases of rape, incest, or where the life of the mother was in danger; (c) allowed in more cases, but only if a clear need was established; or (d) in all cases. I dichotomized the responses, categorizing the first two as pro-life or anti-abortion and the last two as pro-choice or pro-abortion. The third choice admittedly is somewhat ambiguous, but it seems to fit better into the pro-choice camp. People who consider themselves to be pro-life rarely favor allowing abortion except for a very limited set of cases, if they would allow it at all. To measure religious commitment, I used church attendance, which is a widely used measure of this concept, and one for which data are readily available. I classified those who attend church weekly as high in attendance, those who attend at least once a month (but not every week) as medium, and those who attend only a few times a year or not at all as low. The analysis in this chapter, as in the other chapters, is limited to white voters because that is the focus of this study.

Table 5.1 shows the relationship between attitude on abortion and church attendance for white voters from 1996 to 2016. As I did in the previous chapter, I combined the data for 2000 and 2004 to create a larger number of cases, since the ANES surveys for these years (especially 2004) had fewer respondents than was the case for the other years. As we can see, voters who are more religious have been more opposed to abortion for some time. At the beginning of this century, for example, only about one-fourth of those who attended church infrequently or less held pro-life attitudes, but around 70 percent of those who attended weekly did so. That substantial difference has continued and seems to even have widened a bit in more recent years.

In addition to these differences based on religious commitment, there also are differences across denominations among those who have a religious affiliation. Evangelical Protestants are more opposed to abortion than are mainline Protestants or Catholics, even when the level of church attendance is taken into account. The

**TABLE 5.1** Attitude on Abortion by Church Attendance, 1996–2016

| | Church Attendance | | |
|---|---|---|---|
| *Percent Opposed to Abortion:* | *High* | *Medium* | *Low* |
| 2016 | 76.0 | 53.4 | 21.3 |
| 2012 | 73.5 | 49.5 | 19.7 |
| 2008 | 74.5 | 31.2 | 27.8 |
| 2000–2004 | 71.1 | 46.6 | 25.1 |
| 1996 | 72.2 | 38.1 | 21.4 |

Source: ANES surveys, 1996–2016.
Note: Only white, major-party voters are included in the table. Individuals who attend religious service weekly are classified as high in church attendance; those who attend less than weekly but at least once a month are classified as medium; those who attend a few times a year or less are classified as low. See the text for further details on the variables.

vast majority of white voters who have a religious affiliation classify themselves as evangelical Protestant, mainline Protestant, or Catholic. Only a small proportion of whites are some other type of Christian (e.g., Mormons) or are a member of some non-Christian religion (e.g., Jews), so relatively few respondents in the ANES surveys fall into these groups. For that reason, this analysis will focus only on the three major Christian groups identified above, along with those without any religious affiliation, a group that forms a significant share of those who are low in church attendance.

As gay rights issues have captured greater public attention and debate, more questions on this issue have been asked in recent ANES surveys. The 2016 survey asked a number of questions, some of which were not asked in earlier surveys. Table 5.2 displays responses to five different questions involving the rights of LGBT individuals by level of church attendance. For each question, there is a substantial difference between white voters who are low and those who are high in religious commitment. The greatest difference, about 50 points, is on same-sex marriage; the smallest difference, about 28 points, is on protecting gays against employment discrimination. There also are differences based on religious affiliation, with evangelical Protestants less favorable toward gay rights than are Catholics and mainline Protestants.

We cannot analyze changes in the relationships between religious commitment and attitudes on this whole set of gays rights issues because the ANES surveys did not ask all of the questions in all of the earlier years. The issue of gay marriage has been asked in each survey from 2004 to 2016, and an analysis of this question shows two things. First, there has been a remarkable change in public opinion on this issue. Among white voters, approval of legalizing same-sex marriage went from 33 percent in 2004 to 59 percent in 2016. Second, in every year, those with a higher level of church attendance were more likely to oppose legalization. As

**TABLE 5.2** Attitudes on Gay and Transgender Rights by Church Attendance, 2016

|  | Church Attendance | | |
|---|---|---|---|
|  | *High* | *Medium* | *Low* |
| % in favor of same-sex marriage | 24.9 | 46.3 | 73.6 |
| % in favor of allowing gays to adopt children | 44.9 | 72.5 | 85.4 |
| % in favor of laws to protect gays against job discrimination | 47.1 | 61.9 | 74.7 |
| % in favor of requiring businesses to serve gays | 21.2 | 34.6 | 55.8 |
| % in favor of allowing transgender bathroom choice | 25.2 | 41.3 | 59.0 |

Source: ANES survey, 2016.
Note: Only white, major-party voters are included in the table. Individuals who attend religious service weekly are classified as high in church attendance; those who attend less than weekly but at least once a month are classified as medium; those who attend a few times a year or less are classified as low. See the text for further details on the variables.

Table 5.2 shows, there was about a 50-point difference in 2016 between those high and those low in church attendance, with about 25 percent of the former group and about 74 percent of the latter group favoring legalization. The difference in 2004 was about 35 points, which shows that attitudes on this issue are becoming even more strongly aligned with religious commitment. As with abortion, there also are differences by affiliation, with evangelical Protestants more opposed to gay marriage than mainline Protestants or Catholics are.

Another question that has repeatedly been asked in the ANES surveys is the feeling thermometer toward gay and lesbian individuals. The feeling thermometer measures how warmly individuals feel toward a person or a group by asking them to express their feelings on a scale that runs from zero to 100 degrees, with zero defined as the coldest possible feeling, 100 as the warmest possible, and 50 as neither warm nor cold. Scores on the feeling thermometer toward gays correlate quite well with a wide range of specific questions about gay rights, making it a useful overall measure of attitudes toward gays, one that has been used by other researchers. Table 5.3 shows the mean scores on this item by church attendance over the past 20 years. As we can see, mean scores have gone up from 1996 to 2016 for each category of church attendance, but in each year, white voters who are more religious are cooler toward gays and lesbians than are those who are less religious. Moreover, the difference between those high and those low in religiosity has increased somewhat over the past 20 years, from about a 10- to 15-point difference in the earlier years to over a 20-point difference in 2016.

There are other cultural or moral issues besides abortion and gay rights, as the previous section outlined. One effective way of measuring overall orientations on this broad set of cultural issues is to use responses to several very general questions concerning what can be termed moral traditionalism. Four such questions have

**TABLE 5.3** Feelings Toward Gays by Church Attendance, 1996–2016

| Mean Score on the Feeling Thermometer Toward Gays: | Church Attendance | | |
|---|---|---|---|
| | High | Medium | Low |
| 2016 | 45.9 | 56.5 | 68.5 |
| 2012 | 40.0 | 47.7 | 57.6 |
| 2008 | 43.5 | 49.8 | 54.0 |
| 2000–2004 | 38.9 | 48.3 | 50.8 |
| 1996 | 31.3 | 40.5 | 45.3 |

Source: ANES surveys, 1996–2016.
Note: Only white, major-party voters are included in the table. Individuals who attend religious service weekly are classified as high in church attendance; those who attend less than weekly but at least once a month are classified as medium; those who attend a few times a year or less are classified as low. See the text for further details on the variables.

been included in the ANES surveys for the past several elections. The questions ask respondents whether they agree with the following statements: (a) the world is always changing and we should adjust our view of moral behavior to those changes; (b) the newer lifestyles are contributing to the breakdown of our society; (c) we should be more tolerant of people who choose to live according to their own moral standards, even if they are very different from our own; and (d) this country would have many fewer problems if there were more emphasis on traditional family ties. These four rather abstract questions all tap into the underlying value conflict that ties most if not all of these cultural or moral issues together: namely, whether or a society is better off adhering to a set of traditional moral values that are absolute and timeless in nature.

The possible responses to the above questions are on a five-point scale that ranges from strongly agree to strongly disagree. I formed an index from these four questions by scoring each item from one to five, with five being the most conservative response, and then taking the mean score for the four items. The index scores thus range from 1.0 to 5.0, with a higher score indicating a greater degree of moral traditionalism. Scores on this index of moral traditionalism correlate quite well with responses on a wide range of cultural and moral issues. Individuals who are high in moral traditionalism are more likely to oppose abortion, gay marriage, gays serving in the military, an equal role for women, and other more liberal social policies. On both theoretical and empirical grounds, this index is a good overall measure of cultural conservatism.

Table 5.4 shows that feelings of moral traditionalism are strongly related to religious commitment. For ease of presentation, I dichotomized the scores on this index, dividing the respondents roughly in half. The difference in moral traditionalism between those who are low in church attendance versus those who are high is huge. Moreover, the difference has been increasing. For example, during 2000–2004, over 70 percent of those with a high level of church attendance scored

TABLE 5.4 Moral Traditionalism Attitudes by Church Attendance, 1996–2016

| Percent High on the Moral Traditionalism Index: | Church Attendance | | |
| --- | --- | --- | --- |
| | High | Medium | Low |
| 2016 | 82.4 | 63.1 | 37.0 |
| 2012 | 79.6 | 61.5 | 37.8 |
| 2008 | 69.0 | 52.7 | 34.5 |
| 2000–2004 | 71.5 | 56.7 | 37.6 |
| 1996 | 69.9 | 54.4 | 32.3 |

Source: ANES surveys, 1996–2016.
Note: Only white, major-party voters are included in the table. Individuals who attend religious service weekly are classified as high in church attendance; those who attend less than weekly but at least once a month are classified as medium; those who attend a few times a year or less are classified as low. See the text for further details on the variables.

high in moral traditionalism, whereas less than 40 percent with a low level of church attendance were high in moral traditionalism, a difference of over 30 points. That difference widened in each subsequent year, reaching a 45-point difference in 2016.[2] This pattern matches the ones in the previous tables: the difference in attitudes on cultural issues between those who are high in religious commitment and those who are low, a difference that was quite substantial 20 years ago, has steadily increased. While the most important differences are by religiosity, there also are differences between evangelical Protestants and mainline Protestants or Catholics, with evangelical Protestants displaying higher levels of moral traditionalism.

## Cultural Issues, Voting Behavior, and Social Class

Cultural issues have been identified as one reason why white working-class voters have moved toward the Republican Party in recent decades. To examine the validity of this explanation, we need to analyze how much voting behavior is affected by attitudes on these issues and whether these attitudes are related to social class. Moreover, if cultural issues are a source of the change that has taken place in this century in the relationship between social class and voting behavior, then there must have been a change in the effect of these attitudes on voting or a change in the connection between these attitudes and social class. The following analysis will answer these questions.

First of all, we can examine how attitudes on abortion, which has been a prominent cultural issue for decades, are related to voting. Table 5.5 presents the vote for the Republican presidential candidate for pro-life and pro-choice white voters. Pro-life voters have been substantially more Republican for some time. In the George W. Bush years, they were about 25 points more Republican in their presidential voting than were pro-choice voters. That already substantial difference widened to the point that there was a 45-point difference in 2016. That might

**TABLE 5.5** Presidential Vote by Attitude on Abortion, 1996–2016

| | Abortion Attitude | |
|---|---|---|
| *Presidential Vote:* | *Pro-Life* | *Pro-Choice* |
| 2016: % for Trump | 84.7 | 39.9 |
| 2012: % for Romney | 82.5 | 41.6 |
| 2008: % for McCain | 77.4 | 45.5 |
| 2000–2004: % for Bush | 61.7 | 45.8 |
| 1996: % for Dole | 64.5 | 35.6 |

Source: ANES surveys, 1996–2016.
Note: Only white, major-party voters are included in the table. Figures are the percent of the major-party vote for the Republican candidate. See the text for details on the variables.

seem surprising, since Bush was more clearly identified than was Donald Trump as pro-life and as religiously committed. The explanation for this odd result lies not in the candidates but in the fact that attitudes on abortion have become more strongly tied to party identification. In 2016, almost 60 percent of Republican identifiers were pro-life; only 15 percent of Democrats were. Voting behavior in recent presidential elections has been strongly along party lines, so any Republican candidate surely would have done very well among pro-life voters; some probably would have done even better than Trump did.

It is not just attitudes on abortion that have become highly related to party identification. The same pattern is true for attitudes toward gays and lesbians. The feeling thermometer, discussed above, is a good general measure of attitudes on a range of gay rights issues. Table 5.6 shows the mean scores on this measure for Democrats, independents, and Republicans. Independent leaners have been classified as Democrats or Republicans, depending on the party that they lean toward. Only pure independents are classified as such. For the surveys prior to 2012, the number of independents is low, so we should be very cautious in interpreting the percentages for this group. However, the important comparison is between Democrats and Republicans, and the Ns for these groups are large in every year. Over the past 20 years, white Americans have become significantly warmer toward gays, but in each year, there is a clear difference between Democrats and Republicans, a difference that has increased somewhat over time.

Another general attitude discussed above is moral traditionalism; attitudes on this issue correlate with a wide range of cultural issues, making it a good proxy for a variety of specific issues. Table 5.7 presents the mean score on the moral traditionalism index by partisanship. The pattern here is the same as we see in Table 5.6: Democrats and Republicans already differed on this issue 20 years ago, and that difference has increased in this century. All of this reflects a widely

**TABLE 5.6** Feelings Toward Gays by Party Identification, 1996–2016

| Mean Feeling Thermometer Score Toward Gays: | Party Identification | | |
| --- | --- | --- | --- |
| | Democrat | Independent | Republican |
| 2016 | 74.3 | 66.7 | 50.7 |
| 2012 | 63.6 | 49.4 | 42.7 |
| 2008 | 60.3 | 54.1 | 41.9 |
| 2000–2004 | 56.0 | 43.5 | 40.3 |
| 1996 | 47.5 | 41.7 | 32.1 |

Source: ANES surveys, 1996–2016.
Note: Only white, major-party voters are included in the table. For party identification, Democrats and Republicans include independents who lean toward the party. See the text for further details on the variables.

**TABLE 5.7** Moral Traditionalism Attitudes by Party Identification, 1996–2016

| Mean Score on the Moral Traditionalism Index: | Party Identification | | |
|---|---|---|---|
| | Democrat | Independent | Republican |
| 2016 | 2.47 | 3.15 | 3.70 |
| 2012 | 2.73 | 3.36 | 3.85 |
| 2008 | 2.91 | 3.20 | 3.68 |
| 2000–2004 | 2.94 | 3.36 | 3.56 |
| 1996 | 3.25 | 3.41 | 3.91 |

Source: ANES surveys, 1996–2016.
Note: Only white, major-party voters are included in the table. For party identification, Democrats and Republicans include independents who lean toward the party. A higher score on the moral traditionalism index represents a more conservative orientation. See the text for further details on the variables.

studied aspect of American electoral politics: voters are increasingly sorting themselves out ideologically, so that Democrats have become more consistently liberal and Republicans more consistently conservative (Abramowitz 2010; Levendusky 2009). This ideological sorting of voters is matched by increasingly clear ideological differences among party activists and elected officials (Brownstein 2007; Ensley, Tofias, and de Marchi 2014; Jackson and Green 2011; Shor 2014).

Since attitudes on cultural or moral issues are strongly related to religiosity, it is not surprising that voting behavior and party identification are related to church attendance. Table 5.8 presents this analysis for presidential voting. As we would expect, white voters who are more religious are more likely to vote for Republicans. There

**TABLE 5.8** Presidential Vote by Church Attendance, 1996–2016

| Presidential Vote: | Church Attendance | | |
|---|---|---|---|
| | High | Medium | Low |
| 2016: % for Trump | 80.7 | 64.5 | 46.7 |
| 2012: % for Romney | 77.1 | 66.7 | 46.0 |
| 2008: % for McCain | 75.5 | 60.2 | 44.2 |
| 2000–2004: % for Bush | 68.2 | 61.2 | 47.0 |
| 1996: % for Dole | 62.5 | 49.4 | 35.4 |

Source: ANES surveys, 1996–2016.
Note: Only white, major-party voters are included in the table. Figures are the percent of the major-party vote for the Republican candidate. Individuals who attend religious service weekly are classified as high in church attendance; those who attend less than weekly but at least once a month are classified as medium; those who attend a few times a year or less are classified as low. See the text for further details on the variables.

was a substantial difference between those who are high and those who are low in church attendance in 1996, and that difference seems to have widened a bit in the 21st century. The same pattern appears when we analyze the relationship between party identification and religious commitment.

These data show that attitudes on cultural issues have become more strongly related to voting behavior and to party identification over the past 20 years. The next question concerns the relationship between social class and attitudes on cultural issues. Some analysts argue that working-class whites have been drawn to the Republican Party because of their conservative views on cultural or moral issues. Middle-class whites supposedly are more liberal on these issues and thus prefer the Democratic Party on these issues. Since abortion has been a hotly debated issue for some time, it makes sense to start with this issue. Table 5.9 shows how attitudes on abortion differ by social class over the past two decades. Social class is measured here, as it was in the previous chapter, by adjusted household income, which is described in Chapter 2. This analysis looks at voters who are at least 30 years old because income is a poor measure of social class for young people, as Chapter 2 explained.

Among whites, working-class voters are somewhat more likely than are middle-class voters to be opposed to abortion, as we can see from the analysis presented in Table 5.9. Interestingly, the difference is about the same now as it was 20 years ago. The same is true for feelings toward gays, as Table 5.10 shows. Middle-class voters are somewhat more favorable toward gays, but the class differences on this issue are modest and have not changed much over the past two decades. Both working-class and middle-class whites have developed more favorable views of gays in this century, but the class difference in attitudes has remained fairly constant. The same pattern is present if we look at the measure of moral traditionalism that is used earlier in this chapter. Overall, working-class voters are somewhat more conservative on cultural and moral issues than middle-class voters are, and this difference has existed for some time.

Finally, we can look at social class and religion. Previous research has found that individuals of lower socio-economic status are more likely to be religious and

**TABLE 5.9** Attitude on Abortion by Social Class, 1996–2016

| Percent Opposed to Abortion: | Working Class Voters | Middle Class Voters |
|---|---|---|
| 2016 | 46.1 | 32.2 |
| 2012 | 45.5 | 29.7 |
| 2008 | 40.3 | 39.9 |
| 2000–2004 | 49.6 | 35.5 |
| 1996 | 50.8 | 34.3 |

Source: ANES surveys, 1996–2016.
Note: Only white, major-party voters are included in the table. See the text for details on the variables.

**TABLE 5.10** Feeling Toward Gays by Social Class, 1996–2016

| Mean Score on the Feeling Thermometer Toward Gays: | Working Class Voters | Middle Class Voters |
| --- | --- | --- |
| 2016 | 56.4 | 64.9 |
| 2012 | 47.4 | 54.1 |
| 2008 | 46.7 | 48.5 |
| 2000–2004 | 41.6 | 49.8 |
| 1996 | 36.5 | 41.6 |

Source: ANES surveys, 1996–2016.
Note: Only white, major-party voters are included in the table. See the text for details on the variables.

more likely to be evangelical Protestants, both factors that lead to more conservative attitudes on cultural issues (Green 2007, 102–104). Table 5.11 presents the relationship between church attendance and social class from 1996 to 2016. Working-class voters are somewhat more religious, at least as measured by church attendance, but the difference between middle-class and working-class whites in the percentage who attend at least once a month is modest—usually less than 10-points—and there does not seem to be any clear trend toward an increasing or decreasing class difference in religious commitment. Working-class whites also are more likely to be evangelical Protestants: 30 percent of working-class voters were evangelical Protestants in 2016, compared to 20 percent of middle-class voters. The relationship between social class and religion seems consistent with the analysis of the relationship between social class and attitudes on cultural issues. Working-class voters are moderately more religious, which leads them to be moderately more conservative on social issues. To the extent that these issues influence voting, they make the GOP more appealing to working-class white voters and the Democrats more appealing to middle-class whites.

**TABLE 5.11** Church Attendance by Social Class, 1996–2016

| Percent Who Attend Religious Services at Least Once a Month: | Working Class Voters | Middle Class Voters |
| --- | --- | --- |
| 2016 | 49.2 | 38.1 |
| 2012 | 46.0 | 40.3 |
| 2008 | 48.4 | 53.3 |
| 2000–2004 | 56.2 | 53.6 |
| 1996 | 63.9 | 55.1 |

Source: ANES surveys, 1996–2016.
Note: Only white, major-party voters are included in the table. See the text for details on the variables.

## Conclusions

A variety of cultural or moral issues—abortion, gay rights, changing sexual norms, and the role of religion in public life—all have become more important in American politics since the 1960s. The political parties have been divided on these issues since the 1980s. The GOP has appealed more to cultural conservatives and moral traditionalists, while Democrats have taken more liberal and secular positions. These party differences on these issues have increased over time, including in this century. Attitudes on these issues have become woven into party identification and thus are consistently related to voting behavior across elections. Moreover, the impact of cultural issues on the vote has increased somewhat in this century. For example, attitudes on abortion were more closely related to the presidential vote in 2016 than they were 20 years earlier.

Attitudes on cultural and moral issues are related to religion, at least among white voters. Those who are more religious tend to be more conservative on cultural and moral issues. Also, evangelical Protestants are more conservative than are mainline Protestants or Catholics. The result is that Democratic candidates do better among those who are less religious and those who are not evangelical or fundamentalist in their religious orientations. Republicans find their greatest support among evangelical Protestants who have a strong religious commitment. This relationship also has strengthened in this century, to the point that Trump won 80 percent of the vote from voters who attend church regularly, over 10 points better than what George W. Bush received from these voters in 2000–2004.

Among whites, attitudes on cultural and moral issues are related to social class. Working-class voters are somewhat more conservative than middle-class voters are. Working-class voters also are somewhat higher in religious commitment, and they are more likely to be evangelical Protestants. These social class differences in religious orientations largely explain the class differences in attitudes on cultural and moral issues. Class differences in attitudes on these issues have been stable in this century. Working-class whites were moderately more conservative at the start of the century, and that difference has remained about the same through 2016. However, the influence of cultural issues on voting has increased somewhat in this century; what was already a strong relationship has become even stronger.

Cultural and moral issues cut across class lines and have helped to weaken the traditional relationship between social class and voting that has characterized American politics since the New Deal realignment of the 1930s. Working-class voters who prefer the Democrats on economic issues nevertheless may vote for Republican candidates because of the pull of cultural issues. At the same time, middle-class voters with relative liberal and secular views on moral issues may support Democrats even though they favor Republicans on economic matters. And since these issues seem to have an even greater impact on voting now that they did two decades ago, this helps to explain why the relationship between social class and voting behavior has changed in this century.

The qualification made at the end of the previous chapter needs to be restated here. In order to make the presentation simple, I have presented and discussed bivariate relationships in this chapter. Not surprisingly, attitudes on cultural issues are related to many other attitudes, so the bivariate relationships might not represent the true causal effect of these attitudes. In Chapter 7, the results of a multivariate analysis of the vote in 2016 and 2012 will be presented, which will allow for a better estimation of the true effects of the various factors examined in this study. As we will see, those results are consistent with the analysis in this chapter, so the reader can be assured that the analysis in this chapter is not misleading.

## Notes

1  For a list of churches that are considered to be evangelical Protestant, see Green (2007, 178–179).
2  In this analysis, I have divided the respondents into two approximately equal groups in each year. Thus, the analysis reported in Table 5.4 tells us the proportion of individuals in each category of church attendance who are above average in moral traditionalism for that year. The table does not show changes in the absolute level of moral traditionalism over time. There has been some change: the mean index score for moral traditionalism was 3.19 in 2000, and it declined to 2.85 in 2016. Thus, white voters held views that were somewhat less morally traditional in 2016 than they did at the start of the century. That change did not diminish the relationship between church attendance and moral traditionalism, however.

## References

Abramowitz, Alan I. 1995. "It's Abortion, Stupid: Policy Voting in the 1992 Presidential Election." *Journal of Politics* 57(1): 176–186.

Abramowitz, Alan I. 2010. *The Disappearing Center: Engaged Citizens, Polarization, and American Democracy.* New Haven, CT: Yale University Press.

Arana, Gabriel. 2019. "Does the Civil Rights Act Protect Gay Employees? The Court Will Decide." *The American Prospect*, May 22. https://prospect.org/article/does-civil-rights-act-protect-gay-employees-court-will-decide.

Bitzer J., Michael, and Charles Prysby. 2018. "North Carolina." In *The New Politics of the Old South*, 6th edition, eds Charles S. Bullock III, and Mark J. Rozell, 186–213. Lanham, MD: Rowman and Littlefield.

Blanchard, Dallas A. 1994. *The Anti-Abortion Movement and the Rise of the Religious Right: From Polite to Fiery Protest.* New York: Twayne.

Brewer, Mark D., and Jeffrey M. Stonecash. 2007. *Split: Class and Cultural Divides in American Politics.* Washington, DC: CQ Press.

Brisbin, Richard A., Jr. 2001. "From Censorship to Ratings: Substantive Rationality, Political Entrepreneurship, and Sex in the Movies." In *The Public Clash of Private Values: The Politics of Morality Policy*, ed. Christopher Z. Mooney, 91–114. New York: Chatham House Publishers/Seven Bridges Press.

Brownstein, Ronald. 2007. *The Second Civil War: How Extreme Partisanship Has Paralyzed Washington and Polarized America.* New York: Penguin.

Craig, Barbara Hinkson, and David M. O'Brien. 1993. *Abortion and American Politics*. Chatham, NJ: Chatham House.

DelFattore, Joan. 2004. *The Fourth R: Conflicts Over Religion in America's Public Schools*. New Haven: Yale University Press.

D'Emilio, John. 2007. "Will the Courts Set us Free: Reflections on the Campaign for Same-Sex Marriage." In *The Politics of Same-Sex Marriage*, eds Craig A. Rimmerman, and Clyde Wilcox. Chicago: University of Chicago Press.

Eck, Beth A. 1996. "Cultural Conflict and Art: Funding of the National Endowment for the Arts." In *The American Culture Wars: Current Contests and Future Prospects*, ed. James L.Nolan, Jr, 89–114. Charlottesville: The University Press of Virginia.

Ensley, Michael J., Michael W. Tofias, and Scott de Marchi. 2014. "Are These Boots Made for Walking? Polarization and Ideological Change among U.S. House Members." In *The State of the Parties: The Changing Role of Contemporary American Parties*, 7th edition, eds John C. Green, Daniel J. Coffey, and David B. Cohen. Lanham, MD: Rowman and Littlefield.

Epstein, Lee, and Thomas G. Walker. 2019. *Constitutional Law for a Changing America: Rights, Liberties, and Justice*. Thousand Oaks, CA: CQ Press.

Flowers, Ronald B. 1994. *That Godless Court? Supreme Court Decisions on Church-State Relationships*. Louisville, KY: Westminster John Knox Press.

Frank, Thomas. 2004. *What's the Matter with Kansas?*. New York: Metropolitan Books.

Gallup. 2019. "Gay and Lesbian Rights." www.news.gallup.com/poll/1651/gay-lesbian-rights.aspx.

Goldstein, Leslie F., Judith A. Baer, Courtenay W. Daum, and Terri Susan Fine. 2019. *The Constitutional and Legal Rights of Women*, 4th edition. St Paul, MN: West Academic.

Green, John C. 2007. *The Faith Factor: How Religion Influences American Elections*. Westport, CT: Praeger.

Greenawalt, Kent. 2006. *Religion and the Constitution*. Princeton, NJ: Princeton University Press.

Grinberg, Emanuella. 2019. "How the Stonewall Riots Inspired Today's Pride Celebrations." *CNN*, June 29. www.cnn.com/2019/06/28/us/1969-stonewall-riots-history/index.html.

Gunter, Barrie. 2002. *Media Sex What Are the Issues?*. Mahwah, NJ: Erlbaum.

Hansen, Susan B. 2014. *The Politics of Sex: Public Opinion, Parties, and Presidential Elections*. New York: Routledge.

Hartig, Hannah. 2018. "Nearly Six–in–Ten Americans Say Abortion Should be Legal in All or Most Cases." Pew Research Center, October 17. www.pewresearch.org/fact-tank/2018/10/17/nearly-six-in-ten-americans-say-abortion-should-be-legal/.

Hull, N. E. H., and Peter Charles Hoffer. 2010. *Roe V. Wade: The Abortion Rights Controversy in American History*. 2nd edition, revised and expanded. Lawrence, KA: University Press of Kansas.

Hunter, James Davison. 1991. *Culture Wars: The Struggle to Define America*. New York: Basic Books.

Irvine, Janice M. 2002. *Talk About Sex: The Battles Over Sex Education in the United States*. Berkeley: University of California Press.

Jackson, John S., and John C. Green. 2011. "The State of Party Elites: National Convention Delegates, 1992–2008." In *The State of the Parties: The Changing Role of Contemporary American Parties*, 6th edition, eds John C. Green and Daniel J. Coffey, 55–77. Lanham, MD: Rowman and Littlefield.

Jones, Jeffrey M. 2018. "U.S. Abortion Attitudes Remain Closely Divided." *Gallup*. https://news.gallup.com/poll/235445/abortion-attitudes-remain-closely-divided-aspx.

Jurinski, James. 1998. *Religion in the Schools: A Reference Handbook.* Santa Barbara, CA: ABC-CLIO.

Layman, Geoffrey. 2001. *The Great Divide: Religious and Cultural Conflict in American Party Politics.* New York: Columbia University Press.

Levendusky, Matthew. 2009. *The Partisan Sort: How Liberals Became Democrats and Conservatives Became Republicans.* Chicago: University of Chicago Press.

Levin, Dan 2019. "North Carolina Reaches Settlement in 'Bathroom Bill'." *New York Times,* July 23.

Liptak, Adam. 2018. "In Narrow Decision, Supreme Court Sides With Baker Who Turned Away Gay Couple." *New York Times,* June 4.

Masci, David. 2018. "American Religious Groups Vary Widely in Their Views of Abortion." Pew Research Center, January 22. www.pewresearch.org/fact-tank/2018/01/22/american-religious-groups-vary-widely-in-their-views-of-abortion/.

McAnallen, Katherine. 2015. "Sexual Orientation in Employment Discrimination Laws." National Conference of State Legislatures. www.ncsl.org/research/labor-and-employment/sexual-orientation-in-employment-discrimination-laws.aspx.

Moran, Jeffrey P. 2000. *Teaching Sex: The Shaping of Adolescence in the 20th Century.* Cambridge, MA: Harvard University Press.

Munson, Ziad. 2018. *Abortion Politics.* Cambridge, MA: Polity Press.

Nolan, James L. (ed.). 1996. *The American Culture Wars: Current Contests and Future Prospects.* Charlottesville: University Press of Virginia.

Oldfield, Duane M. 1996. *The Right and the Righteous: The Christian Right Confronts the Republican Party.* Lanham, MD: Rowman and Littlefield.

Oyez. 2015. "Obergefell v. Hodges."www.oyez.org/cases/2014/14-556.

Oyez. 2017. "Masterpiece Cakeshop, Ltd. V. Colorado Civil Rights Commission." www.oyez.org/cases/2017/16-111.

Pew Research Center. 2015. "Same-Sex Marriage, State by State." June 26. www.pewforum.org/2015/06/26/same-sex-marriage-state-by-state/.

Pew Research Center. 2019. "Majority of Public Favors Same-Sex Marriage, But Divisions Persist." May 14. www.people-press.org/2019/05/14/majority-of-public-favors-same-sex-marriage-but-divisions-persist/.

Rimmerman, Craig A. 2007. "The Presidency, Congress, and Same-Sex Marriage." In *The Politics of Same-Sex Marriage,* eds Craig A. Rimmerman, and Clyde Wilcox, 273–290. Chicago: University of Chicago Press.

Rom, Mark Carl. 2007. "Introduction: The Politics of Same-Sex Marriage." In *The Politics of Same-Sex Marriage,* eds Craig A. Rimmerman, and Clyde Wilcox, 1–38. Chicago: University of Chicago Press.

Shaffner, Brian. 2016. "White Support for Donald Trump Was Driven by Economic Anxiety, but Also by Racism and Sexism." *Vox,* November 16. www.vox.com/mischiefs-of-faction/2016/11/16/13651184/trump-support-economic-anxiety-racism-sexism.

Shor, Boris. 2014. "Party Polarization in America's State Legislatures: An Update." In *The State of the Parties: The Changing Role of Contemporary American Parties,* 7th edition, eds John C. Green, Daniel J. Coffey, and David B. Cohen, 121–136. Lanham, MD: Rowman and Littlefield.

Sides, John, Michael Tesler, and Lynn Vavreck. 2018. *Identity Crisis: The 2016 Presidential Campaign and the Battle for the Meaning of America.* Princeton, NJ: Princeton University Press.

White, John Kenneth. 2003. *The Values Divide: American Politics and Culture in Transition.* New York: Chatham House Publishers/Seven Bridges Press.

Wilcox, Clyde, and Carin Robinson. 2011. *Onward Christian Soldiers? The Religious Right in American Politics*, 4th edition. Boulder, CO: Westview Press.

Wolbrecht, Christina. 2000. *The Politics of Women's Rights: Parties, Positions, and Change.* Princeton, NJ: Princeton University Press.

# 6

# ECONOMIC ISSUES, SOCIAL CLASS, AND VOTING

Many news stories about the 2016 presidential elections campaign argued that Donald Trump was doing well with white working-class voters because of economic issues. These voters were reported to be concerned about the loss of good blue-collar jobs, stagnating wages for those in the working class, and dismal economic prospects for their children. Several of the campaign reports discussed in Chapter 1 emphasized these concerns. For example, Thomas Edsall (2016) interviewed voters in Pottstown, Pennsylvania, and found that many blue-collar voters were motivated to vote for Trump because of economic concerns. Tim Reid (2016) came to similar conclusions after talking to voters in Canton, Ohio. Other political observers echoed these interpretations of blue-collar support for Trump (Confessore 2016; Coontz 2016; Frank 2016; Gest 2017; Greenberg 2017; Murphy 2016).

However, a number of commentators argued that economic concerns were not an important factor in the vote for Trump. Instead, attitudes on race and immigration were cited as the important factors in explaining Trump's victory (Cox, Lienesch, and Jones 2017; McElwee 2016). These accounts emphasized that many white voters felt that blacks and other minorities received preferential treatment, that the culture of the country was being destroyed by high levels of immigration from non-Western countries, and that white Americans were losing their place in society. Several scholarly analyses of the 2016 election support these conclusions (Abramowitz and McCoy 2019; Hooghe and Dassonneville 2018; Mutz 2018; Schaffner, MacWilliams, and Nteta 2018; Sides, Tesler, and Vavreck 2018).

In sum, one interpretation of Trump's success among white working-class voters emphasizes economic concerns, but another interpretation emphasizes social and cultural concerns. Can these divergent interpretations of the 2016 election be reconciled? At the very least, these contradictory conclusions raise some questions about the relationship between social class and voting behavior.

The first question is whether explanations of Trump's success among white working-class voters also apply to previous elections. As Chapter 3 outlined, the long-standing relationship between social class and voting behavior seriously eroded before 2016. White working-class and middle-class voters became more similar in their voting and their party identification in the early years of the 21st century, and the old relationship between class and voting was even reversed in the second decade of this century. In the 2012 presidential election, Mitt Romney did better among white working-class voters than among middle-class voters, although not to the extent that Trump did in 2016. Was Romney's success among working-class voters due to the same factors that explain Trump's success, or were different forces at work prior to 2016?

A second question is whether the relationship between social class and economic issues has changed in recent years. As Chapter 2 discussed, the long-standing tendency for working-class voters to disproportionately support the Democratic Party rested on economic issues. If working-class voters are no longer more supportive of Democrats, is it because economic issues matter less now, or is it because white working-class voters no longer differ from middle-class voters in their attitudes on economic issues? Many interpretations of the 2016 election emphasize the former possibility, arguing that voters were motivated largely by social and cultural issues in 2016. But the other possibility also may be important, so it should not be dismissed too quickly. In order to understand the changing relationship between social class and voting in the 21st century, we need to examine both possible reasons for this development in American politics. The previous two chapters analyzed social and cultural issues. This chapter will focus on economic issues as a possible source of the changing relationship between social class and voting behavior.

In analyzing the role that economic issues may have played in the changing relationship between social class and voting behavior, we must consider the types of economic issues that led to Democratic Party strength among working-class voters throughout much of the 20th century. Chapter 2 identified three sets of issues that were important in this relationship, and that discussion can be briefly summarized here. First, issues involving social welfare and income security policies have been important. The Democratic Party from the 1930s on has favored more government action to reduce economic inequality. For example, the party has advocated more extensive social welfare programs, from Social Security in the 1930s, to Medicare in the 1960s, to Obamacare most recently. All of these were opposed by Republicans. Second, the Democratic Party has been far more supportive of labor unions on labor-management issues from the 1930s on, and organized labor has responded with consistent support for Democrats. Republicans, on the other hand, have generally sought to make it more difficult for unions to organize and bargain collectively. Finally, the Democratic Party has, at least in the past, enjoyed the image of being the party that is better able to manage the economy, especially for the benefit of the working class. Among

other things, this has meant that Democrats have traditionally been more concerned about unemployment, while Republicans have been more concerned
about inflation.

Before analyzing these economic issues, one important point needs to be stressed: we need to analyze the relevant attitudes on these issues to determine what
role economic concerns continue to play in contemporary voting behavior. Some
analyses of the Trump vote in 2016 dismissed economic concerns as a significant
source of his vote because they found that Trump voters were not economically or
financially worse off than other voters. For example, one study found that white
working-class voters who reported that they were in good financial shape were
more supportive of Trump than those who were not (Cox, Lienesch, and Jones
2017). Other studies concluded that the personal economic situation of the voter
had little effect on the vote in 2016 (Mutz 2018; Rothwell 2016). And a study of
voters who switched from Barack Obama in 2012 to Trump in 2016 determined
that those with declining family incomes were only slightly more likely to be
switchers (Remy, Collingwood, and Valenzuela 2019).

The problem with these studies is that they assume that if white working-class
voters for Trump were not worse off financially, then their vote was not motivated by economic concerns. But inferring economic attitudes from the self-
reported financial situation of individuals is problematic. There are a variety of
reasons why individuals may be worse off now than a year ago, which is the
question often asked in these surveys, but in many of these cases the individuals
would not blame government policies or actions for their worsening personal
situations. A divorce may leave both parties financially worse off. A disability may
force someone to retire early from a well-paying job. The closing of a restaurant
may result in the chef being unemployed for a substantial period of time. Unex-
pected expensive repairs to a married couple's home or cars may strain their
family budget. In these and many similar cases, the affected individuals probably
do not see much political relevance to their economic woes and thus would not
be looking for government policies to improve their situation.

Similarly, individuals whose personal financial situation has been improving do
not necessarily credit government policies for their good fortune. An individual
may be better off economically because he or she took a new job. A married
couple may be better off because a spouse has returned to work after being home
with young children for a few years. A divorced mother may be better off now
because she has finished paying for the college education of her children. We
could add changes in marital status, health status, and other factors to this list. In
many, perhaps most of these cases, the individuals would not feel that government policy is responsible for their improved situation. Some might feel that they
would have been even better off if the government pursued what they felt were
better economic policies.

It is when individuals see a connection between their personal financial situation and government policy that their situation becomes politically relevant

(Campbell *et al.* 1960, 381–401; Kramer 1983). That, of course, can happen in a variety of circumstances. During a recession, individuals who are laid off may, fairly or unfairly, blame the economic policies of the current administration for their job loss. The same individuals probably would be less likely to blame government policy if they lost their job during a period when the economy was doing quite well. Individuals who are having difficulty in obtaining health insurance or in paying medical bills may support a stronger role for the government in health care. Those who are struggling to pay the cost of a college education for their children similarly may feel that the government should do more to help with this problem. What matters is how individuals perceive and interpret their economic situation and how that affects the opinions they form about what government policy should be. In the end, what matters for voting behavior are the attitudes that the voter has on economic matters, not the voter's economic circumstances.

As indicated above, the past connection between social class and voting behavior involved three groups of issues: those involving social welfare and related policies; those concerned with labor-management policies; and those regarding management of the economy. These are different types of issues, so it makes sense to analyze each of them separately, as the old relationships may have changed for one set, but not for others. The remainder of this chapter does exactly that, first considering social welfare issues, then moving on to labor-management issues, and concluding with concerns about the management of the economy, including trade policy. In each case, the analysis will focus on two factors: (a) whether the effect that attitudes on economic issues have on voting behavior has changed during this century, at least for white voters; and (b) whether the relationship between social class and attitudes on economic issues has changed in recent years among white voters. The data analysis will again rely on the American National Election Studies (ANES) surveys of the American electorate.

## Social Welfare Issues

From the 1930s on, Democrats have been more supportive of a variety of policies that would disproportionately benefit less affluent Americans and reduce economic inequality in the nation. Some social welfare programs, such as food stamps or Medicaid, are means tested, so they would seem to obviously benefit those who are struggling economically. But social welfare programs that are not means tested, such as Social Security or Medicare, also tend to reduce economic inequality. Social Security, for example, disproportionately benefits lower-income individuals because, on average, their Social Security payments are a greater share of their retirement income, and they receive back proportionately more than what they contributed, compared to higher-income individuals (Brewer and Stonecash 2007, 61–65). In addition to programs that provide direct benefits to individuals, there are other government policies that aim at helping those who are less well-off. One such policy is the national minimum wage, and proposals to increase that wage have been debated considerably in recent years.

Social welfare and income security issues have not retreated from the American political landscape in the 21st century. Democrats and Republicans continue to debate and differ on these issues, with Democrats continuing to push for more government action to reduce economic inequality and Republicans generally opposed. These recent differences and conflicts are apparent from examinations of the content of party platforms, the behavior of different presidential administrations, and the voting of members of Congress. A few examples will illustrate these continuing partisan differences.

Social Security is one of the oldest social welfare programs in the country, and it has achieved widespread popularity. Attempts to touch those benefits have been considered to be so politically lethal to those who try that the program has been labeled the "third rail" of American politics. Nevertheless, President George W. Bush proposed in 2005 to drastically change the program by partially privatizing it. Bush's proposal would have allowed workers to divert some of their contributions to the program into their own personal investment accounts (Hiltzik 2005, 1–3). This proposal had long been supported by some conservative groups, and it was part of the Republican Party platform in 2004. After his reelection in 2004, Bush made this his top domestic priority, and he traveled around the country attempting to build support for his initiative (Galston 2007). Bush's proposal received initial support from Republicans in Congress, but Democrats were uniformly opposed, arguing that the change would weaken the program. When it appeared that public support for such a change was declining, congressional Republicans backed away from the proposal (Hiltzik 2005, 218–219). Still, the 2008 Republican Party platform called for reforming Social Security by allowing for personal retirement accounts (Republican Party 2008).

Health care policy has sharply divided the two parties for some time. They divided over President Bill Clinton's proposed national health care plan in the early 1990s, and the strong opposition of congressional Republicans was instrumental in defeating the bill (Johnson and Broder 1996; Skocpol 1996). When President Barack Obama proposed a national health can plan after his election in 2008, he too met with widespread GOP opposition. The Affordable Care Act was Obama's signature legislative accomplishment, and it passed the House and the Senate without a single Republican vote (Ballotpedia 2019). Following its enactment, Republicans pledged to repeal Obamacare, a promise that was in their party platforms in both 2012 and 2016 (Republican Party 2012; 2016). Their attempts to fully repeal the act failed for a variety of reasons, including the fact that there was considerable public support for some parts of the law, but they were successful in weakening the law in a variety of ways (Bacon 2018; Gluck 2017).

Medicare, like Social Security, is a highly popular program. Yet Republicans have proposed to move the program over time to one where seniors would effectively receive a voucher that they could use to purchase health care insurance, either from the traditional government plan or from a private plan. This proposed change was pushed by Paul Ryan, one of the Republican leaders in the House and the 2012 vice-presidential nominee of the party, and it was included in the 2012 GOP platform (Pear 2011; Republican Party 2012). Moving Medicare to a "premium support" system fit with the general conservative goal of relying more on the private marketplace for health care and reducing spending on entitlement programs. Democrats criticized the plan, arguing that the vouchers could easily be insufficient for individuals to purchase adequate coverage, leaving them with greater out-of-pocket costs than with the current system (Pear 2016). When the proposed legislation was introduced in Congress in 2011, Democrats controlled the Senate and the White House, so the bill had little chance of being enacted. Nevertheless, Republicans continued to support the idea, particularly after the 2016 election put them in control of the White House and Congress, but when the Democrats won control of the House in 2018, that temporarily ended Republican hopes for success (Pear 2016).

The minimum wage is another policy that Democrats and Republicans have divided over in recent years (Bartels 2008, 235–239). The national minimum wage, which currently stands at $7.25 per hour, was last increased in 2009, on the basis of legislation passed in 2007, when Democrats had control of both houses of Congress (Bartels 2008, 223; Roof 2011, 210). Since then, Democrats have repeatedly called for substantial increases in the minimum wage, and Republicans have consistently stymied efforts to raise it. In 2014, President Obama proposed raising it in stages to $10.10 per hour, but he was unsuccessful in getting Congress to pass the legislation (Huetteman 2014). More recently, congressional Democrats proposed raising the minimum wage to $15.00 per hour, and their Raise the Wage Act passed the House in 2019 on an almost completely party line vote, but Senate Republicans made it clear that the bill would not even be considered (Campbell 2019). Republicans argued that such an increase would hurt poor people because many employers would respond by hiring fewer workers, and they cited studies in support of that conclusion, including a report from the nonpartisan Congressional Budget Office that estimated that 1.3 million workers would lose their jobs if the minimum wage were raised to $15.00 per hour, a report that also estimated that 17 million workers would receive a raise from such an increase (Congressional Budget Office 2019).

In sum, the Democratic and Republican Parties have continued to differ on a large set of issues involving social welfare and income security policies, all of which are intended to reduce economic inequalities. In order to determine the influence of this set of economic issues on voting behavior in recent elections, I analyzed several questions from recent ANES surveys. There are two very general questions that have been asked for years by the ANES surveys, both of which ask respondents to place their attitudes on a seven-point scale. For one question, the scale runs from wanting a great increase in government services and spending to wanting a great decrease in both; for the other question, the scale runs from having the government make sure that everyone has a job and a good living standard to having individuals provide for themselves. In both cases, few respondents choose the extreme ends of the scale, but they do spread themselves out quite well. Responses to these two questions correlate well with responses to other, more specific, questions dealing with social welfare and income security measures, and they can be regarded as good overall measures of how liberal or conservative voters are with regard to government programs and policies in this area.

In 2016, attitudes on both issues were strongly associated with the presidential choices of white voters. The relevant data are in Tables 6.1 and 6.2. For ease of presentation, I have collapsed the seven-point scales for these two variables into three categories by classifying the three most liberal responses as liberal, the middle response as moderate, and the three most conservative responses as conservative. For both variables, white voters with more liberal attitudes were far more likely to vote for Hillary Clinton. If we compare the vote for Clinton

**TABLE 6.1** Presidential Vote by Attitudes Toward Government Services and Spending, 2016

| Presidential Vote: | Government Services and Spending | | |
| | Increase Services | Same level of Services | Decrease Services |
| --- | --- | --- | --- |
| % for Clinton | 79.9 | 52.8 | 13.6 |
| % for Trump | 20.1 | 47.2 | 86.4 |
| Total | 100% | 100% | 100% |
| (N) | (507) | (369) | (744) |

Source: ANES 2016 survey.
Note: Only white, major-party voters are included in the table. See the text for details on the variables.

**TABLE 6.2** Presidential Vote by Attitudes Toward Government Role in Ensuring Employment and a Good Standard of Living, 2016

| Presidential Vote: | Ensuring Employment and Good Living Standards | | |
| | Government Should Ensure | Mixed Opinion | Individuals on Their Own |
| --- | --- | --- | --- |
| % for Clinton | 76.7 | 56.0 | 21.4 |
| % for Trump | 23.3 | 44.0 | 78.6 |
| Total | 100% | 100% | 100% |
| (N) | (446) | (334) | (880) |

Source: ANES 2016 survey.
Note: Only white, major-party voters are included in the table. See the text for details on the variables.

among those with a liberal attitude on the issue with those with a conservative attitude, there is a 66-point difference in one table and a 55-point difference in the other. Overall, it appears that Democrats have a roughly 60-point advantage among liberals on these issues—or, to put it another way, Republicans have a roughly 60-point advantage among conservatives. Some commentators may have argued that economic concerns were unimportant in the 2016 presidential election, but these data indicate otherwise.

For a broader look at how attitudes on social welfare and related issues influence the vote, we can analyze more issues and compare 2016 to 2012. These were quite different presidential elections, with strikingly different Republican candidates, so any similarities in the relationships should point to fundamental differences between Democrats and Republicans. Table 6.3 reports these data. In addition to the two questions discussed above, I included data for two questions dealing with health care, a general question about how much the federal government should take action to reduce inequality, and a general question about how much government should regulate business.[1] All of these questions were asked in both the 2012 and the 2016 ANES surveys. I also included a question on raising the minimum wage, which was only asked in 2016, and a question about increasing or decreasing spending on unemployment insurance, which was only asked in 2012, when the nation was still recovering from the Great Recession and unemployment was at almost 8 percent that fall.[2] For each item, I calculated the Democratic advantage among those with a liberal attitude on the issue, which, of course, is the same as the Republican advantage among those with a conservative attitude. For example, white voters with a liberal response to the question about government services

**TABLE 6.3** Democratic Advantage in the Presidential Vote Among Voters with Liberal Attitudes on Selected Economic Issues, 2012 and 2016

| Economic Issue: | 2012 | 2016 |
|---|---|---|
| Government services and spending | 63.5 | 66.3 |
| Government role regarding jobs and a good standard of living | 47.3 | 55.3 |
| Government role in health care insurance | 63.2 | 59.5 |
| Government assistance with health care costs | 50.4 | 57.3 |
| Government action to reduce inequality | 46.6 | 50.1 |
| Minimum wage | — | 38.4 |
| Spending on unemployment insurance | 43.0 | — |
| Government regulation of business | 63.2 | 50.6 |

Source: ANES 2012 and 2016 surveys.
Note: Figures are the percent voting Democratic among voters with a liberal attitude on the issue minus the percent voting Democratic among those with a conservative attitude on the issue. Only white, major-party voters are included in the table. See the text for details on the variables.

and spending were about 64 points more likely to vote for Obama in 2012 than were white voters with a conservative attitude.

The patterns for 2012 and 2016 are both remarkably similar and consistent across a wide variety of issues that deal with reducing economic inequalities and insecurities. The Democratic advantage among liberals on these issues ranges from a low of about 40 points for the minimum wage item in 2016 to a high of 66 points for the government services and spending item in 2016. The average difference between liberals and conservatives in their vote across all seven issues is about 54 points in both years. Attitudes on social welfare and related issues were just as strongly related to the presidential vote among whites in 2016 as they were in 2012.

If we look at data for earlier years in this century, an interesting pattern emerges. The relationship between presidential voting and attitudes on social welfare issues among whites has increased over time. Table 6.4 reports the Democratic advantage from 2000 to 2016 among liberals on the two general questions examined above: the item about increasing or decreasing government services and spending and the item about whether the government should ensure that everyone has a job and a good living standard. As explained above, attitudes on these two issues are good general measures of how liberal or conservative a voter is overall on questions of social welfare and related policies, and they have been asked in each ANES survey for some time. As I did in the analyses reported in previous chapters, I have combined the data for 2000 and 2004 to create a larger number of cases because the ANES surveys for these two years (especially 2004) had fewer respondents than was the case for the other years.

During the early years of this century, there was a strong relationship between voting and attitudes on these issues. During the Bush elections, 2000 and 2004, white voters with a liberal attitude were 40 to 50 points more likely

**TABLE 6.4** Democratic Advantage in the Presidential Vote Among Voters with Liberal Attitudes on Selected Economic Issues, 2000–2016

|  | Economic Issue | |
| --- | --- | --- |
| Presidential Election: | Government Services and Spending | Government Role Regarding Jobs and Good Living Standards |
| 2016 | 66.3 | 55.3 |
| 2012 | 63.5 | 47.3 |
| 2008 | 41.3 | 44.2 |
| 2000–2004 | 49.4 | 40.5 |

Source: ANES surveys, 2000–2016.
Note: Figures are the percent voting Democratic among voters with a liberal attitude on the issue minus the percent voting Democratic among those with a conservative attitude on the issue. Only white, major-party voters are included in the table. See the text for details on the variables.

to cast a Democratic vote than were those with a conservative attitude. That already strong relationship became even stronger in subsequent elections. Much of the explanation for this change can be attributed to the growing ideological and partisan polarization in the country, a development in American politics that has been widely analyzed by many scholars (Abramowitz 2010; Levandusky 2009). Attitudes on a wide variety of issues have become more strongly aligned with party identification as voters increasingly sort themselves into partisan camps based on their ideology. To quickly show how this has worked out for the issues analyzed here, Table 6.5 displays mean scores for Democrats and Republicans on the two questions analyzed in the previous table. These mean scores are based on the full seven-point scale used for these questions. In 2000–2004, Democrats were, on average, substantially more liberal than Republicans were. The difference in mean scores between Democrats and Republicans is over 1.2 points for both questions. This already sizable difference increased over time, and by 2016, there is roughly a two-point difference.

In every presidential election in this century, voting has been heavily along party lines, so the strong relationship between party identification and attitudes on social welfare issues is translated into a strong relationship between these attitudes and the vote. If the parties had nominated different presidential candidates in 2016, we probably would have found similarly strong relationships between the vote and attitudes on social welfare issues because these attitudes have been so thoroughly incorporated into party identification. People are Democrats or Republicans in large part because of their orientations on economic matters. That has been true for years, and it seems no less true today.

**TABLE 6.5** Attitudes on Selected Economic Issues by Party Identification, 2000–2016

| | Economic Issue | | | |
| | Government Services and Spending | | Government Role Regarding Jobs and Good Living Standards | |
| | Party Identification | | | |
| | Democrats | Republicans | Democrats | Republicans |
|---|---|---|---|---|
| 2016 | 3.19 | 5.31 | 3.57 | 5.47 |
| 2012 | 3.55 | 5.32 | 3.78 | 5.45 |
| 2008 | 3.11 | 4.75 | 3.91 | 5.36 |
| 2000–2004 | 3.23 | 4.52 | 4.03 | 5.25 |

Source: ANES surveys, 2000–2016.
Note: Entries are mean scores. Attitudes on both economic issues are measured on a scale that runs from 1 to 7, with a higher score indicating a more conservative attitude. Only white, major-party voters are included in the table. For party identification, Democrats and Republicans include independent leaners. Pure independents are not included in the table. See the text for further details on the variables.

For the analysis reported so far in this chapter to be relevant to the focus of this study, we need to connect attitudes on social welfare issues to social class. Table 6.6 does that by presenting the mean scores on the two general questions that are used in the previous analysis for working and middle-class voters; these mean scores are based on the seven-point scales, with a lower score representing a more liberal orientation. As I pointed out before, attitudes on these two issues are strongly related to attitudes on more specific social welfare issues, so they indicate what general relationships exist in this area. Social class is measured here, as in the previous chapters, by adjusted household income, which is described in Chapter 2. This analysis looks at voters who are at least 30 years old because income is a poor measure of social class for young people, as Chapter 2 explained.

Perhaps surprisingly, the differences between working-class and middle-class whites were modest at the start of this century—only about 0.2 points on the seven-point scales. Class differences on these issues increased in 2008 to about one-half point on average, suggesting that economic conditions in the country can influence the relationship, but class differences declined after 2008. In 2016, working-class whites were at best only slightly more liberal on these issues.

In sum, these data indicate that social welfare and income security issues have not become less important to voters in this century. Just the opposite is the case. Attitudes on these issues are more strongly related to voting now than they were two decades ago, largely because these attitudes have become more closely tied to party identification. However, attitudes on these issues have become less related to social class among whites, to the point that there is little difference between working-class and middle-class whites. Social welfare issues now provide white working-class voters with little reason to be more supportive of Democratic candidates than middle-class voters are.

**TABLE 6.6** Attitudes on Selected Economic Issues by Social Class, 2000–2016

| | Economic Issue | | | |
| | Government Services and Spending | | Government Role Regarding Jobs and Good Living Standards | |
| | Working-class Voters | Middle-class Voters | Working-class Voters | Middle-class Voters |
|---|---|---|---|---|
| 2016 | 4.39 | 4.38 | 4.57 | 4.68 |
| 2012 | 4.40 | 4.65 | 4.58 | 4.88 |
| 2008 | 3.85 | 4.28 | 4.56 | 5.16 |
| 2000–2004 | 3.91 | 4.12 | 4.64 | 4.87 |

Source: ANES surveys, 2000–2016.
Note: Entries are mean scores. Attitudes on both economic issues are measured on a scale that runs from 1 to 7, with a higher score indicating a more conservative attitude. Only white, major-party voters are included in the table. See the text for further details on the variables.

It may seem odd that working-class white voters are not more supportive of government measures to reduce economic inequality and help those who are less well off. Working-class individuals presumably would benefit more than middle-class individuals from such government actions as raising the minimum wage, increasing Social Security benefits, providing more extensive unemployment benefits, and helping people with their health care costs. One likely explanation of this seeming paradox involves the combination of racial attitudes and beliefs about who deserves government help. Several research studies have found that Americans are not necessarily opposed to helping the poor. Americans generally support government help to those who need and deserve it (Page and Jacobs 2009, 56–74; Piston 2018, 3–4). On the other hand, there is considerable opposition to the government providing benefits to people who should be able to take care of themselves (Gilens 1999, 31–67). These attitudes tie into race-related attitudes, particularly feelings of racial resentment. As Chapter 4 explained, racial resentment involves the belief that blacks could do better if they tried harder. Thus, individuals with higher levels of racial resentment are less likely to support social welfare and related programs because they are more likely to see these programs as giving benefits to those who do not deserve them.

Chapter 4 showed that working-class whites tend to have higher levels of racial resentment than do middle-class whites. Moreover, the relationship between racial attitudes and attitudes on at least some economic issues seems to have strengthened during the Obama administration (Tesler 2016, 117–118). Thus, one possible reason why working-class whites are not more liberal than their middle-class counterparts on these economic issues is that they are more likely to see blacks, and perhaps other minorities, as taking unfair advantage of such programs. Beliefs that racial minorities unfairly benefit from so-called government handouts did not originate in the 21st century. Such beliefs have been described in earlier studies. For example, Edsall and Edsall (1991) argued that attitudes on race and welfare contributed to the movement of whites toward the GOP in the 1970s and 1980s. Gilens (1999) presents considerable data to show that racial stereotypes present in the mass media have helped to shape public attitudes toward welfare from the 1960s on. Moreover, there appears to be an increased racialization of attitudes on economic issues after 2008. For example, Tesler (2016, 94–104) found that attitudes on health care among whites were more clearly related to attitudes on race after Obama became president. However, class differences on racial issues are not that great, so they could not fully explain why working-class whites are no longer more liberal on economic issues than are middle-class whites. Other factors must be involved as well.

This analysis should make it clear that what ultimately matters is what attitudes voters have regarding various government programs or policies, not whether or not they would be likely to directly benefit from those programs or policies. We need to understand what voters think is fair or desirable. Of course, self-interest frequently influences beliefs about what is fair or desirable, but it is far from the sole determinant of these beliefs. Furthermore, individuals differ in how they perceive their economic interests. Sometimes they believe that they would benefit from policies even if most objective analyses indicate otherwise.

## Labor-Management Relations

Labor unions have a long relationship with the Democratic Party, one that dates back to the 1930s. Unions have consistently supported the Democratic Party, providing campaign funds, campaign workers, and candidate endorsements. Among the policies that directly affect labor unions are federal laws and actions that affect how easy it is for them to organize workers and engage in collective bargaining. For example, unions have continued to press for eliminating the provision in the 1947 Taft-Hartley Law that allows states to enact "right-to-work" laws, which exist in about one-half of the states and which prevent workers in a company from being required to pay dues to a union that represents the workers at that company (Roof 2011, 100–101). Unions also have sought changes in labor laws that would make it easier for them to organize and represent workers at a company, including stiffer penalties for employers who illegally impede union organizing efforts. These issues have continued to be important to organized labor, and the parties continue to differ over them. Democrats, especially northern Democrats, have generally supported these union goals, while Republicans have consistently opposed them.

A recent major legislative goal of organized labor was the Employee Fair Choice Act (EFCA). This law would have made it easier for unions to organize a workplace by instituting a "card check" procedure, which would have certified a union as the collective bargaining agent once it obtained the signatures of a majority of the employees at the workplace (Roof 2011, 211). The EFCA also would have established stiffer penalties for employers who violate labor laws, a measure pushed by unions because they felt that existing penalties were so weak that employers often would knowingly violate laws to impede union organizing efforts. Democrats, who were in control of Congress in 2007, brought the bill up for a vote in both houses of Congress. The EFCA passed the House on an almost completely party-line vote: all but two congressional Democrats voted for it, while 93 percent of Republicans voted against it (Roof 2011, 211). The bill failed in the Senate, however, because Senate Democrats lacked the votes to override a Republican filibuster. On a vote to end the filibuster, every Democrat voted for cloture and all but one of the Republicans voted against it, indicating how strongly positions on this issue aligned with the two parties (Roof 2011, 212). In 2009, when the Democrats controlled the White House and both house of Congress, including briefly holding a veto-proof 60 seats in the Senate, the EFCA was reintroduced, with the support of President Obama. However, a few Democratic senators opposed the legislation, making it impossible to prevent a Republican filibuster (Francia 2010).

Differences on labor-management issues also exist for the appointments and executive actions of recent presidents. President George W. Bush was widely considered to be unfavorable toward unions, and his appointments to the National Labor Relations Board (NLRB) were not supported by the major labor unions (Doyle 2010). President Obama, on the other hand, appointed individuals to the NLRB who were supported by organized labor, and the NLRB subsequently issued rules that made it easier for unions to organize (Roof 2011, 226). Obama also reinstituted project labor agreements, which had been banned by President Bush, for federal construction projects (Francia 2010). These agreements gave unions more power to negotiate favorable working conditions for these projects, and they were strongly supported by construction unions. And, as Chapter 2 described, President Obama tried to expand the number of employees who would be eligible for overtime pay, although he was unsuccessful in this attempt. President Trump was more favorable to business interests in his appointments to the NLRB, which then resulted in the NLRB issuing regulations that were more pro-business (Johnson 2018).

Conflict over the rights of unions has appeared in state politics as well. The most notable example of this involves Wisconsin after the election of Republican Governor Scott Walker in 2010. Early in 2011, Walker proposed major changes in state law that would almost eliminate the ability of state workers to engage in collective bargaining (Tumulty 2011). The Republican controlled state legislature passed the legislation, which also included significant reductions in the health and pension benefits that state employees received, but only after a contentious battle with the affected unions and state workers, who were supported by Democrats. The conflict received considerable coverage in the national news, especially when tens of thousands of protesters demonstrated in and around the Capitol, filling the building for days (Davey and Greenhouse 2011). Four years later, Governor Walker signed into law a bill that made Wisconsin a right-to-work state (Hall 2015). Like the 2011 legislation, this was passed by the Republican-controlled state legislature over the bitter opposition of Democrats and labor unions.

While labor unions remain strong allies of the Democratic Party, union membership has declined substantially since its high point in the early 1950s, when about one-third of workers belonged to a union (Panagopoulos and Francia, 2008). Only about 11 percent of workers currently are union members, although the share of voters who are in a household with at least one union member has been around 20 percent in recent elections, which still constitutes an important voting bloc (Francia 2012). The decline in union membership might help to explain the changing relationship between social class and voting behavior, since unionized blue-collar workers have been strongly Democratic. One reason for the strong support for Democrats from unionized working-class voters is that union membership makes voters more likely to focus on economic issues in deciding their vote (Francia and Bigelow 2010). But the particular concern of this analysis is how voters feel about policies that directly affect unions.

Individuals who have more favorable attitudes toward unions when it comes to labor-management issues should be more supportive of Democrats, and working-class individuals traditionally have been more favorable toward unions, especially if they are in a union. We can see if these relationships persist in recent elections.

Recent ANES surveys do not contain specific questions about labor-management issues, such as the ones discussed above. However, these surveys have routinely included a feeling thermometer question about labor unions. On this question, respondents are asked to place their feeling toward labor unions on a scale that runs from zero to 100 degrees, with zero being the coldest possible feeling, 100 the warmest possible, and 50 representing a neutral feeling. It is reasonable to assume that individuals who feel warmer toward labor unions would be more likely to favor policies that would make it easier for unions to organize workers and engage in collective bargaining. Interestingly, even though there has been a substantial decline in labor union membership, there has been little change in feelings toward unions. For example, the average thermometer rating for unions was about 57 degrees in the 1960s, about 54 degrees in the 1990s, and about 55 degrees in the early years of this century (Panagopoulos and Francia 2008). In the two most recent presidential election years, the average thermometer rating was about 55 degrees, with white voters being slightly cooler.

Feelings toward labor unions are strongly related to the vote. Table 6.7 shows the vote in presidential elections from 2000 through 2016 by how white voters felt toward unions. For ease of presentation, I classified voters as warm, neutral, or cool, depending on whether their thermometer rating was above 50, exactly 50, or below 50, respectively. As we can see, in every presidential election in this century, whites who feel cooler toward labor unions have been more likely to vote for the Republican candidate. The difference in voting between those who are warm and those who are cool usually has been around 40 percent, with a somewhat greater difference in 2012. Overall, the relationship between

**TABLE 6.7** Presidential Vote by Attitude Toward Unions, 2000–2016

| Presidential Vote: | Feeling Toward Unions | | |
| --- | --- | --- | --- |
| | Warm | Neutral | Cool |
| 2016: % for Trump | 42.1 | 61.2 | 81.0 |
| 2012: % for Romney | 29.3 | 55.8 | 80.3 |
| 2008: % for McCain | 36.7 | 62.8 | 74.0 |
| 2000–2004: % for Bush | 41.8 | 59.3 | 78.5 |

Source: ANES surveys, 2000–2016.
Note: Only white, major-party voters are included in the table. Figures are the percent of the major-party vote for the Republican candidate. The feeling toward unions is measured by a feeling thermometer that runs from zero to 100, with a higher score indicating a warmer feeling. See the text for details on the variables.

presidential voting and feelings toward labor unions appears just as strong now as it was earlier in the century. Moreover, further analysis of these data show that those with favorable attitudes toward unions are about as likely to vote for Democrats regardless of whether they are a union member. What matters most are the attitudes, not the union membership per se.

What has changed, however, is how working-class and middle-class whites feel about unions. In the first decade of this century, working-class voters were somewhat warmer than middle-class voters were in their feelings toward unions. In 2000–2004, for example, working-class whites had a mean feeling thermometer score of about 57 degrees, compared to about 52 degrees for middle-class whites. But in the two most recent elections, there has been almost no difference in mean feeling thermometer scores between working-class and middle-class white voters. Thus, it appears that while feelings toward unions continue to affect voters, they no longer make working-class voters more inclined than middle-class voters to support Democrats.

## Management of the Economy

The state of the economy clearly plays an important role in American elections. Considerable research shows that voters tend to blame the incumbent president for a bad economy and credit him for a good one (Erikson 1989. Kiewiet 1983; Lewis-Beck and Paldam 2000). That phenomenon is illustrated by the fact that the last two presidents who failed to win reelection—Jimmy Carter in 1980 and George H. W. Bush in 1992—lost in large part because the nation was in a recession at the time of the election (McDonald 1981; Frankovic 1993). Furthermore, it is not just the incumbent president who is affected by the state of the economy. Blame or reward extends to the president's party as well. In 2008, for example, the Great Recession was beginning, and, as a result, the approval ratings of president George W. Bush plummeted. But even though Bush was not on the ballot in 2008, the Republican presidential nominee, John McCain, was hurt by the deteriorating economy (Crotty 2009; Schier and Box-Steffensmeier 2009). These effects apply to congressional elections as well, which helps to explain why the Republican Party lost 21 House and eight Senate seats in the 2008 congressional elections (Jacobson 2010).

Existing research has extensively investigated this relationship between the economy and voting behavior, and there seems to be a consensus on several points. First, voters respond more to the condition of the national economy, not to their personal financial situation (Feldman 1982; Kiewiet 1983, 14–25, 81–117). They are not "pocketbook voters" in the narrow sense, despite frequent depictions to the contrary in the popular media. Numerous studies have found little relationship between a voter's personal financial situation and how that person votes, especially when evaluations of the national economy are included in the analysis (Feldman 1982; Kinder and Kiewiet 1979). While this might seem surprising, it is consistent with the discussion earlier in this chapter about how individuals perceive and interpret their economic situation. As that discussion explained, there are many reasons why a voter might be better or worse off financially, and in many cases a voter would not feel that his or her economic situation was the result of government actions. On the other hand, most voters feel that government actions play a decisive role in determining the state of the national economy, so it seems logical for voters to evaluate a president's performance on this basis. Of course, the voter's recent financial situation and experiences may play a role in the formation of assessments of the national economy, but so do other factors, including the actual conditions of the national economy (Conover, Feldman, and Knight 1986; Lewis-Beck 2006; Lewis-Beck, Martini, and Kiewiet 2013).

In evaluating the condition of the national economy, voters tend to focus on a few major macroeconomic variables, particularly unemployment, inflation, and growth in the economy. These, of course, are the economic statistics most commonly reported by the news media. In evaluating the state of the economy, voters tend to have a short time horizon. Most studies conclude that what happened in the last year has the biggest effect on the voters (Bloom and Price 1975; Healy and Lenz 2014; Hellwig and Marinova 2015). Two examples may illustrate this tendency. During President Ronald Reagan's first term, the nation suffered what at that time was its worst economic recession in the post–World War II era. Reagan's approval rating dropped substantially, and the GOP suffered significant losses in the 1982 midterm congressional elections (Hunt 1983). But by 1984, the economy was in excellent shape, and Reagan won a landslide reelection (Kiewiet and Rivers 1985). The opposite situation happened to Reagan's successor, President George H. W. Bush. The economy did rather well during Bush's first three years in office, but in 1992 the nation slipped into a recession, and Bush lost his reelection bid (Frankovic 1993).

While retrospective assessments of the president's handling of the economy are important, the ultimate determinant of the vote surely is a prospective evaluation of which party would do a better job of managing the economy (Kinder and Kiewiet 1979; Lewis-Beck 1988; MacKuen, Erikson, and Stimson 1992). Indeed, it is hard to imagine that a voter who thinks that Party A would do a better job than Party B in managing the economy in the future would nevertheless vote for Party B on the basis that Party A did a poor job in the past. For many voters, it is likely that this prospective performance judgment is influenced by their retrospective evaluations of recent economic performance, but in the end, the vote should be affected by the prospective judgments about which party would be better at managing the economy (Fiorina 1981, 169; Kuklinski and West 1981).

These questions about how economic assessments affect voting are relevant for the concerns of this study only if working-class and middle-class voters differ in their evaluations of the parties as managers of the economy. As it turns out, there are reasons to think that is true. As Chapter 2 outlined, working-class individuals tend to be more concerned than middle-class individuals are about unemployment

(Hibbs 1977; 1987, 138–141; Weatherford 1978). Blue-collar workers are more likely to be laid off and less able to deal with the subsequent loss of income than are middle-class workers, who tend to be more concerned about inflation. These social class differences in economic priorities have led, at least in the past, to differences in the evaluation of the political parties as managers of the economy. Throughout much of the post-World War II era, Democrats were viewed as the party that was more concerned with reducing unemployment, while the Republicans were seen as more concerned with fighting inflation (Kiewiet 1983, 111–116; Tufte 1978, 72–76; Weatherford 1978).

An examination of past party platforms shows these differences in economic priorities, as Chapter 2 reported. So too do the economic records of the parties. An analysis of economic data from 1948 through 2005 shows that unemployment averaged about 4.8 percent during Democratic administrations, compared to about 6.3 percent during Republican administrations (Bartels 2008, 48). Growth in the per-capita GNP also was better under Democratic administrations by over a full percentage point. Inflation was lower during Republican administrations, but not by much: it averaged about 3.8 percent under Republican presidents and about 4.0 percent under Democratic ones (Bartels 2008, 48). Given those statistics, it is not surprising that in the last half of the twentieth century, the Democratic Party generally was viewed as better able to manage the economy (Hibbs 1977; Weatherford 1978; Brewer 2009, 11–17). Moreover, working-class voters were more likely than middle-class voters were to see the Democrats as better when it came to the economy (Brewer 2009, 26–29).

The question is whether these past patterns regarding evaluations of the parties as managers of the economy remain today. One possible source of change in these relationships concerns recent free trade policies, which have generated considerable attention in recent decades. The North American Free Trade Association (NAFTA), which was negotiated under the administration of President George H. W. Bush and supported by President Clinton, was opposed by major labor unions, who argued that it would result in a loss of manufacturing jobs to Mexico, where prevailing wages were much lower than in the U.S. (Kilborn 1993). President Clinton was able to get the trade agreement ratified by Congress in 1993 only with significant help from Republican members of Congress, as many members of his own party opposed the measure (Kessler 2016). Over two decades after NAFTA went into effect, it remained controversial, with labor unions still staunchly opposed (Lowrey 2014). A 2013 report by the Economic Policy Institute, an organization linked to labor unions, claimed that 700,000 American jobs were lost as a result of the trade agreement (Faux 2013). However, estimates by many economists concluded that NAFTA had a modest positive impact on the U.S. economy (McBride and Sergie 2018).

Disputes over trade policies appeared to escalate in this century, perhaps because of changing economic conditions. The economy performed very well during the 1990s, and the unemployment rate was 4.1 percent in the fall of 2000, a 30-year low, which may have muted criticism of NAFTA (Bureau of Labor Statistics 2000). During the administration of George W. Bush, China was admitted to the World Trade Organization, which then resulted in a sharp increase in imports of manufactured goods from China into this country. An analysis in 2018 by the pro-labor Economic Policy Institute estimated that 3.4 million jobs were lost as a result of the trade deficit with China (Scott and Mokhiber 2018). Concerns over the loss of manufacturing jobs in this century may have been heightened by the extent of the Great Recession and the subsequent slow recovery. President Obama proposed a new trade agreement in 2015, the Trans-Pacific Partnership (TPP), which resulted from talks that were started during the George W. Bush administration. The TPP also was opposed by major labor unions, and it was never ratified by the Congress, as President Trump withdrew the U.S. from the agreement in 2017 (Amadeo 2019).

The result of this support for free trade policies by Democratic and Republican administrations alike may have been to weaken working-class views of the Democratic Party as more concerned with fighting unemployment, particularly among blue-collar workers. As has been discussed above, unemployment is a matter of considerable concern to working-class voters. The effects of unemployment are greater than might seem to be the case from the unemployment rate. Estimates are that in a given year, the proportion of workers who experience unemployment at some point will be two to three times the unemployment rate (Hibbs 1979). Thus, an unemployment rate of 8 percent for the year would mean that as much as one-fourth of the labor force would be directly affected. Additionally, there are employees who fear losing their job but do not, employees who are only able to work part-time, and people in a household in which someone else has lost a job, even if temporarily. Thus, a sizable share of the electorate may be highly concerned about deteriorating employment prospects. It should be noted, however, that the existence of unemployment benefits and the growth of two-earner households may make the existence of an unemployed household member less financially devastating than it was decades ago (Schlozman and Verba 1979, 48–53).

Questions about the value of free trade policies were particularly salient in 2016. In the Democratic presidential nomination contests, Senator Bernie Sanders provided an unexpectedly strong challenge to Hillary Clinton, and an important part of his message was his attack on what he referred to as the disastrous free trade policies of the past (Sargent 2017). His message resonated so well with Democratic primary voters that Clinton retracted her support for the TPP. In the Republican presidential nomination, Trump railed against all of these free trade agreements, claiming that they had greatly harmed the U.S. and promising to change trade arrangements, particularly those regarding Mexico and China, so that the U.S. would no longer be taken advantage of. Unlike previous presidential elections, voters in 2016 were presented with clearer differences between the candidates on trade issues, and that may have influenced their views of which party was better able to manage the economy.

To determine how these issues of economic policy affect the current relationship between social class and voting, we need to answer two questions. First, what difference is there between working-class and middle-class voters in their attitudes regarding the parties as managers of the economy? Second, how much do attitudes about the parties as managers of the economy affect the vote. This analysis is complicated by the fact that party identification strongly shapes evaluations of the parties as managers of the economy (Evans and Anderson 2006). Democrats are highly likely to see the Democratic Party as better at handling the economy; Republicans are very likely to have the opposite view. The strength of this relationship is shown by the data in Table 6.8, which presents data from two different years, 2008 and 2016.

In 2016, Republicans were more likely to be viewed by white voters as better able to manage the economy: nearly half thought that the Republican Party would be better, but only about 30 percent thought that of the Democratic Party (black and Latino voters were more favorable to the Democrats). But a breakdown by party identification shows that few white Democrats thought that the GOP would be better for the economy, and hardly any Republicans thought that the Democrats would be better, although there were some in each party who saw no difference on this question. Opinions of the Democrats as managers of the

**TABLE 6.8** View of the Parties as Managers of the Economy by Party Identification, 2008 and 2016

| View of the Parties as Managers of the Economy | Party Identification | | | |
| --- | --- | --- | --- | --- |
| | Democrat | Independent | Republican | All Voters |
| *2016* | | | | |
| Democrats better | 66.1 | 9.4 | 1.3 | 28.6 |
| No difference | 27.1 | 59.4 | 19.1 | 25.2 |
| Republicans better | 6.8 | 31.3 | 79.7 | 46.2 |
| Total | 100% | 100% | 100% | 100% |
| (N) | (746) | (128) | (934) | (1,808) |
| *2008* | | | | |
| Democrats better | 74.2 | 13.2 | 5.7 | 35.4 |
| No difference | 23.5 | 83.0 | 33.7 | 31.7 |
| Republicans better | 2.3 | 3.8 | 60.6 | 32.9 |
| Total | 100% | 100% | 100% | 100% |
| (N) | (472) | (53) | (578) | (1,103) |

Source: ANES surveys, 2008 and 2016.
Note: Only white, major-party voters are included in the table. For party identification, Democrats and Republicans include independent leaners. See the text for further details on the variables.

economy were more favorable in 2008, but the same pattern emerges when attitudes are broken down by party identification: both Democrats and Republicans were far more likely to see their own party as best. Thus, the absolute level of support for either party as best able to handle the economy changes over time as economic circumstances change, but within each year, there always are large differences by party identification.

Recognizing that party identification exerts considerable influence on assessments of which party will be better at handling the economy, we can examine the effect that these assessments have on the vote by including all three variables in the analysis. Table 6.9 shows the presidential vote from 2000 to 2016 by party identification and the view of which party would better handle the economy. To simplify the analysis, I combined the Democrats who saw no difference between the parties with the small number who saw the Republicans as better, and I did the same for the Republicans. As we can see, in every presidential election, Democrats who thought that their party would be better at managing the economy voted overwhelmingly for the Democratic presidential candidate, but there were significant defections among those Democrats who did not see their party as better able to manage the economy. In 2016, about one-third of Democrats felt that about their party, and about 30 percent of this group voted for Trump. A similar pattern is present for Republicans, although they were somewhat less likely to defect in their vote when they did not feel that the GOP was better on this question.

Attitudes on trade influenced how voters perceived the parties as managers of the economy in 2016. Table 6.10 shows the relationship between the assessments that voters had of the parties regarding the management of the economy and their attitude on trade. For 2016, I measured attitudes on trade by forming an

**TABLE 6.9** Presidential Vote by View of the Parties as Managers of the Economy and Party Identification, 2000–2016

| | Party Identification | | | |
| | Democrat | | Republican | |
| | View of the Parties as Managers of the Economy | | | |
| Presidential Vote: | Democrats Better | No Diff. or Rep. Better | Republicans Better | No Diff. or Dem. Better |
|---|---|---|---|---|
| 2016: % for Trump | 3.0 | 30.2 | 97.7 | 74.7 |
| 2012: % for Romney | 3.7 | 22.8 | 98.1 | 78.3 |
| 2008% for McCain | 5.1 | 32.8 | 96.6 | 83.8 |
| 2000–2004: % for Bush | 6.1 | 26.2 | 97.7 | 80.8 |

Source: ANES surveys, 2000–2016.
Note: Only white, major-party voters are included in the table. Figures are the percent of the major-party vote for the Republican candidate. For party identification, Democrats and Republicans include independent leaners. See the text for further details on the variables.

**TABLE 6.10** View of the Parties as Managers of the Economy by Attitude on Trade and Party Identification, 2012–2016

| View of the Parties as Managers of the Economy: | Party Identification | | | |
| | Democrat | | Republican | |
| | Attitude on Trade | | | |
| | Favorable | Unfavorable | Favorable | Unfavorable |
| --- | --- | --- | --- | --- |
| *2016:* | | | | |
| Democrats better | 70.2 | 60.3 | 2.2 | 0.8 |
| No difference | 25.3 | 29.1 | 21.5 | 17.5 |
| Republicans better | 4.5 | 10.6 | 76.3 | 81.7 |
| *2012:* | | | | |
| Democrats better | 70.7 | 66.6 | 1.5 | 0.9 |
| No difference | 24.4 | 29.7 | 11.6 | 24.5 |
| Republicans better | 4.9 | 3.7 | 86.9 | 74.6 |

Source: ANES surveys, 2012–2016.
Note: Only white, major-party voters are included in the table. For party identification, Democrats and Republicans include independent leaners. See the text for further details on the variables.

index from three questions about trade: (a) whether imports should be limited to preserve U.S. jobs; (b) whether trade had good or bad effects; and (c) whether the voter favored or opposed free trade agreements. To make the analysis simple, I dichotomized the trade index so that those who had more positive than negative responses on the three questions were classified as being favorable to free trade, and those with more negative than positive responses were considered to be unfavorable. Overall, about 60 percent of the white voters in 2016 had favorable attitudes on trade, using this measure.

In looking at the relationship between attitudes on free trade and evaluations of the parties as managers of the economy, I controlled for party identification because of its strong effect on the latter variable. In 2016, Democrats who held favorable attitudes toward free trade were more likely than Democrats with unfavorable attitudes to see the Democratic Party as better able to manage the economy. Among Republicans, there was almost no relationship between attitudes on free trade and assessments of the parties as managers of the economy; if anything, there was a slight tendency for those with unfavorable attitudes on trade to be more positive in their assessments of the GOP.

Table 6.10 also include data for 2012. For that year, the ANES survey included just one relevant question on trade, which was whether foreign imports should be limited to protect U.S. jobs. The 2012 patterns for both Democrats and Republicans differ from the 2016 patterns. Among Democrats in 2012, there is no relationship between attitude on free trade and assessment of the parties as managers of the economy. Democrats who wanted to limit imports were just as likely to say that the Democratic Party was better able to manage the economy as were Democrats who opposed limits. For Republicans, there is a relationship: those who did not want to limit imports were more likely to see the Republican Party as better able to manage the economy. The likely explanation for the difference between the 2012 and 2016 patterns is that in 2016 the GOP was seen as the party that was opposed to free trade, whereas in 2012 it was not.

Table 6.11 brings social class into the analysis. We can see how working-class and middle-class white voters differed in their attitudes toward trade, controlling for party identification. Among Democrats, there has been little change. Throughout this century, working-class white Democrats have been more unfavorable in their attitudes on trade, relative to middle-class white Democrats, and that difference has widened a bit in the most recent years. Among Republicans, there has been striking change. In the early years of this century, working-class white Republicans and Democrats were rather similar in their attitudes toward free trade. The same was true for middle-class whites. As late as 2012, class differences in attitudes on trade were clear, but party differences were not. Working-class Republicans were almost as opposed to free trade as were working-class Democrats. In 2016, however, party differences were enormous. Republicans went from a majority in favor of free trade in 2012 to over 60 percent opposed in 2016, with the change especially great among middle-class Republicans. It appears that many Republican voters changed their attitudes on trade to bring them more in line with the positions of their party's presidential nominee. No such change appeared among Democrats, however; their 2016 attitudes on trade hardly differed from their 2012 attitudes.

This leads us to the most important question for this analysis: do working-class and middle-class voters differ in their views of which party is better at managing

**TABLE 6.11** Attitude Toward Foreign Trade by Social Class and Party Identification, 2000–2016

| Percent with an Unfavorable View of Foreign Trade: | Party Identification | | | |
| | Democrat | | Republican | |
| | Social Class | | | |
| | Working Class | Middle Class | Working Class | Middle Class |
| 2016 | 49.7 | 30.5 | 68.7 | 61.8 |
| 2012 | 49.3 | 30.3 | 43.8 | 33.9 |
| 2008 | 45.8 | 27.4 | 41.6 | 37.7 |
| 2000–2004 | 44.6 | 31.8 | 42.4 | 30.2 |

Source: ANES surveys, 2000–2016.
Note: Only white, major-party voters are included in the table. For party identification, Democrats and Republicans include independent leaners. See the text for further details on the variables.

the economy. Table 6.12 presents these data for recent elections. Since these assessments of the parties are strongly influenced by party identification, Democrats and Republicans are analyzed separately. Among white Democrats, there is little change in this century in class differences in these economic assessments. In every presidential election, working-class and middle-class Democrats have very similar assessments of the Democratic Party. Democrats who see their party as better able to manage the economy are less likely to defect from their partisanship in their presidential vote, but since working-class Democrats are no more likely than their middle-class counterparts to feel that way, these economic assessments do not give working-class Democrats greater reason to vote for the Democratic candidate. Exactly the same pattern is true for Republicans now, but it was not that way earlier in this century. From 2000 through 2008, working-class white Republicans were less likely than middle-class white Republicans to see the GOP as better able to manage the economy. To the extent that these assessments affect voting behavior, that gave working-class Republicans more reason to vote for a Democratic presidential candidate. They no longer have more reason to defect, at least for these concerns.

There may be a variety of reasons why working-class whites are no longer more likely to view the Democratic Party as better able to manage the economy, but these data suggest that free trade issues have contributed to this development. Working-class voters are more opposed to free trade than are middle-class voters. In the past three decades, Democratic presidents have supported free trade agreements just as much as Republican presidents have. It would not be surprising if many working-class voters came to see both parties as largely the same on this issue, at least before 2016, giving them fewer reasons than they once had to vote for Democrats. Similarly, middle-class voters also may have felt that Democrats

**TABLE 6.12** View of the Parties as Managers of the Economy by Social Class and Party Identification, 2000–2016

| | Party Identification | | | |
| | Democrat | | Republican | |
| | Social Class | | | |
| Percent Who See Their Party as Better at Managing the Economy: | Working Class | Middle Class | Working Class | Middle Class |
|---|---|---|---|---|
| 2016 | 66.1 | 68.0 | 81.7 | 80.1 |
| 2012 | 66.8 | 64.4 | 77.3 | 79.9 |
| 2008 | 72.4 | 76.0 | 52.9 | 65.7 |
| 2000–2004 | 66.6 | 64.4 | 54.7 | 63.3 |

Source: ANES surveys, 2000–2016.
Note: Only white, major-party voters are included in the table. For party identification, Democrats and Republicans include independent leaners. See the text for further details on the variables.

supported free trade just as much as Republicans. Again, other factors also may have contributed to these lack of class differences in assessments of the parties, but the important point is that when it comes to managing the economy, neither party currently enjoys an advantage with either social class.

It is, of course, true that the assessments of the parties change from one election to the next, largely because of changes in national economic conditions. For example, in 2004, 36 percent of all voters thought that the Democrats would be better at managing the economy, while 26 percent felt that Republicans would. In 2008, that increased to 40 percent feeling that Democrats would be better, but in 2012 it dropped to 32 percent, which made the two parties tied on this question. But while national assessments of the parties as managers of the economy shift from one election to the next, that does not necessarily mean that social class differences in these assessments change, and class differences are what this study is concerned with. Class differences could increase or decrease from one election to the next if working-class and middle-class voters respond differently to changes in national economic conditions, but these data do not show much fluctuation in class differences over time, at least in this century. Among white Democrats, there is little variation in the difference between working-class and middle-class assessments of the parties as managers of the economy, a difference that is small in each of the years. Among white Republicans, there is only one shift in class differences in these assessments: between 2008 and 2012, class differences essentially evaporated. Otherwise, class differences remained stable across elections for Republicans.

## Conclusion

Attitudes on economic issues continue to influence voting behavior, and the effects are just as strong now as they were at the start of this century. White voters with more liberal attitudes on social welfare issues are much more likely to vote for Democrats, and attitudes on these issues are deeply imbedded into party identification. Feelings toward labor unions also are clearly related to voting among whites. Those who have favorable views of labor unions, regardless of whether they are a union member, continue to be more supportive of Democrats than are those with unfavorable views. When it comes to evaluating the parties in terms of their ability to manage the economy, both Democrats and Republicans are likely to think that their party would be better, but the minority of partisans who do not feel that way about their party are significantly more likely to defect in their presidential vote.

What has changed is how these attitudes on economic issues are connected to social class among white voters. At one time, working-class whites were more liberal or more favorable toward Democrats on all of these economic issues. Those class differences began to diminish in the latter part of the 20th century, and whatever differences remained at the beginning of this century have almost disappeared by now. For example, during the Bush elections, 2000–2004, working-class voters were moderately more liberal than middle-class voters on social welfare issues; by 2016, that difference had almost disappeared. Working-class voters used to be more favorable toward unions than middle-class voters were. Today there is no difference; both groups are equally supportive. When it comes to assessing the parties as managers of the economy, the old Democratic advantage among working-class voters had already largely disappeared by the start of this century, and by 2016 it was completely gone. The disappearance of class differences is not mostly the result of working-class whites becoming more conservative on economic issues. An increased economic liberalism among middle-class whites has contributed equally to this development. But regardless of the source of this diminished class difference in economic attitudes, the implications for voting are clear: if middle-class and working-class whites had voted in 2016 solely on the basis of economic issues, there would have been little class difference in the vote.

The same qualification that I made in the previous two chapters applies here as well. In order to make the presentation simple, I have presented and discussed bivariate relationships in this chapter. However, the bivariate relationships might not represent the true causal effect of these attitudes. The next chapter will present the results of a multivariate analysis of the vote in 2016 and 2012, which will allow for a better estimation of the true effects of the various factors examined in this study. As we will see, those results are basically consistent with the analysis in this chapter.

## Notes

1  One question about health care asked respondents to place themselves on a seven-point scale that ran from having a complete government plan for health care insurance to relying solely on private plans. The other question about health care asked respondents whether they wanted to increase government spending on health care, decrease it, or keep it the same. The question about government action to reduce inequality asked respondents to place themselves on a seven-point scale that ran from having the government make every effort to reduce inequality to having it make no special effort at all. The question about government regulation of business asked respondents whether regulation of business should be increased, decreased, or kept the same.

2  The question about the minimum wage asked respondents whether the national minimum wage should be increased, decreased, or kept the same. The question about spending on unemployment benefits asked respondents whether the spending should be increased, decreased, or kept the same.

## References

Abramowitz, Alan I. 2010. *The Disappearing Center: Engaged Citizens, Polarization, and American Democracy*. New Haven, CT: Yale University Press.

Abramowitz, Alan, and Jennifer McCoy. 2019. "United States: Racial Resentment, Negative Partisanship, and Polarization in Trump's America." *The ANNALS* 681 (January): 137–156.

Amadeo, Kimberly. 2019. "Trans-Pacific Partnership Summary, Pros and Cons." *The Balance*, March 11. www.thebalance.com/what-is-the-trans-pacific-partnership-3305581.

Bacon, Perry Jr. 2018. "Republicans Killed Much of Obamacare Without Repealing It." *FiveThirtyEight*, December 18. https://fivethirtyeight.com/features/republicans-killed-much-of-obamacare-without-repealing-it/.

Ballotpedia. 2019. "Obamacare Overview." https://ballotpedia.org/Obamacare_overview.

Bartels, Larry M. 2008. *Unequal Democracy: The Political Economy of the New Gilded Age.* Princeton, NJ: Princeton University Press.

Bloom, Howard S., and H. Douglas Price. 1975. "Voter Response to Short-run Economic Conditions: The Asymmetric Effect of Prosperity and Recession." *American Political Science Review* 69: 1240–1254.

Brewer, Mark D. 2009. *Party Images in the American Electorate.* New York: Routledge.

Brewer, Mark D., and Jeffrey M. Stonecash. 2007. *Split: Class and Cultural Divides in American Politics.* Washington, DC: CQ Press.

Bureau of Labor Statistics. 2000. "TED: The Economics Daily." United States Department of Labor, March 29. www.bls.gov/opub/ted/2000/Mar/wk4/art03.htm.

Campbell, Alexia Fernandez. 2019. "The Minimum Wage Bill Has All but Died in the Senate." *Vox*, August 16. www.vox.com/2019/8/16/20807610/raise-the-wage-act-15-minimum-wage-bill.

Campbell, Angus, Philip E. Converse, Warren E. Miller, and Donald E. Stokes. 1960. *The American Voter.* New York: John Wiley & Sons.

Confessore, Nicholas. 2016. "How G.O.P. Elites Lost the Party's Base to Trump." *New York Times*, November 9.

Congressional Budget Office. 2019. "The Effects on Employment and Family Income of Increasing the Federal Minimum Wage." Congress of the United States. www.cbo.gov/system/files/2019-07/CBO-55410-MinimumWage2019.pdf.

Conover, Pamela Johnston, Stanley Feldman, and Kathleen Knight. 1986. "Judging Inflation and Unemployment: The Origins of Retrospective Evaluations." *Journal of Politics* 48(3): 565–588.

Coontz, Stephanie. 2016. "Working-class Whites Give Trump the White House." *CNN*, November 11. www.cnn.com/2016/11/10/opinions/how-clinton-lost-the-working-class-coontz/index.html.

Cox, Daniel, Rachel Lienesch, and Robert P. Jones. 2017. "Beyond Economics: Fears of Cultural Displacement Pushed the White Working Class to Trump." *PRRI/The Atlantic Report.* Public Religion Research Institute, May 9. www.prri.org.

Crotty, William J. 2009. "Electing Obama: The 2008 Campaign." In *Winning the Presidency 2008*, ed. William J. Crotty, 20–47. Boulder, CO: Paradigm Publishers.

Davey, Monica, and Steven Greenhouse. 2011. "Angry Demonstrations in Wisconsin as Cuts Loom." *New York Times*, February 16.

Doyle, Daniel J. 2010. "Labor Relations Under the Bush Administration." *Inquiries* 2(5): 1.

Edsall, Thomas B. 2016. "Measuring the Trump Effect." *New York Times*, June 19.

Edsall, Thomas Byrne, and Mary D. Edsall. 1991. *Chain Reaction: The Impact of Race, Rights, and Taxes on American Politics.* New York: W. W. Norton.

Erikson, Robert S. 1989. "Economic Conditions and the Presidential Vote." *The American Political Science Review* 83(2): 567–573.

Evans, Geoffrey, and Robert Anderson. 2006. "The Political Conditioning of Economic Perceptions." *Journal of Politics* 68(1): 194–207.

Faux, Jeff. 2013. "NAFTA's Impact on U.S. Workers." *Working Economics Blog*. Economic Policy Institute, December 9. www.epi.org/blog/naftas-impact-workers/.

Feldman, Stanley. 1982. "Economic Self-Interest and Political Behavior." *American Journal of Political Science* 26(3): 446–466.

Fiorina, Morris P. 1981. *Retrospective Voting in American National Elections*. New Haven, CT: Yale University Press.

Francia, Peter L. 2010. "Assessing the Labor-Democratic Party Alliance: A One-Sided Relationship?." *Polity* 42(3): 293–303.

Francia, Peter L. 2012. "Do Unions Still Matter in U.S. Elections? Assessing Labor's Political Power and Significance." *The Forum* 10(1): Article 3. www.degruyter.com/view/j/for.2012.10.issue-1/1540–8884.1497/1540–8884.1497.xml?lang=en.

Francia, Peter L., and Nathan S. Bigelow. 2010. "What's the Matter with the White Working Class? The Effects of Union Membership in the 2004 Presidential Election." *Presidential Studies Quarterly* 40(1): 140–158.

Frank, Thomas. 2016. "Millions of Ordinary Americans Support Donald Trump. Here's Why." *The Guardian*, March 7. www.theguardian.com/commentisfree/2016/mar/07/donald-trump-why-americans-support.

Frankovic, Kathleen A. 1993. "Public Opinion in the 1992 Campaign." In *The Election of 1992*, ed. Gerald M. Pomper, 110–131. Chatham, NJ: Chatham House.

Galston, William A. 2007. "Why the 2005 Social Security Initiative Failed and What it Means for the Future." *Brookings*. www.brookings.edu/research/why-the-2005-social-security-initiative-failed-and-what-it-means-for-the-future/.

Gest, Justin. 2017. "The Two Kinds of Trump Voters." *Politico*. February 8. www.politico.com/magazine/story/2017/02/trump-voters-white-working-class-214754.

Gilens, Martin. 1999. *Why Americans Hate Welfare: Race, Media, and the Politics of Antipoverty Policy*. Chicago: University of Chicago Press.

Gluck, Abbe R. 2017. "How the G.O.P. Sabotaged Obamacare." *New York Times*, May 25.

Greenberg, Stanley. 2017. "The Democrats' Working-Class Problem." *The American Prospect*, June 1. https://prospect.org/article/democrats'-'working-class-problem'.

Hall, Dee J. 2015. "Scott Walker Signs Bill, Makes Wisconsin 25th Right-to-Work State." *Wall Street Journal*, March 9.

Healy, Andrew, and Gabriel S. Lenz. 2014. "Substituting the End for the Whole: Why Voters Respond Primarily to the Election-Year Economy." *American Journal of Political Science* 58(1): 31–47.

Hellwig, Timothy, and Dani M. Marinova. 2015. "More Misinformed than Myopic: Economic Retrospections and the Voter's Time Horizon." *Political Behavior* 37(4): 865–887.

Hibbs, Douglas A., Jr. 1977. "Political Parties and Macroeconomic Policy." *American Political Science Review* 71(4): 1467–1487.

Hibbs, Douglas A., Jr. 1979. "The Mass Public and Macroeconomic Policy: The Dynamics of Public Opinion Toward Unemployment and Inflation." *American Journal of Political Science* 23(3): 705–773.

Hibbs, Douglas A., Jr. 1987. *The American Political Economy: Macroeconomics and Electoral Politics*. Cambridge, MA: Harvard University Press.

Hiltzik, Michael A. 2005. *The Plot Against Social Security: How the Bush Plan is Endangering Our Financial Future*. New York: HarperCollins.

Hooghe, Marc, and Ruth Dassonneville. 2018. "Explaining the Trump Vote: The Effect of Racist Resentment and Anti-Immigrant Sentiments." *PS: Political Science & Politics* 51(3): 528–534.

Huetteman, Emmarie. 2014. "Obama Calls for Minimum Wage Rise and Equal Pay as Elections Approach." *New York Times*, September 1.

Hunt, Albert R. 1983. "National Politics and the 1982 Campaign." In *The American Elections of 1982*, eds Thomas E. Mann and Norman J. Ornstein, 1–43. Washington, DC: American Enterprise Institute.

Jacobson, Gary C. 2010. "Congress: The Second Democratic Wave." In *The Elections of 2008*, ed. Michael Nelson, 100–121. Washington, DC: CQ Press.

Johnson, Haynes, and David S. Broder. 1996. *The System: The American Way of Politics at the Breaking Point*. Boston: Little, Brown and Company.

Johnson, Katie. 2018. "Under Trump, Labor Protections Stripped Away." *Boston Globe*, September 3. www.bostonglobe.com/business/2018/09/02/under-trump-labor-protec tions-stripped-away/jbr9aClCWyca8SbQCdtKJP/story.html.

Kessler, Glenn. 2016. "History Lesson: More Republicans than Democrats Supported NAFTA." *Washington Post*, May 9.

Kiewiet, D. Roderick. 1983. *Macroeconomics & Micropolitics: The Electoral Effect of Economic Issues*. Chicago: University of Chicago Press.

Kiewiet, D. Roderick, and Douglas Rivers. 1985. "The Economic Basis of Reagan's Appeal." In *The New Direction in American Politics*, eds John E. Chubb and Paul E. Peterson, 69–90. Washington, DC: The Brookings Institution.

Kilborn, Peter T. 1993. "Unions Gird for War Over Trade Pact." *New York Times*, October 4.

Kinder, Donald R., and D. Roderick Kiewiet. 1979. "Economic Discontent and Political Behavior: The Role of Personal Grievances and Collective Economic Judgements in Congressional Voting." *American Journal of Political Science* 23(3): 495–517.

Kramer, Gerald H. 1983. "The Ecological Fallacy Revisited: Aggregate- versus Individual-level Findings on Economics and Elections, and Sociotropic Voting." *American Political Science Review* 77(1): 92–111.

Kuklinski, James H., and Darrell M. West. 1981. "Economic Expectations and Voting Behavior in United States House and Senate Elections." *The American Political Science Review* 75(2): 436–447.

Levandusky, Matthew. 2009. *The Partisan Sort: How Liberals Became Democrats and Conservatives Became Republicans*. Chicago: University of Chicago Press.

Lewis-Beck, Michael S. 1988. "Economics and the American Voter: Past, Present, Future." *Political Behavior* 10(1): 5–21.

Lewis-Beck, Michael S. 2006. "Does Economics Still Matter? Econometrics and the Vote." *Journal of Politics* 68(1): 208–212.

Lewis-Beck, Michael S., Nicholas F. Martini, and D. Roderick Kiewiet. 2013. "The Nature of Economic Perceptions in Mass Publics." *Electoral Studies* 32(3): 524–528.

Lewis-Beck, Michael S., and Martin Paldam. 2000. "Economic Voting: An Introduction." *Electoral Studies* 19(2): 113–121.

Lowrey, Annie. 2014. "Nafta Still Bedevils Unions." *New York Times*, March 27. https://economix.blogs.nytimes.com/2014/03/27/nafta-still-bedevils-unions/.

MacKuen, Michael B., Robert S. Erikson, and James A. Stimson. 1992. "Peasants or Bankers? The American Electorate and the U.S. Economy." *American Political Science Review* 86(3): 597–611.

McDonald, Stephen L. 1981. "Economic Issues in the Campaign." In *A Tide of Discontent: The 1980 Elections and Their Meaning*, eds Ellis Sandoz and Cecil V.Crabb, Jr, 139–156. Washington, DC: CQ Press.

McElwee, Sean. 2016. "Yep, Race Really Did Trump Economics: A Data Dive on His Supporters Reveals Deep Racial Animosity." *Salon*, November 13. www.salon.com/2016/11/13/yep-race-really-did-trump-economics-a-data-dive-on-his-supporters-reveals-deep-racial-animosity/.

McBride, James, and Mohammed Aly Sergie. 2018. "NAFTA's Economic Impact." Council on Foreign Relations. www.cfr.org/backgrounder/naftas-economic-impact.

Murphy, Patricia. 2016. "Why These Union Members and Lifelong Democrats Are Voting Trump." *Daily Beast*, July 26. www.thedailybeast.com/why-these-union-members- and-lifelong-democrats-are-voting-trump.

Mutz, Diana C. 2018. "Status Threat, Not Economic Hardship, Explains the 2016 Presidential Vote." *Proceedings of the National Academy of Sciences* 115(19): 4330–4339. www.pnas.org/cgi/da/10,1073/pnas.1718155115.

Page, Benjamin I., and Lawrence R. Jacobs. 2009. *Class War? What Americans Really Think About Economic Inequality*. Chicago: University of Chicago Press.

Panagopoulos, Costas, and Peter L. Francia. 2008. "Poll Trends: Labor Unions in the United States." *Public Opinion Quarterly* 72(1): 134–159.

Pear, Robert. 2011. "G.O.P. Blueprint Would Remake Health Policy." *New York Times*, April 4.

Pear, Robert. 2016. "A Battle to Change Medicare Is Brewing, Whether Trump Wants It or Not." *New York Times*, November 24.

Piston, Spencer. 2018. *Class Attitudes in America*. Cambridge: Cambridge University Press.

Reid, Tim. 2016. "Ohio's Dirty Little Secret: Blue-Collar Democrats for Trump." *Reuters*, March 12. www.reuters.com/article/us-usa-election-trump-ohio-insight/ohios-dirty-little-secret-blue-collar-democrats-for-trump-idUSKCN0WC19Q.

Remy, Tyler T., Loren Collingwood, and Ali A. Valenzuela. 2019. "Vote Switching in the 2016 Election: How Racial and Immigration Attitudes, Not Economics, Explain Shifts in White Voting." *Public Opinion Quarterly* 83(1): 91–113.

Republican Party. 2008. "2008 Republican Party Platform." *The American Presidency Project*. www.presidency.ucsb.edu/documents/2008-republican-party-platform.

Republican Party. 2012. "2012 Republican Party Platform." *The American Presidency Project*. www.presidency.ucsb.edu/documents/2012-republican-party-platform.

Republican Party. 2016. "2016 Republican Party Platform." *The American Presidency Project*. www.presidency.ucsb.edu/documents/2016-republican-party-platform.

Roof, Tracy. 2011. *American Labor, Congress, and the Welfare State, 1935–2010*. Baltimore, MD: The Johns Hopkins University Press.

Rothwell, Jonathan. 2016. "Economic Hardship and Favorable Views of Trump." *Gallup*, July 22. https://news.gallup.com/opinion/polling-matters/193898/economic-hardship-favorable-views-trump.aspx.

Sargent, Greg. 2017. "'Feel the Bern:' Hillary's Agonizing Loss and the Future of the Democratic Party." In *Trumped: The Election That Broke All the Rules*, eds Larry J. Sabato, Kyle Kondike, and Geoffrey Skelley, 112–122. Lanham, MD: Rowman and Littlefield.

Schaffner, Brian F., Matthew MacWilliams, and Tatishe Nteta. 2018. "Understanding White Polarization in the 2016 Vote for President: The Sobering Role of Racism and Sexism." *Political Science Quarterly* 133(1): 9–34.

Schier, Steven E., and Janet M. Box-Steffensmeier. 2009. "The General Election Campaign." In *The American Elections of 2008*, eds Janet M. Box-Steffensmeier and Steven E. Schier, 55–78. Lanham, MD: Rowman and Littlefield.

Schlozman, Kay, and Sidney Verba. 1979. *Injury to Insult.* Cambridge, MA: Harvard University Press.

Scott, Robert E., and Zane Mokhiber. 2018. "The China Toll Deepens." Economic Policy Institute. www.epi.org/files/pdf/156645.pdf.

Sides, John, Mark Tesler, and Lynn Vavreck. 2018. *Identity Crisis: The 2016 Presidential Election and the Battle for the Meaning of America.* Princeton, NJ: Princeton University Press.

Skocpol, Theda S. 1996. *Boomerang: Health Care Reform and the Turn Against Government.* New York: W. W. Norton.

Tesler, Michael. 2016. *Post-Racial or Most-Racial? Race and Politics in the Obama Era.* Chicago: University of Chicago Press.

Tufte, Edward R. 1978. *Political Control of the Economy.* Princeton, NJ: Princeton University Press.

Tumulty, Karen. 2011. "Wisconsin Governor Wins Battle with Unions on Collective Bargaining." *Washington Post,* March 10.

Weatherford, M. Stephen. 1978. "Economic Conditions and Electoral Outcomes: Class Differences in the Political Response to Recession." *American Journal of Political Science* 22(4): 917–938.

# 7

# ANALYZING THE 2012 AND 2016 PRESIDENTIAL ELECTIONS

The relationship between social class and voting behavior has changed in the 21st century, at least among white voters. White working-class voters no longer are more likely to support Democrats, a marked change in what had been a long-standing relationship in American politics. The Democratic advantage among white working-class voters began to evaporate in the first decade of this century. In the second decade, it reversed. The Republican candidate did better among white working-class voters than among white middle-class voters in the 2012 and 2016 presidential elections. Both scholars and media commentators have offered explanations for this change, and the previous three chapters have analyzed the possible sources of this change. Those chapters found that several factors appear to have contributed to this development in electoral politics.

Chapter 4 found that attitudes regarding race and immigration help to explain the change in the relationship between social class and voting behavior among whites. Working-class whites currently have somewhat more unfavorable views of blacks and immigrants than their middle-class counterparts do. Both of these attitudes are related to voting behavior, with Republicans doing much better among those with more negative attitudes. Over the past two decades, class differences in these attitudes have emerged, from what were very weak differences to the currently moderate differences, and the impact of these attitudes on the vote has increased. The combination of these two changes in the electorate provides one explanation for the increased support for Republicans among white working-class voters, relative to middle-class white voters.

Chapter 5 found that attitudes on moral issues also help to explain the change in how social class and voting behavior are related among whites. Middle-class and working-class white voters differ in their attitudes on abortion, gay rights, and other moral issues that are tied to religion. Middle-class voters tend to be more liberal on these moral issues than working-class voters are, a difference that has been fairly stable in this century. What has changed in recent decades is the influence of these moral issues on voting behavior. That effect has strengthened, with Republicans doing significantly better among voters with more conservative attitudes on moral issues, which is another reason why the white working class is now more Republican than is the white middle class.

Chapter 6 found that attitudes on economic issues are a third factor that has contributed to the changing relationship between social class and voting behavior. For economic issues, what is most significant is that social class differences on these issues have become very small. Working-class voters used to prefer the Democratic Party on economic issues, but that has changed in this century. Currently, working-class whites differ very little from middle-class whites in their attitudes toward social welfare issues and toward labor unions, two sets of issues that used to be prime motives for working-class voters to prefer Democrats. Additionally, white working-class voters no longer are more likely than middle-class voters to see the Democrats as better able to manage the economy, a development that seems related to attitudes on trade. Attitudes on economic issues still affect the vote, but they no longer make working-class voters more likely to support Democrats or middle-class voters more likely to support Republicans.

Most of the analysis presented in the previous three chapters was a straightforward bivariate analysis, where I simply presented the relationships between attitudes and the vote without controlling for other variables. That was done to make the analysis easy to understand by readers unfamiliar with more advanced statistical methods. However, the bivariate analyses could be misleading. Attitudes on all of these issues are interrelated, so some of the bivariate relationships might not reflect the true effects of these variables on the vote. Rather, the associations might reflect the confounding effects of other variables. For a better understanding of the true effects of each of these variables, a more sophisticated statistical analysis is needed.

This chapter will extend the analysis done so far by looking at the results of multivariate analyses of the vote, which will show us the independent effect of each variable on the vote with the others held constant. Furthermore, both the 2012 and the 2016 presidential elections will be analyzed. These were quite different elections, with very different candidates, so any similarities that we see across these two elections probably will represent more fundamental relationships, not just effects that are specific to the candidates involved. By conducting similar analyses of the vote in 2012 and 2016, we will see the extent to which Romney appealed to working-class and middle-class voters on the same basis that Trump did, as well as seeing the unique appeals of Trump.

Many interpretations of the 2016 presidential election stressed Donald Trump's ability to appeal to white working-class voters, an appeal that other Republicans supposedly lacked. But earlier analysis in this book has shown that Mitt Romney in 2012 also did better among white working-class voters than he did among white middle-class voters, albeit not to the extent that Trump did. While Trump may have been a very unusual Republican presidential candidate, especially regarding the concerns of this book, that cannot be said about Romney. The 2012 presidential election was, at least in terms of the issue positions of the candidates, a contest between a fairly typical Democrat and a fairly typical Republican. Moreover, in the 2012 presidential election campaign, Romney was characterized by Democrats as a wealthy capitalist who had little understanding of the economic difficulties encountered by ordinary Americans. Those portrayals received considerable media attention, and many voters gave Romney low marks on empathy (Holian and Prysby 2015, 144–145). Romney contributed to these perceptions with some of his own statements during the campaign. Particularly damaging were comments that he made to a group of supporters and that were subsequently widely reported in the national news. In that gathering, Romney stated that 47 percent of the people would not vote for him because they wanted government handouts and that he would "never convince them that they should take personal responsibility and care for their lives" (Balz 2013, 6). If anything, Romney would seem to be a Republican who would be less appealing to working-class voters than previous Republican presidential candidates, such as John McCain or George W. Bush. This makes it especially interesting to see what similarities exist in the reasons for class differences in the presidential vote in 2012 and 2016.

The following analyses of voting in the 2012 and 2016 presidential elections rely on the American National Election Study (ANES) surveys of the American electorate. Only major-party voters are included in the analyses in this chapter, as was the case in the previous chapters, so the dependent variable, presidential vote, is dichotomous (i.e., Democratic or Republican). That makes logistic regression the appropriate statistical method (King 1989, 97–110; Meyers, Gamst, and Guarino 2006, 221–240). The independent variables used in the analysis for each year are described in the appendix. First of all, party identification is included because extensive research shows that it has a powerful influence on the vote (Campbell *et al.* 1960, 120–145; Lewis-Beck *et al.* 2008, 111–137). For economic attitudes, I included four variables: assessments of which party would better handle the economy, attitudes on trade policies, attitudes on social welfare issues, and attitudes toward labor unions. Also included in the analysis are attitudes toward blacks, attitudes on immigration, and attitudes on two moral issues, abortion and gay rights. All of these attitudes on economic, social, and cultural issues are discussed in earlier chapters, and, as the above summary of those chapters shows, all were found to be relevant factors that affect the vote and help to explain the changing relationship between social class and voting behavior.

Whenever possible, I measured the attitudes with indices that combined responses to two or more questions; using an index built from multiple items should produce a more accurate measure of the attitude in question. Attitudes on almost all of the issues are measured on four-point scales, with a lower score representing a more liberal or pro-Democratic attitude. The two variables that are not measured on a four-point scale are: (a) party identification, where respondents are classified as Democrats, independents, or Republicans (with independent leaners counted as Democrats or Republicans); and (b) assessment of which party would better handle the economy, where respondents are classified as believing the Democrats would be better, Republicans would be better, or neither party would be better.

## The 2016 Presidential Election

This analysis of the presidential vote in 2016 shows that many attitudes influenced white voters. Table 7.1 presents the results of a logistic regression of the vote using all of the variables discussed above, along with one other variable. Since Trump's campaign emphasized how he was an outsider who would be able to accomplish goals that elected officials from both parties had failed to achieve, it seemed worthwhile to include a variable that measured trust in politicians. The hypothesis is that voters with low trust in politicians in general would be more inclined to vote for Trump. That variable is described in the appendix, along

**TABLE 7.1** Analysis of the Presidential Vote, 2016

| Independent Variable: | Model A | | Model B | |
|---|---|---|---|---|
| | Coeff. | (S.E.) | Coeff. | (S.E.) |
| Party identification | 1.173** | (.143) | | |
| Best party for economy | 1.540** | (.185) | | |
| Attitude on social welfare issues | .474* | (.206) | 1.808** | (.158) |
| Attitude toward labor unions | .104 | (.157) | .461** | (.123) |
| Attitude toward free trade | .318** | (.128) | .372** | (.101) |
| Attitude toward blacks | .998** | (.187) | .876** | (.142) |
| Attitude on immigration issues | 1.130** | (.223) | 1.448** | (.181) |
| Attitude on moral issues | .656** | (.138) | .927** | (.110) |
| Trust in politicians | .395* | (.190) | .190 | (.151) |
| Nagelkerke $R^2$ | .858 | | .761 | |
| % of cases correctly. predicted | 93.2 | | 88.8 | |
| (N) | (1633) | | (1635) | |

Source: ANES 2016 survey.
Note: Entries are logistic regression coefficients, with standard errors in parentheses. Positive coefficients indicate that a Republican vote is related to a Republican party identification, more favorable assessment of Republicans as the best party to manage the economy, more conservative attitudes on social welfare and moral issues, more negative attitudes toward free trade policies, labor unions, blacks, and immigration, and a low trust in politicians. Only white, major-party voters are included in the analysis. See the text for information on how the variables are measured.

with all of the other variables used in the analysis. The results of two different logistic regressions are presented in Table 7.1. Model A uses all of the variables to predict the vote, while Model B excludes party identification and assessment of the parties as managers of the economy.

The results for Model A show that the vote for president was affected by a number of attitudes. Party identification and assessment of which party would better manage the economy both have a strong effect on the vote. As Chapter 6 explained, the assessment of the parties as managers of the economy is strongly influenced by party identification, but the fact that this assessment influences the vote even after controlling for party identification and all of the other variables in the analysis confirms what Chapter 6 concluded, which is that if partisans do not see their party as better able to manage the economy, then they are less likely to vote for their party's presidential candidate. Furthermore, if independents see one party as better able to handle the economy, then they are more likely to vote for that party. Other economic issues appear to exert less influence on the vote, once other attitudes are controlled for. Attitudes on social welfare issues and on trade have a statistically significant effect on the vote, but the coefficients for these variables are not as large as those for other variables, and attitudes toward labor unions have a weak and statistically insignificant effect. All of the variables except the first two are measured on four-point scales, so the coefficients provide a good indication of the relative impact of each variable.[1]

Attitudes toward blacks and on immigration issues stand out as particularly important influences on the vote in 2016. That confirms the findings in Chapter 4 and is in line with many of the interpretations of the 2016 presidential election that were discussed in Chapter 1. Trump emphasized such issues in his campaign, and voters clearly were influenced by these considerations. Attitudes on moral issues, such as abortion or gay rights, did not receive very much attention in media coverage of the 2016 campaign, but this analysis shows that they too affected the vote, although not as much as did attitudes on race and immigration.

Perhaps one surprising finding in this analysis is that trust in politicians had only a modest effect on the vote. During the 2016 campaign, many commentators speculated that part of Trump's appeal was his emphasis on his being an outsider and his criticism of the elites from both parties. That supposedly struck a responsive chord among the many Americans who were "fed up" with the way things were being run in the country, who thought that the system was "rigged" for the benefit of a wealthy and influential elite, and who thought both parties were to blame for the "mess in Washington." Indeed, Trump talked about "draining the swamp" in Washington if he were elected. These data indicate that those feelings played only a minor role in Trump's appeal. Furthermore, the three questions that were used to build this index seem to directly tap into the feelings that commentators talked about in 2016, so the weak effect of trust in politicians on the vote cannot be attributed to a poor measure of that attitude.

The results of Model A may mask the effects of some of the variables because that model includes party identification in the analysis. Some of the attitudes on issues might have strong effects on party identification, thus indirectly affecting the vote in that manner, even if the direct effect of these variables on the vote is smaller. Attitudes that shape party identification do ultimately affect the vote because voting is very much along party lines, especially in recent elections. In 2016, for example, about 90 percent of Democrats voted for Clinton and about 90 percent of Republicans voted for Trump. Voting in congressional elections also is highly related to party identification. Thus, anything that has a large impact on party identification will have a substantial effect on the vote. To allow for an examination of possible indirect effects on the vote, Model B repeats the analysis without party identification and assessment of the parties as managers of the economy, a variable that is very closely linked to party identification.

What stands out in Model B is the strong effect of attitudes on social welfare issues. They have a very strong effect on the vote, much of which is through party identification. Once party identification is removed from the analysis, that effect is clear. It should not be surprising that attitudes on social welfare issues are highly related to party identification. The Democratic and Republican parties have differed on these matters for many decades, creating clear images of the parties for voters to respond to. Furthermore, as Chapter 6 showed, voters increasingly base their party identification on their ideological orientations, and party differences on these issues have been sharpening, producing a stronger relationship between attitudes on social welfare issues and party identification.

In addition to attitudes on social welfare issues, attitudes toward labor unions and attitudes on moral issues have substantially stronger effects on the vote in Model B, indicating that they also have strong indirect effects on the vote through their effect on party identification, even if their direct effects on the vote are more modest. As earlier chapters have recounted, the ties between labor unions and the Democratic Party have been strong since the 1930s, so we would expect that voters with more favorable views of unions, which would include most union members, would be more likely to identify as Democrats. Regarding moral issues, the two parties have clearly divided on these matters at least since the 1980s. From that decade on, for example, in every presidential election, the Democratic candidate has supported legalized abortion and the Republican candidate has always opposed it (except perhaps allowing it in limited cases, such as rape or incest). With voters more likely now to base their party identification on their ideological orientations, and with clear party differences on abortion, it is not surprising that attitudes on abortion help to shape party identification. The same logic applies to other moral issues, such as gay rights or religious freedom.

The results of the analysis reported in Table 7.1 shows that when we take into account both the direct effects on the vote and the indirect effects through party identification, a range of attitudes influenced the presidential vote in 2016. Attitudes on race, immigration, and moral issues all were important. Economic issues also were important, largely through their effects on party identification, but through some direct effects as well. The fact that the direct effects of the economic variables are not that strong indicates that they did not play the leading role in getting partisans to defect from their party or in influencing the vote of independents in 2016. In particular, the relatively modest direct effect on the vote of attitudes toward trade undercuts the argument that many Democratic or independent voters decided to support Trump because they were concerned about the loss of manufacturing jobs in their community.

Although economic issues may not be the primary reason that Trump was able to win votes from Democrats or independents in so-called rustbelt states, some voters in these states may have been motivated largely by these concerns. I ran the analysis in Table 7.1 separately for two groups of states: (a) the northeastern and north central states, which are more likely to be the places where manufacturing jobs were in greatest decline; and (b) the southern and border states, which are less likely to experience "rustbelt" problems. The effect of trade attitudes on the vote is greater in the northern states, as is the effect of assessments of the parties as managers of the economy. On the other hand, the effect of attitudes on race and immigration on the vote is greater in the southern states. Thus, there may be some validity to the stories cited in Chapter 1 that claimed that voters in northern industrial towns, including some who voted for Obama in 2012, were motivated by economic concerns to vote for Trump. But it also should be noted that even in the northern industrial states, this analysis finds that attitudes on race and immigration were quite important, even if not as important as they were in the South.

The focus of this study is on how and why social class is related to voting behavior. For that, we need to connect the above analysis to social class. The first question is whether working-class and middle-class voters base their vote decision on similar concerns. To investigate that question, I ran the analysis reported in Table 7.1 separately for working-class and middle-class white voters. Social class is measured here, as it is in the other chapters, by adjusted household income, which is described in Chapter 2. This analysis is limited to voters who are at least 30 years old because income is a poor measure of social class for young people, as Chapter 2 explained. The results of this analysis are presented in Table 7.2.

For the most part, working-class and middle-class voters were motivated by the same factors in 2016. Party identification and assessments of the parties as managers of the economy, two highly related attitudes, have a strong effect for both groups. The combined effect of these two variables is very similar for working and middle-class voters. Other economic attitudes also affect the vote for both groups of voters, although largely through their indirect effects on party identification. If we compare the coefficients in Model B for both groups, which capture the direct and indirect effects of the variables on the vote, they do not differ very much. The one notable difference when it comes to economic issues is that middle-class voters were significantly more influenced by attitudes on social welfare issues, especially regarding their direct effect on the vote. For both groups of voters, those with more conservative attitudes on social welfare issues were more likely to vote for Trump, but this was particularly true for middle-class voters.

**TABLE 7.2** Analysis of the Presidential Vote, by Social Class, 2016

| Independent Variable: | Working Class | | Middle Class | |
|---|---|---|---|---|
| | Model A | Model B | Model A | Model B |
| Party identification | 1.015** | | 1.364** | |
| Best party for economy | 2.176** | | 1.575** | |
| Attitude on social welfare issues | .413 | 1.724** | 1.614** | 2.751** |
| Attitude toward labor unions | .408 | .778** | .152 | .433* |
| Attitude toward free trade | .554** | .378** | .700** | .550** |
| Attitude toward blacks | .790** | .497* | 1.346** | 1.300** |
| Attitude on immigration issues | 1.001** | 1.816** | 1.363** | 1.228** |
| Attitude on moral issues | .662** | .888** | .556* | .895** |
| Trust in politicians | .224 | .201 | .314 | .062 |
| Nagelkerke $R^2$ | .868 | .735 | .899 | .821 |
| % of cases correctly. Predicted | 94.2 | 87.7 | 94.8 | 90.4 |
| (N) | (669) | (670) | (683) | (683) |

Source: ANES 2016 survey.

Note: Entries are logistic regression coefficients. Positive coefficients indicate that a Republican vote is related to a Republican party identification, more favorable assessment of Republicans as the best party to manage the economy, more conservative attitudes on social welfare and moral issues, more negative attitudes toward free trade policies, labor unions, blacks, and immigration, and a low trust in politicians. Only white, major-party voters who are at least 30 years old are included in the analysis. See the text for information on how the variables are measured.

The impact of social and cultural issues on the vote in 2016 also is largely similar for working-class and middle-class voters. Attitudes on immigration were very important for both groups. Attitudes on moral issues also were important, although not as much as were attitudes on immigration. There is a clear difference when it comes to attitudes toward blacks. Both working-class and middle-class whites were more likely to vote for Trump if they had more negative attitudes toward blacks, but that effect was much stronger for middle-class voters. Finally, it is interesting to note that neither group was significantly influenced by their level of trust in politicians. While some media accounts of Trump's appeal argued that working-class voters liked his populist message, these data provide little support for that conclusion.

Overall, it appears that working-class and middle-class white voters were influenced by the same attitudes in their presidential vote in 2016. There are some class differences in the strength of the effect of some of the variables, but what is notable is that when we look at the independent effect of each variable on the vote, with all of the other variables held constant, and we take into account both direct and indirect effects on the vote, both groups of voters were substantially influenced by economic concerns, by attitudes on race and immigration, and by attitudes on moral issues—but not by trust in politicians.

The next question then is how middle-class and working-class voters differ on these issues. To answer that question, I calculated the mean scores for each variable for each group. The results of that analysis are in Table 7.3, and the data make it clear why working-class whites were more likely to vote for Trump than middle-class whites were. On social and cultural issues, working-class whites are more conservative. The biggest differences are on moral issues. Differences on race and immigration are more modest. As Table 7.1 shows, all of these social and cultural attitudes strongly affected the vote, therefore making them reasons why Trump did better among white working-class voters. Working-class whites were only slightly more Republican than middle-class whites in their party identification and assessment of the parties as managers of the economy, but the combined effect of these two highly related attitudes on the vote is very strong, so even the small difference in attitudes translates into a difference in voting. Finally, attitudes on economic issues fail to provide a reason for working-class whites to be more supportive of Democrats. There is virtually no class difference on social welfare orientations or on feelings toward labor unions, two factors that once provided solid reasons for working-class voters to support the Democratic Party. And when it comes to attitudes on trade, it is working-class voters who are more skeptical of the benefits of free trade, thus making them more attracted to Trump on this issue, although attitudes on trade had a weaker effect on the vote than did the other attitudes in this analysis. Overall, economic issues did not pull working-class voters in a Democratic direction; if anything, they may have nudged them a bit toward Trump.

**TABLE 7.3** Political Attitudes by Social Class, 2016

|  | Social Class | |
| --- | --- | --- |
| *Political Attitude:* | *Working Class* | *Middle Class* |
| Party identification | 2.16 | 2.06 |
| Best party for economy | 2.22 | 2.14 |
| Attitude on social welfare issues | 2.66 | 2.69 |
| Attitude toward labor unions | 2.33 | 2.37 |
| Attitude toward free trade | 2.56 | 2.25 |
| Attitude toward blacks | 2.88 | 2.65 |
| Attitude on immigration issues | 2.48 | 2.21 |
| Attitude on moral issues | 2.15 | 1.79 |
| Trust in politicians | 2.81 | 2.66 |

Source: 2016 ANES survey.
Note: Figures are the mean scores for the indicated variables. Only major-party, white voters 30 years of age or older are included in the table. A higher mean score indicates a more conservative or more pro-Republican attitude. See the text for information on how the variables are measured.

## The 2012 Presidential Election

The 2012 presidential election featured quite different candidates and a campaign with a very different tone than what voters saw in 2016. Nevertheless, Romney did better among working-class white voters than he did among middle-class whites, although not to the extent that Trump did. By repeating the 2016 analysis reported above with 2012 data, we can see the similarities and differences in the basis of the Republican appeal to working and middle-class voters in these two presidential elections. Table 7.4 shows the results of the analysis of all white voters, using the same variables that were used in the 2016 analysis, except for the measure of trust in politicians, which only seemed relevant in 2016, and which turned out not to be important in that year. Because some of the variables may have strong indirect effects on the vote through effects on party identification, I ran the analysis with and without party identification and assessment of the parties as managers of the economy, just as I did in the 2016 analysis.

There are both similarities and difference in the analysis results from 2012 and 2016. In 2012, as in 2016, voters were affected by economic concerns, attitudes on race and immigration, and attitudes on moral issues. There are some differences in the strength of these effects, however. In 2012, as in 2016, voters were strongly influenced by party identification and assessment of the parties as managers of the

**TABLE 7.4** Analysis of the Presidential Vote, 2012

| Independent Variable: | Model A Coeff. | (S.E.) | Model B Coeff. | (S.E.) |
|---|---|---|---|---|
| Party identification | 1.199** | (.097) | | |
| Best party for economy | 1.716** | (.147) | | |
| Attitude on social welfare issues | .955** | (.158) | 2.103** | (.125) |
| Attitude toward labor unions | .450** | (.114) | .829** | (.090) |
| Attitude toward free trade | .070 | (.080) | –.017 | (.058) |
| Attitude toward blacks | .692** | (.140) | .677** | (.104) |
| Attitude on immigration issues | .508** | (.133) | .646** | (.102) |
| Attitude on moral issues | .923** | (.108) | 1.224** | (.083) |
| Nagelkerke $R^2$ | .840 | | .699 | |
| % of cases correctly. predicted | 92.5 | | 85.3 | |
| (N) | (2,759) | | (2,775) | |

Source: ANES 2012 survey.

Note: Entries are logistic regression coefficients, with standard errors in parentheses. Positive coefficients indicate that a Republican vote is related to a Republican party identification, more favorable assessment of Republicans as the best party to manage the economy, more conservative attitudes on social welfare and moral issues, and more negative attitudes toward free trade policies, labor unions, blacks, and immigration. Only white, major-party voters are included in the analysis. See the text for information on how the variables are measured.

economy. In both years, voting fell very much along party lines, and when partisan defected in their vote, it often was because they did not see their party as better able to manage the economy. Attitudes on social welfare issues and toward labor unions had a somewhat greater effect in 2012 than they did in 2016. Attitudes toward free trade, which had a modest effect on the vote in 2016, had no effect in 2012. As Chapter 6 explained, this can be explained by the lack of clear party differences on this issue in 2012. Regarding social and cultural issues, voters in 2012 were significantly influenced by attitudes on race, immigration, and moral issues, just as they were in 2016. However, immigration attitudes had a noticeably smaller effect in 2012, while moral issues had a significantly bigger effect. These differences easily reflect the differences in what the candidates emphasized in these two years.

The above analysis was repeated separately for working-class and middle-class white voters to see if there were significant differences in the types of attitudes that influence the voting of these two groups. Table 7.5 presents the result of that analysis, and the results show that there is very little difference. Only attitudes on trade had a notable class difference in the effect on the vote. Working-class voters were somewhat more likely to vote for Romney if they had a more favorable attitude toward free trade, while middle-class voters were unaffected by this issue. Even here, the class difference is not large. Overall, working-class and middle-class voters based their vote decision on the same factors.

**TABLE 7.5** Analysis of the Presidential Vote, by Social Class, 2012

| Independent Variable: | Working Class | | Middle Class | |
|---|---|---|---|---|
| | Model A | Model B | Model A | Model B |
| Party identification | 1.455** | | 1.038** | |
| Best party for economy | 1.618** | | 1.915** | |
| Attitude on social welfare issues | 1.151** | 1.862** | .910** | 2.451** |
| Attitude toward labor unions | .210 | .790** | .665** | 1.025** |
| Attitude toward free trade | -.042 | -.258** | .070 | .150 |
| Attitude toward blacks | .161 | .603** | .856** | .640** |
| Attitude on immigration issues | .776** | .729** | .430* | .629** |
| Attitude on moral issues | .843** | 1.058** | .597** | 1.181** |
| Nagelkerke $R^2$ | .833 | .640 | .844 | .737 |
| % of cases correctly. Predicted | 93.1 | 82.6 | 92.5 | 88.1 |
| (N) | (1,108) | (1,111) | (1,212) | (1,217) |

Source: ANES 2012 survey.
Note: Entries are logistic regression coefficients. Positive coefficients indicate that a Republican vote is related to a Republican party identification, more favorable assessment of Republicans as the best party to manage the economy, more conservative attitudes on social welfare and moral issues, and more negative attitudes toward free trade policies, labor unions, blacks, and immigration. Only white, major-party voters who are at least 30 years old are included in the analysis. See the text for information on how the variables are measured.

Finally, we can compare the attitudes of working and middle-class voters in 2012 and compare them to the 2016 patterns. Table 7.6 presents the mean scores for all of the variables used in the 2012 analysis of the vote for working-class and middle-class white voters. There are considerable similarities between the 2012 class differences and those for 2016, which are displayed in Table 7.3, but there are some differences as well. First of all, there is no real class difference in 2012 on party identification or on assessment of the parties as managers of the economy, two highly related variables. In 2016, working-class voters were somewhat more Republican on these two orientations. Also, working-class whites in 2012 were slightly more liberal on social welfare issues than were middle-class whites, which was not the case in 2016. The only economic issue where working-class whites were more conservative than middle-class whites in 2012 was on trade, but attitudes on trade had little effect on the vote in 2012. Thus, in 2012, economic issues would have given the Democrats a slight advantage among working-class voters, largely because these voters were somewhat more liberal on social welfare issues. In 2016, economic issues failed to provide the Democrats with any working-class advantage.

While economic issues may have worked to make working-class voters more Democratic in their 2012 presidential vote, social and cultural issues were working in the opposite direction, and the pull of these issues outweighed that of economic issues. First of all, class differences on social and cultural issues were relatively large, larger than the differences on economic issues (except for attitudes on trade, which had little effect on the vote in 2012). Working-class whites were more conservative on moral issues, more opposed to immigration, and slightly

**TABLE 7.6** Political Attitudes by Social Class, 2012

| Political Attitude: | Social Class | |
| --- | --- | --- |
| | Working Class | Middle Class |
| Party identification | 2.11 | 2.13 |
| Best party for economy | 2.15 | 2.18 |
| Attitude on social welfare issues | 2.81 | 2.90 |
| Attitude toward labor unions | 2.64 | 2.69 |
| Attitude toward free trade | 2.96 | 2.57 |
| Attitude toward blacks | 3.06 | 2.93 |
| Attitude on immigration issues | 2.67 | 2.40 |
| Attitude on moral issues | 2.30 | 1.97 |

Source: 2012 ANES survey.
Note: Figures are the mean scores for the indicated variables. Only major-party, white voters 30 years of age or older are included in the table. A higher mean score indicates a more conservative or more pro-Republican attitude. See the text for information on how the variables are measured.

more negative in their attitudes toward blacks—all attitudes that considerably affected the vote in 2012. The combined impact of these issues on the vote pulled working-class voters in a Republican direction, relative to middle-class voters. While economic issues were pushing in the opposite direction, their effect on class differences in voting was outweighed by the impact of social and cultural issues in 2012. In 2016, social and cultural issues again pulled working-class voters more toward the GOP, and economic issues exerted no countervailing push, for two reasons: by 2016 working-class whites were no longer more liberal on some of these economic issues, and attitudes on trade had more of an impact on the vote in 2016 than they did in 2012.

While there were more reasons for working-class whites to be Republican in 2016 than in 2012, it is interesting to note that these data do not show that working-class whites became more conservative between these two elections. For example, attitudes on social welfare issues, toward labor unions, and toward blacks were measured with exactly the same questions in both years. On all three attitudes, working-class whites were more liberal in 2016 than they were in 2012. Attitudes on trade, immigration, and moral issues were not measured with exactly the same questions, so the mean scores for these variables are not directly comparable across the years, but attitudes for some specific issues, such as gay rights, also show increased liberal orientations. But while working-class whites in 2016 were more liberal than they were in 2012, that was even more true for middle-class whites. In 2016, working-class whites may have been more liberal in an absolute sense than they were in 2012, but they were more conservative in a relative sense, and that is what helps to explain the change in class differences in voting.

## Summary

The analysis in this chapter supports the conclusions in the previous three chapters. Those chapters mostly presented fairly simple bivariate analyses to show the effects of different variables on the vote. This chapter uses a multivariate analysis to examine the independent effect of each variable, controlling for all of the other variables. This more advanced statistical analysis provides stronger evidence that the variables identified in the earlier chapters as factors that influence the vote do indeed have those effects. Moreover, the relative importance of the variables can be ascertained more accurately. In both the 2012 and the 2016 presidential elections, social and cultural issues had a clear effect on the vote, with attitudes on moral issues being most important in 2012, and attitudes on immigration being most important in 2016. The tendency for working-class whites to be more conservative on social and cultural issues helps to explain why they have become more supportive of Republicans.

Economic concerns also were important in both elections, with attitudes on social welfare issues having strong indirect effects on the vote through effects on party identification. Attitudes toward labor unions also were of some importance in both elections, with much of that influence being through indirect effects on party identification. Both of these economic attitudes had a bigger effect on the vote in 2012 than in 2016. In contrast, attitudes on trade did have some effect on the vote in 2016, but no effect in 2012. While attitudes on economic issues affect the vote, working-class whites no longer are more liberal on economic issues than middle-class whites were, so they now have no reason to favor the Democratic Party on economic issues. In fact, working-class voters tend to be more opposed to free trade agreements, which inclined them to be a little more supportive of Trump in 2016 than they otherwise would have been.

The comparison of 2012 to 2016 also indicates that there was change in the underlying relationship of social class to partisan choice, not just change regarding presidential voting. The Republican advantage among white working-class voters was greater in 2016 than it was in 2012. Some of that increased advantage was due to the unique effects of Trump. He did better than Romney did in motivating working-class Democrats to defect in their presidential vote. But some of that increased advantage was due to the fact that working-class whites were more Republican in their party identification than were middle-class whites, something that was not true in 2012. Party identification is a relatively fundamental and durable orientation that affects voting at all levels, so the Republican working-class advantage in party identification, if it continues, indicates that the GOP is likely to do relatively better among working-class whites even after Trump, and not just in presidential elections.

## Note

1  Because party identification and assessments of the parties as managers of the economy are measured on three-point scales, that will make the coefficients for these two variables larger than they would be if they were measured on a four-point scale. Had these variables been measured on a four-point scale, their coefficients would have been about two-thirds of what they are.

## Appendix

The various measures of attitudes and orientations used in the analysis of the 2012 and 2016 ANES data in this study are described below.

### Analysis Variables for 2016

*Party identification* is measured by a three-point scale, with respondents classified as Democrats, independents, or Republicans. Independents who lean toward the Democrats or Republicans are classified as Democrats or Republicans, respectively, so the independent category includes only those voters who do not lean toward either of the two parties. A high score indicates a Republican party identification.

*Assessment of which party would be better for the economy* is measured by a question about which party would better handle the economy. This variable also is a three-point scale, with respondents classified as thinking that the Democratic Party would be better, neither party would be better than the other, or that the Republican Party would be better. A high score indicates a more favorable assessment of Republicans.

*Attitude toward trade policies* is measured by an index formed from three items: whether imports should be limited to protect jobs; whether trade with other countries has been good for the U.S.; and whether the U.S. should make free trade agreements with other countries. The index is scaled to run from 1.0 to 4.0, with a high score representing a more negative attitude toward free trade.

*Attitude on social welfare issues* is measured by an index formed from four items: whether the government should provide more or fewer services; whether the government should see that everyone has a job and a good standard of living; whether the government should have a health insurance plan to cover everyone; and whether the government should take measures to reduce income inequality. The index is scaled to run from 1.0 to 4.0, with a high score representing a more conservative attitude.

*Attitude toward labor unions* is measured by a feeling thermometer that is scaled down to run from 1.0 to 4.0, with a higher score representing a more negative attitude toward unions.

*Attitude on immigration policy* is measured by an index constructed from four items about immigration policy: what U.S. policy should be toward unauthorized immigrants; whether the immigration level should be increased or decreased; whether immigration takes jobs away from those already here; and an index formed from three questions that measure tolerance toward immigrants. The index is scaled to run from 1.0 to 4.0, with a high score representing a more negative orientation toward immigrants.

*Attitude toward blacks* is measured by an index formed from four questions: whether blacks should be able to work their way up without special favors; whether past slavery and racial discrimination makes it more difficult for blacks to work their way up; whether blacks have received less than they deserved; and whether blacks need to try harder to work their way up. The index is scaled to run from 1.0 to 4.0, with a high score representing a more negative attitude toward blacks.

*Attitude on moral issues* is measured by an index formed from two questions: one asking about the circumstances under which abortion should be legal (from never to always) and one asking whether gays should be allowed to marry. The index is scaled to run from 1.0 to 4.0, with a high score representing a more conservative attitude.

*Trust in politicians* is an index constructed from three items: whether most politicians care about people; whether most politicians are trustworthy; and whether politicians are the main problem in the U.S. The index is scaled to run from 1.0 to 4.0, with a high score representing a more negative attitude toward politicians.

## Analysis Variables for 2012

For the analysis of the 2012 ANES data, a few of the variables are measured with different items from the ones used for the 2016 analysis because the 2012 ANES survey asked somewhat different questions on these issues than the 2016 ANES survey did. The following variables are measured in the same way that they were in 2016: party identification, assessment of which party would be better for the economy, attitude on social welfare issues, attitude toward labor unions, and attitude toward blacks. The variables that are measured in a somewhat different manner for 2012 than they were for 2016 are described below. While these three variables are not measured in exactly the same way as they were for 2016, they are measured using very similar questions, so they should be very comparable. One 2016 variable, trust in politicians, was not measured at all because no appropriate questions were asked in 2012.

*Attitude toward trade policies* is measured by a single item that asked whether imports should be limited to protect jobs. The variable is scaled to run from 1.0 to 4.0, with a high score representing a more negative attitude toward free trade.

*Attitude on immigration policy* is measured by an index constructed from five items about immigration policy: what U.S. policy should be toward unauthorized immigrants; whether there should be a path to citizenship for unauthorized immigrants who were brought to the country as children; whether the immigration level should be increased or decreased; whether immigration takes jobs away from those already here; and whether state laws should require state and local police officers to determine the immigration status of a person if they find that there is reasonable suspicion that he or she is an undocumented immigrant? The index is scaled to run from 1.0 to 4.0, with a high score representing a more negative orientation toward immigration.

*Attitude on moral issues* is measured by an index formed from two components: a question asking about abortion and an index of attitudes on gay rights formed from four questions. The gay rights questions asked respondents whether they thought that gays should be protected against job discrimination, allowed to serve in the military, allowed to adopt children, and allowed to marry. The moral issues index is scaled to run from 1.0 to 4.0, with a high score representing a more conservative attitude.

## References

Balz, Dan. 2013. *Collision 2012: Obama vs. Romney and the Future of Elections in America.* New York: Viking.

Campbell, Angus, Philip E. Converse, Warren E. Miller, and Donald E. Stokes. 1960. *The American Voter.* New York: John Wiley.

Holian, David B., and Charles L. Prysby. 2015. *Candidate Character Traits in Presidential Elections.* New York: Routledge.

King, Gary. 1989. *Unifying Political Methodology: The Likelihood Theory of Statistical Inference.* New York: Cambridge University Press.

Lewis-Beck, Michael S., William G. Jacoby, Helmut Norpoth, and Herbert F. Weisberg. 2008. *The American Voter Revisited.* Ann Arbor: University of Michigan Press.

Meyers, Lawrence S., Glenn Gamst, and A. J. Guarino. 2006. *Applied Multivariate Research: Design and Interpretation.* Thousand Oaks, CA: Sage.

# 8

# CONCLUSION: SOCIAL CLASS AND VOTING IN THE 21ST CENTURY

For decades, the Democratic Party was the party of the working class. That relationship was established in the 1930s, and it persisted throughout the remainder of the 20th century. The relationship between class and voting weakened somewhat after World War II, and there were some regional changes in how social class affected partisan choice. Nevertheless, as late as the 1990s, there were clear class differences in voting behavior. Democratic candidates did relatively better among working-class voters; Republican candidates did relatively better among middle-class voters. Those class differences were stronger among the entire electorate, but they were clear even among white voters.

That long-standing relationship between social class and voting began diminishing among whites in the 21st century. In 2016, the popular media frequently discussed Donald Trump's appeal to working-class whites, often implying that this was a sharp break with past patterns. However, working-class whites began moving away from the Democratic Party well before Trump. That change began early in the 21st century. By 2012, the old relationship between class and voting had not only disappeared but had even reversed. The Republican presidential candidate, Mitt Romney, did better among working-class white voters than he did among their middle-class counterparts. Trump just accentuated a trend that began years earlier. Moreover, the same shifts were present in party identification as well, indicating that this was more than just a pair of deviating presidential elections, due to unique candidates or unusual issues in those years. More fundamental party loyalties, which affect voting at all levels, were being altered as well, although the shifts in party identification lagged behind the changes in presidential voting.

While class differences in voting among whites were weakening in the early 21st century, the Democratic Party still drew relatively more support from working-class voters when the entire electorate was considered. The loss of

Democratic support among white working-class voters was compensated for by strong support from blacks and Hispanics, who are disproportionately working-class. During the first decade of the 21st century, Democratic presidential candidates averaged almost 11 percentage points better among all working-class voters than they did among middle-class voters, even though the Democratic working-class advantage among whites was only around three points. But when the relationship between social class and voting among whites actually reversed in the second decade of this century, with white working-class voters now disproportionately Republican, that reduced and then eliminated the Democratic working-class advantage among all voters. In 2016, Trump did relatively better among working-class voters in the entire electorate, not just among white voters, although his working-class advantage was greater among whites.

The focus of this study is on the change in the relationship between social class and voting behavior among whites. While I often focus on the change in the voting patterns among working-class whites, this study is just as much about middle-class whites. If working-class whites have become relatively more Republican, then it follows that middle-class whites have become relatively more Democratic. The concern here is with the difference between working-class and middle-class voters, not in the absolute level of support that either group provides for either party. Over the past several decades, Democratic support has declined among white voters as a whole, but the decline has been greater among working-class whites. Perhaps that explains why there have been more stories in the popular media about the decline of Democratic support among working-class whites than about the increase in Democratic support from the middle class, but these two changes are just two sides of the same coin. While there has been plenty of discussion of changing class alignments in both the popular media and scholarly research, that coverage has not yet provided an accurate and thorough description and explanation of the recent change in how social class affects voting behavior. The goal of this study has been to provide that thorough description and explanation. Some of the key points of the previous chapters are summarized below, followed by a discussion of future possibilities and implications.

## Measuring Social Class

Most media stories about social class and voting use education to define social class: those with a four-year college degree are considered to be middle-class; all others are classified as working-class. As I argued in Chapter 2, this is not the most accurate way of measuring social class. Only one-third of American adults have a college degree, which would make two-thirds of Americans working-class. That would be a very broad definition of the working class. It does not fit the perceptions of most Americans, over one-half of whom call themselves middle-class. There are many people who lack a college degree yet are clearly middle-class, both in their own eyes and in the eyes of others. They have occupations and incomes that are widely considered to be middle-class, not working-class.

Social class probably is best defined in terms of occupation and income. Most people think of the working class as made up of those in blue-collar jobs or in poorly paid white-collar jobs. Middle-class individuals are those in better-paid and more prestigious white-collar occupations. Unfortunately, good information on occupation is not available in recent surveys of the American electorate. Given the data that are available, I argue that income currently is the best measure of social class, and it is the one more frequently used by political scientists in current research. However, income needs to be adjusted for marital status, since married individuals tend to have a higher household income than single people. Even with this adjustment, which is described in Chapter 2, income is far from a perfect measure of social class. Nevertheless, it seems superior to education, for all of the reasons outlined in Chapter 2.

Income is a much better measure of social class if it is adjusted for marital status, as I have done. Also, it is a better measure of social class when we look at voters who are at least 30 years old. Measuring the social class of young people, many of whom have not competed their education or have not really begun their career, is difficult to do. For that reason, I often confine my analysis to voters who are 30 or older. Failing to consider the effects of age and marital status can lead to misleading results. Unfortunately, that problem plagues many analyses, even scholarly ones. Several studies of voting in the early years of the 21st century concluded that white working-class voters continued to be disproportionately Democratic in their voting. However, those studies based their conclusions on the fact that lower-income whites were more Democratic, without taking into account the confounding effects of marital status and age, and the result was that they failed to realize that class differences in voting were in decline.

To illustrate the potential problem, consider the 2004 presidential election. If we look at all white voters, and if we just compare those with above-average household incomes to those with below-average incomes, without correcting for marital status, we find that the Democratic candidate, John Kerry, did 16 points better among less-affluent white voters than he did among more-affluent ones. That gives the impression that class differences were very strong in that election, which is what many commentators concluded. In fact, that was not the case. Kerry did so much better among lower-income white voters in large part because he did better among both young voters and unmarried voters, for reasons largely unrelated to social class. The complicating factor is that both young and unmarried people are likely to have below-average household incomes, but not because they are really working-class. Quite obviously, a one-person household is likely to have a lower income than a two-person household, and young people often have a lower income because they have yet to really begin their career. If we examine the 2004 data using adjusted household income and restrict the analysis to those over 30, we find that Kerry did just two points better among white working-class voters than among white middle-class voters. That very small class difference in voting seems to be a more accurate description of what happened in the 2004 election, and it is a description that matches up with the results for other measures of social class.

In arguing that income is better than education as a measure of social class, I am not claiming that education is unimportant. In fact, presidential voting in 2016 was more strongly related to education than to income. That is, the difference between college and non-college educated white voters was greater than the difference between more-affluent and less-affluent white voters. But while education may have been related more strongly to the vote in 2016, that does not make it a more accurate measure of social class. Education appears to affect political behavior apart from its connection to income and occupation. Two individuals who are equal in income and occupation, but who differ in education, are likely to differ in their voting behavior. In 2016, for example, Trump did much better among higher-income white voters without a college degree than he did among higher-income white voters with a college degree. There are two possible explanations for this pattern. First, higher education may directly affect the attitudes of voters, making them more liberal on social and cultural issues. Second, within the middle class, even the upper middle class, those without a college degree are likely to be in different occupations than those with a degree.

College-educated voters are not representative of all middle-class voters, and this is not simply because middle-class voters without a degree occupy the bottom rungs of the middle class. There are a significant number of solidly middle-class, even upper middle-class, voters who lack a college degree, as Chapter 2 explained. These two groups of middle-class voters—college versus non-college—differ not only in education but also in occupation. Professional positions in education, law, medicine, and finance almost always require a college degree, something that is not required for success in business, entertainment, or the arts. If we look at college-educated voters, we are examining a group that is not fully representative of the entire middle class, and that may exaggerate class differences. Using income, adjusted as I do in this study, should provide a more accurate estimate of true class differences, albeit not a perfect one.

In 2016, Trump did over 20 points better among whites without a college degree than he did among those with a degree, but he did only about 12 points better among lower-income whites. That college/non-college difference probably exaggerates the true difference between working-class and middle-class white voters. Many of the non-college voters for Trump were people with above-average incomes. Some of these may have been well-paid blue-collar workers, but many probably were solidly middle-class voters who differed in their political attitudes from their college-educated middle-class counterparts. Unfortunately, we lack the necessary data on occupation to verify this hypothesis for 2016, but an analysis of data from earlier years, when data on occupation were available, does reveal differences between college and non-college educated white-collar voters. In contrast to the 2016 patterns, there is little difference in 2012 between using income versus education to measure social class. Romney did about four points better among lower-income whites versus about five points better among non-college whites. In some years, therefore, both measures may yield similar results.

Having argued for using income, properly adjusted, as the best available measure of social class, I hasten to add that all the basic findings of this study hold true regardless of which measure of social class is used. The analysis presented in Chapter 3 examines income, education, class identification, and occupation (through 2004). All four measures show that the class differences that existed in the 1980s and 1990s began to weaken and then to reverse direction in the 21st century. Moreover, the results of the analyses of the reasons for the change in the relationship between social class and voting behavior, which are in Chapters 4–6, remain basically the same if another measure of social class is used, although there are differences in the relative strength of various effects or in the amount of change. Relying on income to measure social class does not yield fundamentally different results, but it should provide at least a somewhat more accurate estimates of differences and effects.

## Explaining the Change in the Relationship Between Class and Voting

Most political scientists love a good mystery novel. In a typical murder mystery, there are several suspects, but just one true culprit in the end. However, in Agatha Christie's *Murder on the Orient Express*, there are a number of suspects, all of whom contributed to the crime. That is the situation here. Many of the stories about the 2016 presidential election that appeared in the popular media emphasized a single reason for Trump's appeal to white working-class voters, some claiming that it was his opposition to free trade, others arguing that it was his stand on immigration, for example. This study finds that no single factor explains Trump's working-class appeal or why the relationship between social class and voting changed during this century. No doubt there were individual voters in 2016 who were motivated primarily by a single issue, but no one factor fully explains the electoral behavior that is the subject of this study. This investigation finds that there were several suspects, and most of them turn out to be guilty.

Racial issues were highlighted by some commentators as the reason why Trump appealed so well to working-class whites. Attitudes on race-related issues did contribute to the change in the relationship between social class and voting that has taken place in this century. At the end of the 20th century, class differences on race-related issues among whites were very small. During the 21st century, modest class differences emerged, with working-class whites becoming more conservative than middle-class whites. Whites overall did not become more conservative. What changed were the class differences on these issues. Moreover, the impact of racial issues on the vote increased over the past two decades from strong to very strong. The combination of the increased class differences on racial issues and the increased impact of these issues on the vote contributed to the white working class becoming relatively more Republican. Nevertheless, the fact that class differences on these issues are small means that this is only a partial explanation.

Attitudes on immigration also played a role in the change in how social class is related to voting. What were weak class differences in immigration attitudes at the end of the 20th century developed into moderate class differences by the second decade of the 21st century. Also, the impact that attitudes on immigration had on the vote increased greatly, from very little in the 1990s to a great deal in 2016. The combined impact of these two changes in the electorate helped to make working-class whites move from being relatively more Democratic in the 1990s to being relatively more Republican in 2016. While these issues were particularly important in the 2016 presidential election, they also contributed to Romney doing better among working-class whites than among middle-class whites.

Moral issues, such as abortion or gay rights, did not receive much news coverage during the 2016 presidential election campaign. However, this study shows that these issues also contributed to the change in the relationship between social class and voting. Working-class whites have been more conservative on these issues for decades, largely because they tend to be more religious and more likely to be evangelical Protestants. Class differences on moral issues remained fairly stable during the first two decades of the 21st century. What did change is the impact that these issues have on the vote. There already was a sizable influence at the start of the century, but that influence became greater, which helped to weaken and then reverse the old relationship between social class and voting. A considerable amount of the impact of moral issues on the vote is through their influence on party identification. Cultural conservatives are more likely to be Republican identifiers, which then leads them to vote for Republican candidates. Those relationships help to explain why Trump did so well among supporters of the Christian Right, even though he seemed to be an unlikely candidate to receive their vote.

While each of the above social and cultural issues—race, immigration, abortion, gay rights—contributed only partly to the change in class voting that took place in this century, the cumulative effect of these issues was considerable. Working-class whites were at least somewhat more conservative than middle-class whites on these social and cultural issues, and for issues of race and immigration, that social class difference represented a change from the late 20th century, when the class differences were minimal. Added to the increased class differences on these issues was the greater impact that social and cultural issues began to have on the vote. These issues already affected voting behavior at the start of the 21st century, but that influence increased over time, both through direct effects on the vote and through effects on party identification. Democrats and Republicans increasingly became divided on these issues.

The above discussion of the impact of social and cultural issues can be recast with a focus on the white middle class. Over the past two decades, class differences on social and cultural issues have increased, with white middle-class voters becoming relatively more liberal. That development, combined with the increasing impact of these issues on the vote, moved white middle-class voters toward the Democrats. Whether the changing relationship between class and voting is described in terms of the working class or the middle class, the point is the same. What matters is the relative difference between the social classes. In some cases, such as on racial issues, whites have become more liberal over the past 20 years, but middle-class whites more so. In other cases, such as on immigration, attitudes overall have become more conservative in this century, but more so for working-class whites. In either case, working-class whites have become relatively more conservative and middle-class whites relatively more liberal. It is the increased class difference in attitudes that has contributed to increased Democratic support among working-class whites—or increased Republican support among middle-class whites.

Economic issues have contributed in a different way to the changing relationship between social class and voting. What happened was a disappearance of class differences on most economic issues. In the 20th century, even as late as the 1990s, working-class voters were relatively more liberal on social welfare issues and more supportive of labor unions. Attitudes on both of these issues strongly affected the vote, in large part through their influence on party identification. Those issues continued to divide the parties and to play a strong role in voting. What changed is how attitudes on these issues connected to social class. Class differences on these economic issues weakened during the 21st century, to the point that by 2016 there was no difference between working-class and middle-class whites in their attitudes on social welfare or toward labor unions. Middle-class whites were just as liberal as working-class whites. A few decades earlier, these issues would have pulled working-class voters toward the Democratic Party. Today they do not.

In the latter half of the 20th century, the Democratic Party was generally regarded as better able to manage the economy, and working-class voters were especially likely to hold that view. That economic orientation also has changed. White working-class voters no longer are more likely to see the Democratic Party as better able to manage the economy. The gradual disappearance of the old class difference is partly due to changes in party identification. Working-class whites have become as Republican in party identification as middle-class whites, if not more so, often because of social and cultural issues. Party identification strongly affects assessments of the parties as managers of the economy: Democrats largely think that their party would do better; Republicans feel the same about their party. Therefore, diminished class differences in party identification work to minimize class differences in assessments of the parties as managers of the economy.

Assessments of the parties as managers of the economy are not completely determined by party identification. In any election, some Democrats and Republicans will not feel that their party is best able to manage the economy. These are the partisans most likely to vote for the candidate of the other party. Also, independents vote in part on how they see the parties as managers of the economy. In the past, social class did influence assessments of the parties as economic managers, even after party identification was taken into account. For example, working-class Republicans were less likely than middle-class Republicans to think that the GOP was the best party to manage the economy. That influence of social class on views of the parties as economic managers has disappeared. The end result is that considerations of which party will best manage the economy no longer pull working-class whites toward the Democratic Party. Middle-class whites are equally likely to see the Democrats as better managers of the economy.

Trade policy may be one reason why working-class voters no longer see the Democratic Party as superior to the GOP when it comes to managing the economy. Working-class voters have been more skeptical than middle-class voters of the benefits of free trade agreements for some time. However, those class differences in attitudes toward trade had little effect on class voting because attitudes on that issue did not affect voting. The likely reason why there was no effect is because voters did not see clear differences between the parties on trade. Republican and Democratic presidents from the 1980s on supported free trade deals, starting with NAFTA. The situation changed in 2016. Trump's loud and strong opposition to trade deals led voters to see party differences on this issue, and attitudes on trade did have some influence on the vote in that election.

Overall, several developments during the 21st century caused the clear class divisions in voting that were present as late as the 1990s to diminish and then reverse direction. Class differences on social and cultural issues increased, as did the influence of these issues on voting. Clear class differences on economic issues that were present at the end of the 20th century began to evaporate, to the point that there were minimal class differences by 2016. Working-class whites used to be more liberal on social welfare issues, more supportive of labor unions, and more inclined to see the Democratic Party as better able to manage the economy. By the second decade of the 21st century, none of those class differences remained among whites. These economic issues still had a strong influence on the vote, especially through effects on party identification. But now working-class whites had no more reason than middle-class whites to vote for Democrats on the basis of these economic issues. The one economic issue where clear class differences remained was on free trade, where working-class voters continued to be more opposed to free trade deals, but attitudes on trade had little effect on the vote until 2016, when they tended to disproportionately pull working-class voters toward the GOP. No one of these economic or social/cultural issues was sufficient to produce the changes in class voting that occurred in this century, but the cumulative effect of all of the changes described above did result in significant change.

While many factors did contribute to the change in how social class is related to voting, there are two suspects that were identified by many media commentators as reasons why Trump appealed so well to working-class whites in 2016, but that turn out not to be guilty. One supposed reason was Trump's appeal as a political outsider, one who was critical of the elites of both parties. Working-class voters supposedly found that very appealing because they were more alienated from the existing system. The analysis in Chapter 7 shows that while working-class whites were somewhat less trusting in politicians, that attitude had little if any impact on the candidate choice of most white voters.

The other reason suggested by some commentators was that working-class whites felt that they were not respected by Democratic elites, who supposedly had condescending views of ordinary people. Working-class voters supposedly thought that Trump was more like them and that Clinton was too elitist. This argument was not only made in 2016, but in earlier elections as well. In particular, numerous analysts claimed that one reason why George W. Bush won his two presidential elections was because ordinary Americans found him more likeable and relatable than his Democratic opponents, Al Gore in 2000 and John Kerry in 2004, both of whom were frequently characterized as too aloof and elitist. However, the data do not support that argument. In all of these elections, the Democratic candidate was seen by the voters as the one who cared more about people like them, according to the data analyzed in this study. That hardly sounds like something people would say about someone whom they thought had a condescending view of them. There probably were some voters who were strongly motivated by anti-elitist attitudes to vote for Trump in 2016, or for Bush in 2000 or 2004, but these data indicate that such voters were a very small part of the electorate.

## Future Possibilities

The relationship between social class and voting behavior has changed considerably during the first two decades of this century. That suggests that it could change in the next decade. The current Republican advantage among the white working class could remain or even strengthen. Alternatively, class divisions in voting might move back to where they were during the 1990s, when Democrats had a significant working-class advantage. And, of course, something between these two alternatives could be what happens. We can explore the likelihood of these possible developments by considering the factors that altered how social class is related to voting and how they might change during the 2020s.

Social and cultural factors contributed significantly to the emerging Republican advantage among white working-class voters. If class differences in attitudes on these issues were to diminish, or if the impact of these issues on voting were to decline, then the GOP working-class advantage would weaken, or even disappear. At this point, neither of these possibilities seems likely, at least in the near future. Attitudes on race and immigration have become more important in American elections in this century, and the best explanation of this is that a considerable number of whites are concerned about the growth of the minority population and feel that their status as the dominant group in society is being threatened. The projections are for the minority population to grow, which should lead to issues of race and immigration remaining or even increasing in importance. Class differences on race and immigration have been increasing, and there seems little reason to think that those differences will decrease in the near future. For one thing, these attitudes are related to education—college educated individuals tend to be more liberal on these questions—and education is becoming a more important determinant of social class. While it is still possible to obtain the occupation and income to be middle-class without a college degree, it probably is more difficult now to do so than it was in the past. All of this suggests that race and immigration will continue to be issues that lead working-class whites to be relatively more Republican in the next decade. In the long run, however, this might change, particularly if younger voters have more liberal attitudes on these issues, as some research has reported.

Declining class differences on economic issues also has played a role in the disappearance of the old Democratic advantage among the white working class. Economic issues still play a strong role in voting behavior, and the two parties remain very divided on these issues, but white working-class voters are no longer more liberal or more pro-Democratic on economic issues. Perhaps that will change. The Democratic Party has continued to stand for economic policies, such as raising the minimum wage or expanding health care, that presumably would disproportionately benefit less-affluent Americans. Perhaps growing concerns over rising inequality and economic insecurity will lead more white working-class voters to become relatively more liberal on economic issues, which then would make them more likely to support the Democratic Party.

Indeed, as this book is being completed in the fall of 2019, many of the Democratic presidential candidates are making an improved effort to appeal to working-class voters, particularly in the battleground Midwestern industrial states. Some of the candidates have explicitly criticized free trade deals, for example. Most have called for making college more affordable; some even want to make public universities tuition free for everyone. Almost all have emphasized the need to address the rising economic inequality in America. If Democrats are successful in convincing white working-class voters that their economic interests are better served by the Democratic Party, that would reduce, or perhaps even eliminate, the current advantage that Republicans have among these voters. Furthermore, if concerns over growing economic inequality translate into growing support for labor unions among working-class voters, that also would strengthen Democratic working-class support. Voters who are union members, or who even have a union member in their household, continue to be more supportive of the Democratic Party.

How these possibilities actually play out will depend on how the political parties respond and on the success of present and future presidents. If Trump is reelected in 2020, and if he finishes his second term with a high approval rating among working-class whites, that should help to solidify the current GOP working-class advantage and ensure that it will continue after Trump leaves the political stage. But if the Trump presidency ends with a low approval rating from white working-class voters, Democrats would gain support from these voters. In the same way, the policies and successes of future Democratic presidents also could alter the existing relationship between social class and voting.

At this point in time, it is unclear how the parties will attempt to appeal to working-class whites. Trump's deviated from Republican orthodoxy in his trade policies, although in other areas of economic policy, such as taxes or business regulation, he did not. Will the post-Trump Republican Party return to its traditional support for free trade? Will future Democratic presidential candidates be more critical of free trade, as many of the 2020 candidates now are? Trade issues did not play a dominant role in the 2016 election, but they had some effect, and the working-class has consistently been less enthusiastic about the benefits of foreign trade.

Trade is not the only economic issue that could affect class differences in voting. Republicans in Congress have supported reductions in popular social welfare programs, such as Medicare, in recent years, as Chapter 6 outlined. If they are able to enact these changes, that might result in a loss of support from less-affluent voters. Democrats have been advocates of a large increase in the minimum wage. If they accomplish that goal, that might increase Democratic support among less-affluent voters. There is every reason to think that economic policies have the potential to influence class differences in voting. Whether they will remains to be seen.

## Conclusion

This study has attempted to provide a more thorough and accurate description and explanation of the changing relationship between social class and voting behavior in contemporary America. That relationship has changed in this century among whites. The reason that it has changed is because white working-class and middle-class voters have changed. The old relationship between class and party rested on economic issues. Working-class voters were more Democratic because they preferred Democrats on economic issues. Economic issues remain important in American elections, and the two parties continue to divide on these issues as they have in the past. What has changed are class differences on these issues, at least among whites. Working-class whites are no longer more liberal or more pro-Democratic than middle-class whites on economic matters. Added to this change is the growth of class differences on social and cultural issues, which have increased in importance. The combination of these two changes has produced a relationship between class and party that is quite different from what it was in the late 20th century.

There are many relevant questions that are beyond the scope of this study. For example, generational differences were not analyzed, but they could be important. If the relationship between class and voting is different for younger voters than it is for older voters, then generational replacement is likely to alter the overall nature of how class and partisan choice are connected, although it will take time for substantial changes to occur. Geographical differences also were largely ignored. A number of studies have emphasized the strong support for the GOP in rural areas, which often have a disproportionate number of less-affluent voters. Do rural working-class voters differ in their political attitudes and behavior from urban working-class voters, and is the same true for middle-class voters? Despite all of the work that has been done on the relationship between social class and voting behavior in contemporary America, more could be done. If this study has advanced our understanding of this aspect of electoral politics, and if it stimulates more research in this area, it will have accomplished its goals.

# INDEX

Page numbers in *italic* refer to tables.